Lecture Notes in Computer Science 6546

Commenced Publication in 1973
Founding and Former Series Editors:
Gerhard Goos, Juris Hartmanis, and Jan van Leeuwen

W0192959

Rex Page Zoltán Horváth
Viktória Zsók (Eds.)

Trends
in Functional
Programming

11th International Symposium, TFP 2010
Norman, OK, USA, May 17-19, 2010
Revised Selected Papers

 Springer

Volume Editors

Rex Page
University of Oklahoma, School of Computer Science
110 West Boyd Street, Norman, OK 73019, USA
E-mail: page@ou.edu

Zoltán Horváth
Eötvös Loránd University, Faculty of Informatics
Department of Programming Languages and Compilers
Pázmány Péter sétány 1/C, 1117 Budapest, Hungary
E-mail: hz@inf.elte.hu

Viktória Zsók
Eötvös Loránd University, Faculty of Informatics
Department of Programming Languages and Compilers
Pázmány Péter sétány 1/C, 1117 Budapest, Hungary
E-mail: zsv@inf.elte.hu

ISSN 0302-9743   e-ISSN 1611-3349
ISBN 978-3-642-22940-4   ISBN 978-3-642-22941-1 (eBook)
DOI 10.1007/978-3-642-22941-1
Springer Heidelberg Dordrecht London New York

Library of Congress Control Number: 2011934807

CR Subject Classification (1998): D.1.1, D.1, D.3.2, F.3.3, D.1-2

LNCS Sublibrary: SL 1 – Theoretical Computer Science and General Issues

Typesetting: Camera-ready by author, data conversion by Scientific Publishing Services, Chennai, India

Printed on acid-free paper

Springer is part of Springer Science+Business Media (www.springer.com)

Preface

The 11th Symposium on Trends in Functional Programming took place on the University of Oklahoma campus in Norman, Oklahoma, May 17-19, 2010. The program included presentations of 26 papers submitted by researchers from six nations and an invited talk by J. Strother Moore on machine reasoning so well received that the question/answer session continued for a full hour beyond the talk, well into the lunch period. Most of the authors submitted revisions of their papers, based in part on responses to their presentations. The revisions were reviewed and discussed in detail by the Program Committee, and 13 of them were accepted for publication in this volume.

A little over half of the revisions accepted for publication were student papers (that is, papers with a student as first author). Following a long-established custom, the Program Committee designated one of them as the best student paper. This year the award went to Stephen Chang for his paper, with co-authors David van Horn and Matthias Felleisen, describing a way to evaluate a call-by-need λ-calculus on the control stack. The Program Committee appreciates the originality and insight in this work and congratulates Stephen Chang on earning the award.

TFP aspires to be a forum for new directions in functional programming research. This year was no exception. Presentations covered new ideas for refactoring, managing source-code complexity, functional language implementation, graphical languages, applications of functional programming in pure mathematics, type theory, multitasking and parallel processing, distributed systems, scientific modeling, domain-specific languages, hardware design, education, and testing.

The editors want to thank the Program Committee and all of the referees for their diligence and for their well-considered reviews. We also want to thank the University of Oklahoma and Erlang Solutions Ltd, for their generous support. Finally, we thank the participants for their lively attention during the symposium. We trust that a good time was had by all.

December 2010

Rex Page
Zoltán Horváth
Viktória Zsók

Organization

Program Committee

Peter Achten	Radboud University Nijmegen, The Netherlands
Emil Axelsson	Chalmers University of Technology, Sweden
Francesco Cesarini	Erlang Training and Consulting, Ltd., UK
John Clements	California Polytechnic State University, USA
Daniel Cooke	Texas Tech University, USA
Nils Anders Danielsson	University of Nottingham, UK
Jared Davis	Centaur Technology, USA
Martin Erwig	Oregon State University, USA
Ruben Gamboa	University of Wyoming, USA
Jurriaan Hage	Utrecht University, The Netherlands
Kevin Hammond	University of St. Andrews, UK
Michael Hanus	Christian Albrechts University zu Kiel, Germany
Zoltán Horváth (symposium co-chair)	Eötvös Loránd University, HU
Garrin Kimmell	University of Kansas, USA
Pieter Koopman	Radboud University Nijmegen, The Netherlands
Hans-Wolfgang Loidl	Heriot-Watt University, UK
Rita Loogen	Philipps University Marburg, Germany
Jay McCarthy	Brigham Young University, USA
Greg Michaelson	Heriot-Watt University, UK
Marco T. Morazán	Seton Hall University, USA
Rodney Oldehoeft	Krell Institute, USA
Rex Page (Chair)	University of Oklahoma, USA
Ricardo Peña	Complutense University of Madrid, Spain
Walid Taha	Rice University, USA
Sam Tobin-Hochstadt	Northeastern University, USA
Simon Thompson	University of Kent, UK
Phil Trinder	Heriot-Watt University, UK
Marko van Eekelen	Radboud University Nijmegen and Open University, The Netherlands
Viktória Zsók (symposium co-chair)	Eötvös Loránd University, HU

Sponsoring Institutions

Erlang Solutions Ltd. (UK)
The University of Oklahoma (USA)

Table of Contents

Evaluating Call-by-Need on the Control Stack

Stephen Chang*, David Van Horn**, and Matthias Felleisen*

PLT & PRL, Northeastern University, Boston, MA 02115, USA

Abstract. Ariola and Felleisen's call-by-need λ-calculus replaces a variable occurrence with its value at the last possible moment. To support this gradual notion of substitution, function applications—once established—are never discharged. In this paper we show how to translate this notion of reduction into an abstract machine that resolves variable references via the control stack. In particular, the machine uses the *static address* of a variable occurrence to extract its current value from the *dynamic control stack*.

1 Implementing Call-by-Need

Following Plotkin [1], Ariola and Felleisen characterize the by-need λ-calculus as a variant of β:

$$(\lambda x.E[x])\ V = (\lambda x.E[V])\ V\ ,$$

and prove that a machine is an algorithm that searches for a (generalized) value via the leftmost-outermost application of this new reduction [2].

Philosophically, the by-need λ-calculus has two implications:

1. First, its existence says that imperative assignment isn't truly needed to implement a lazy language. The calculus uses only one-at-a-time substitution and does not require any store-like structure. Instead, the by-need β suggests that a variable dereference is the resumption of a continuation of the function call, an idea that Garcia et al. [3] recently explored in detail by using delimited control operations to derive an abstract machine from the by-need calculus. Unlike traditional machines for lazy functional languages, Garcia et al.'s machine eliminates the need for a store by replacing heap manipulations with control (stack) manipulations.

2. Second, since by-need β does not remove the application, the binding structure of programs—the association of a function parameter with its value—remains the same throughout a program's evaluation. This second connection is the subject of our paper. This binding structure *is* the control stack, and thus we have that in call-by-need, *static* addresses can be resolved in the *dynamic* control stack.

---

* Partially supported by grants from the National Science Foundation.
** Supported by NSF Grant 0937060 to the CRA for the CIFellow Project.

R. Page, Z. Horváth, and V. Zsók (Eds.): TFP 2010, LNCS 6546, pp. 1–15, 2011.

Our key innovation is the CK+ machine, which refines the abstract machine of Garcia et al. by making the observation that when a variable reference is in focus, the location of the corresponding binding context in the dynamic control stack can be determined by the lexical index of the variable. Whereas Garcia et al.'s machine linearly traverses their control stack to find a specific binding context, our machine employs a different stack organization where indexing can be used instead of searching. Our machine organization also simplifies the hygiene checks used by Garia et al., mostly because it explicitly maintains Garcia et al.'s "well-formedness" condition on machine states, instead of leaving it as a side condition.

The paper starts with a summary of the by-need λ-calculus and the abstract textual machine induced by the standard reduction theorem. We then show how to organize the machine's control stack so that when the control string is a variable reference, the machine is able to use the lexical address to compute the location of the variable's binding site in the control stack.

2   The Call-by-Need λ-Calculus, the de Bruijn Version

The terms of the by-need λ-calculus are those of the λ-calculus [4], which we present using de Bruijn's notation [5], i.e., lexical addresses replace variables:

$$M ::= n \mid \lambda.M \mid M\ M$$

where $n \in \mathbb{N}$. The set of values is just the set of abstractions:

$$V ::= \lambda.M$$

One of the fundamental ideas of call-by-need is to evaluate the argument in an application only when it is "needed," and when the argument *is* needed, to evaluate that argument only once. Therefore, the by-need calculus cannot use the β notion of reduction because doing so may evaluate the argument when it is not needed, or may cause the argument to be evaluated multiple times. Instead, β is replaced with the *deref* notion of reduction:

$$(\lambda.E[n])\ V\ \textbf{need}\ (\lambda.E[V])\ V,\quad \lambda \text{ binds } n \qquad\qquad deref$$

The *deref* notion of reduction requires the argument in an application to be a value and requires the body of the function to have a special shape. This special shape captures the demand-driven substitution of values for variables that is characteristic of call-by-need. In the *deref* notion of reduction, when a variable is replaced with the value V, some renaming may still be necessary to avoid capture of free variables in V, but for now, we assume a variant of Barendregt's hygiene condition for de Bruijn indices and leave all necessary renaming implicit.

Here is the set of evaluation contexts E:

$$E ::= [\,]\mid E\ M \mid (\lambda.E)\ M \mid (\lambda.E'[n])\ E$$

Like all contexts, an evaluation context is an expression with a hole in the place of a subexpression. The first evaluation context is an empty context that is just a hole. The second evaluation context indicates that evaluation of applications proceeds in a leftmost-outermost order. This is similar to how evaluation proceeds in the by-name λ-calculus [1]. Unlike call-by-name, however, call-by-need defers dealing with arguments until absolutely necessary. It therefore demands evaluation within the body of a let-like binding. The third evaluation context captures this notion. This context allows the *deref* notion of reduction to search under applied λs for variables to substitute. The fourth evaluation context explains how the demand for a parameter's value triggers and directs the evaluation of the function's argument. In the fourth evaluation context, the visible λ binds n in $\lambda.E'[n]$. This means that there are n additional λ abstractions in E' between n and its binding λ.

To make this formal, let us define the function $\Delta : E \to \mathbb{N}$ as:

$$\Delta([\,]) = 0 \qquad\qquad \Delta((\lambda.E'[n])\ E) = \Delta(E)$$
$$\Delta(E\ M) = \Delta(E) \qquad\qquad \Delta((\lambda.E)\ M) = \Delta(E) + 1$$

With Δ, the side condition for the fourth evaluation context is $n = \Delta(E')$.

Unlike β, *deref* does not remove the argument from a term when substitution is complete. Instead, a term $(\lambda.M)\ N$ is interpreted as a term M and an environment where the variable (index) bound by λ is associated with N. Since arguments are never removed from a by-need term, reduced terms are not necessarily values. In the by-need λ-calculus, reductions produce "answers" a (this representation of answers is due to Garcia et al. [3]):

$$a ::= A[V] \qquad\qquad\qquad\qquad \text{answers}$$
$$A ::= [\,] \mid (\lambda.A)\ M \qquad\qquad \text{answer contexts}$$

Answer contexts A are a strict subset of evaluation contexts E.

Since both the operator and the operand in an application reduce to answers, two additional notions of reduction are needed:

$$(\lambda.A[V])\ M\ N\ \textbf{need}\ (\lambda.A[V\ N])\ M \qquad\qquad\qquad\qquad \textit{assoc-L}$$
$$(\lambda.E[n])\ ((\lambda.A[V])\ M)\ \textbf{need}\ (\lambda.A[(\lambda.E[n])\ V])\ M,\ \text{if}\ \Delta(E) = n \qquad \textit{assoc-R}$$

As mentioned, some adjustments to de Bruijn indices are necessary when performing substitution in λ-calculus terms. For example, in a *deref* reduction, every free variable in the substituted V must be incremented by $\Delta(E) + 1$. Otherwise, the indices representing free variables in V no longer count the number of λs between their occurrence and their respective binding λs. Similar adjustments are needed for the *assoc-L* and *assoc-R* reductions, where subterms are also pulled under λs.

Formally, define a function $\uparrow$ that takes three inputs: a term M, an integer x, and a variable (index) m, and increments all free variables in M by x, where a free variable is defined to be an index n such that $n \geq m$. In this paper, we use the notation $M{\uparrow}^x_m$. Here is the formal definition of $\uparrow$:

$$n\!\uparrow^x_m = n + x, \text{ if } n \geq m \qquad (M\ N)\!\uparrow^x_m = ((M\!\uparrow^x_m)\ (N\!\uparrow^x_m))$$
$$n\!\uparrow^x_m = n, \qquad \text{if } n < m \qquad \lambda.M\!\uparrow^x_m = \lambda.(M\!\uparrow^x_{m+1})$$

Using the $\uparrow$ function for index adjustments, the notions of reduction are:

$$(\lambda.E[n])\ V \ \textbf{need}\ (\lambda.E[V\!\uparrow^{\Delta(E)+1}_0])\ V, \ \text{ if } \Delta(E) = n \qquad\qquad deref$$

$$(\lambda.A[V])\ M\ N \ \textbf{need}\ (\lambda.A[V\ (N\!\uparrow^{\Delta(A)+1}_0)])\ M \qquad\qquad assoc\text{-}L$$

$$(\lambda.E[n])\ ((\lambda.A[V])\ M) \ \textbf{need}\ (\lambda.A[((\lambda.E[n])\!\uparrow^{\Delta(A)+1}_0)\ V])\ M, \ \text{ if } \Delta(E) = n$$
$$assoc\text{-}R$$

It is acceptable to apply the Δ function to A because A is a subset of E.

3   Standard Reduction Machine

In order to derive an abstract machine from the by-need λ-calculus, Ariola and Felleisen prove a Curry-Feys-style Standardization Theorem. Roughly, the theorem states that a term M reduces to a term N in a canonical manner if M reduces to N in the by-need calculus.

The theorem thus determines a state machine for reducing programs to answers. The initial state of the machine is the program, the collection of states is all possible programs, and the final states are answers. Transitions in the state machine are equivalent to reductions in the calculus:

$$E[M] \longmapsto_{\textbf{need}} E[M'], \text{ if } M \ \textbf{need}\ M'$$

where E represents the same evaluation contexts that are used to define the demand-driven substitution of variables in the $deref$ notion of reduction.

The machine is deterministic because all programs M satisfy the unique decomposition property. This means that M is either an answer or can be uniquely decomposed into an evaluation context and a redex. Hence, we can use the state machine transitions to define an evaluator function:

$$\texttt{eval}_{\textbf{need}}(M) = \begin{cases} a, & \text{if } M \longmapsto\!\!\!\!\!\twoheadrightarrow_{\textbf{need}} a \\ \bot, & \text{if for all } M \longmapsto\!\!\!\!\!\twoheadrightarrow_{\textbf{need}} N, \ N \longmapsto_{\textbf{need}} L \end{cases}$$

Lemma 1. $eval_{need}$ *is a total function.*

Proof. The lemma follows from the standard reduction theorem [2]. $\square$

4   The CK+ Machine

A standard reduction machine specifies evaluation steps at a high-level of abstraction. Specifically, at each evaluation step in the machine, the entire program is partitioned into an evaluation context and a redex. This repeated partitioning is inefficient because the evaluation context at any given evaluation step tends to share a large common prefix with the evaluation context in the previous step. To eliminate this inefficiency, Felleisen and Friedman propose the CK machine [6, Chapter 6], an implementation for a standard reduction machine of a call-by-value language. Consider the following call-by-value evaluation:

$$((\lambda w.w) \; \underline{((\lambda x.(x \; ((\lambda y.y) \; \lambda z.z))) \; \lambda x.x)})$$
$$\longmapsto_v ((\lambda w.w) \; ((\lambda x.x) \; \underline{((\lambda y.y) \; \lambda z.z)}))$$
$$\longmapsto_v ((\lambda w.w) \; \underline{((\lambda x.x) \; \lambda z.z)})$$
$$\longmapsto_v \underline{((\lambda w.w) \; \lambda z.z)}$$
$$\longmapsto_v \lambda z.z$$

In each step, the β_v redex is underlined. The evaluation contexts for the first and third term are the same, $((\lambda w.w) \; [\;])$, and it is contained in the evaluation context for the second term, $((\lambda w.w) \; ((\lambda x.x) \; [\;]))$. Although the evaluation contexts in the first three terms have repeated parts, a standard reduction machine for the call-by-value calculus must re-partition the program at each evaluation step.

The CK machine improves upon the standard reduction machine for the by-value λ-calculus by eliminating redundant search steps. While the standard reduction machine uses whole programs as machine states, a state in the CK machine is divided into separate subterm (C) and evaluation context (K) registers. More precisely, the C in the CK machine represents a control string, i.e., the subterm to be evaluated, and the K is a continuation, which is a data structure that represents an evaluation context in an "inside-out" manner. The original program can be reconstructed from a CK machine state by "plugging" the expression in the C subterm register into the context represented by K. When the control string is a redex, the CK machine can perform a reduction, just like the standard reduction machine. Unlike the standard reduction machine though, the CK machine still remembers the previous evaluation context in the context register and can therefore resume the search for the next redex from the contractum in C and the evaluation context in K.

4.1   CK+ Machine States

We introduce the CK+ machine, a variant of the CK machine, for the by-need λ-calculus. The CK+ machine is also a modification of the abstract machine of Garcia et al. [3]. The machine states for the CK+ machine are specified in figure 1. The core CK+ machine has three main registers, a control string (C), a "renaming" environment (R), and a continuation stack ($\bar{K}$).

In figure 1, the ... notation means "zero or more of the preceding element" and in the stack $\|k, \; K, \; \ldots\|$, the partial stack frame k is the top of the stack. The initial CK+ machine state is $\langle M, (\;), \|\mathtt{mt}\| \rangle$, where M is the given program, $(\;)$ is an empty renaming environment, and $\|\mathtt{mt}\|$ is a stack with just one element, an empty frame.

$$
\begin{array}{llr}
S, T ::= \langle C, R, \bar{K} \rangle & & \text{machine states} \\
C ::= M & & \text{control strings} \\
R ::= (i, \ldots) & & \text{renaming environments} \\
i \in \mathbb{N} & & \text{offsets} \\
\bar{K} ::= \| k, \ K, \ \ldots \| & & \text{continuation stacks} \\
K ::= (\text{bind } M \ R \ k) & & \text{complete stack frames} \\
k ::= \text{mt} \mid (\text{arg } M \ R \ k) \mid (\text{op } \bar{K} \ k) & & \text{partial stack frames}
\end{array}
$$

Fig. 1. CK+ machine states

4.2   Renaming Environment

As mentioned in section 2, substitution requires some form of renaming, which manifests itself as lexical address adjustments when using a de Bruijn representation of terms. Instead of adjusting addresses directly, the CK+ machine delays the adjustment by keeping track of offsets for all free variables in the control string in a separate *renaming environment*. The delayed renaming is forced when a variable occurrence is evaluated, at which point the offset is added to the variable before it is used to retrieve its value from the control stack.

Here we use lists for renaming environments and the offset corresponding to variable n, denoted $R(n)$, is the n-th element in R (0-based). The : function is cons, and the function $M{\Leftarrow}R$ applies a renaming environment R to a term M, yielding a term like M except with appropriately adjusted lexical addresses:

$$
\begin{aligned}
M{\Leftarrow}(\ ) &= M \\
n{\Leftarrow}R &= n + R(n) \\
(\lambda.M){\Leftarrow}R &= \lambda.(M{\Leftarrow}(0{:}R)) \\
(M \ N){\Leftarrow}R &= ((M{\Leftarrow}R) \ (N{\Leftarrow}R))
\end{aligned}
$$

Because the CK+ machine uses renaming environments, the $\uparrow$ function from section 2 is replaced with an operation on R. When the machine needs to increment all free variables in a term, it uses the $\oplus$ function to increment all offsets in the renaming environment that accompanies the term. The notation $R{\oplus}x$ means that all offsets in renaming environment R are incremented by x. Thus, the use of indices in place of variables enables hygiene maintenance through simple incrementing and decrementing of the indices. As a result, we have eliminated the need to keep track of the "active variables" that are present in Garcia et al.'s machine [3, Section 4.5].

4.3   Continuations and the Continuation Stack

Like the CK machine, the CK+ machine represents evaluation contexts as continuations. The [ ] context is represented by the mt continuation. An evaluation context $E[([\ ]\ N)]$ is represented by a continuation $(\text{arg } M\ R\ k)$ where k represents E and $(M{\Leftarrow}R) = N$. An evaluation context $E[(\lambda.[\ ])\ N]$ is represented by a continuation $(\text{bind } M\ R\ k)$ where k represents E and $(M{\Leftarrow}R) = N$. Finally, the $E[(\lambda.E'[n])\ [\ ]]$ context is represented by an $(\text{op } \bar{K}\ k)$ continuation. The E' under the λ in the evaluation context is represented by the nested $\bar{K}$ stack in the continuation and the E surrounding the evaluation context corresponds to the k in the continuation. The op continuation does not need to remember the n variable in the evaluation context because the variable can be derived from the length of $\bar{K}$.

The contents of the $\bar{K}$ register represent the control stack of the program and we refer to an element of this stack as a frame. The key difference between the CK+ machine and Garcia et al.'s machine is in the organization of the frames of the stack. Instead of a flat list of frames like in Garcia et al.'s machine, our control stack frames are groups of nested continuations of a special shape. Thus we also call our control stack a "continuation stack." We use two kinds of frames, partial and complete. The first frame in the continuation stack is always a partial one, while all others are complete. The outermost continuation of a complete frame is a bind and all other nested pieces of a complete frame are op, arg, or mt. Thus, not counting the first partial frame, there is exactly one frame in the control stack for every bind continuation in the program. As a result, the machine can use a variable (lexical address) n to find the bind corresponding to that variable in the control stack.

4.4   Maintaining the Continuation Stack

Each frame of the control stack, with the exception of the top frame, has the shape $(\text{bind } M\ R\ k)$, where k is a partial frame that contains no additional bind frames. In order for the continuation stack to maintain this invariant, CK+ machine transitions must adhere to two conditions:

1. When a machine transition is executed, only the top partial frame of the stack is updated unless the instruction descends under a λ.
2. If a machine transition descends under a λ, the partial frame on top of the stack is completed and a new mt partial frame is pushed onto the stack.

Essentially, the top frame in the stack "accumulates context" until a λ is encountered, at which time the top partial frame becomes a complete frame. Maintaining evaluation contexts for the program in this way implies a major consequence for the CK+ machine:

when the control string is a variable n, then the binding for n is $(n + R(n) + 1)$ stack frames away.

4.5   Relating Machine States to Terms

Figure 2 defines the φ function, which converts machine states to λ-terms. It uses the $M{\Leftarrow}R$ function to apply the renaming environment to the control string and

$$\|k, \ K, \ \ldots\| [M] = \ldots [K[k[M]]]$$

$$\varphi(\langle M, R, \bar{K}\rangle) = \bar{K}[M{\Leftarrow}R]$$

$$\mathtt{mt}[M] = M$$
$$(\mathtt{arg} \ N \ R \ k)[M] = k[(M \ (N{\Leftarrow}R))]$$
$$(\mathtt{op} \ \bar{K} \ k)[M] = k[(\lambda.\bar{K}[\mathtt{len}(\bar{K}) - 1]) \ M]$$
$$(\mathtt{bind} \ N \ R \ k)[M] = k[(\lambda.M) \ (N{\Leftarrow}R)]$$

Fig. 2. φ converts CK+ machine states to λ-calculus terms

then uses a family of "plug" functions, dubbed $\cdot[\cdot]$, to plug the renamed control string into the hole of the context represented by the continuation component of the state. Figure 2 also defines these plug functions, where $K[M]$ yields the term obtained by plugging M into the context represented by K, and $\bar{K}[M]$ yields the term when M is plugged into the context represented by the continuation stack $\bar{K}$.

4.6   CK+ Machine State Transitions

Figure 3 shows the first four state transitions for the CK+ machine. The ++ notation indicates an "append" operation for the continuation stack. Since the purpose of the CK+ machine is to remember intermediate states in the search for a redex, three of the first four rules are search rules. They shift pieces of the control string to the $\bar{K}$ register. For example, the [shift-arg] transition shifts the argument of an application to the $\bar{K}$ register.

The [descend-λ] transition shifts a λ binding to the $\bar{K}$ register. When the control string in the CK+ machine is a λ abstraction, and that λ is the operator

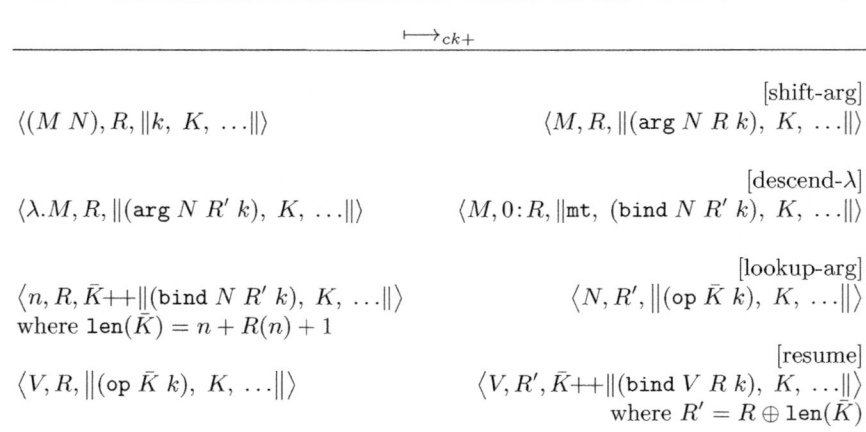

Fig. 3. State transitions for the CK+ machine

in an application term—indicated by an `arg` frame on top of the stack—the body of the λ becomes the control string; the top frame in the stack is updated to be a complete `bind` frame; and a new partial `mt` frame is pushed onto the stack.

The [descend-λ] instruction also updates the renaming environment which, as mentioned, is a list of numbers. There is one offset in the renaming environment for each `bind` continuation in the control stack and the offsets in the renaming environment appear in the same order as their corresponding `bind` continuations. When the machine descends into a λ expression, a new `bind` continuation is added to the top of the control stack so a new corresponding offset is also added to the front of the renaming environment. Since offsets are only added to the renaming environment when the machine goes under a λ, whenever a variable n (a lexical address) becomes the control string, its renaming offset is located at the n-th position in the renaming environment. A renaming offset keeps track of the relative position of a `bind` continuation since it was added to the control stack so a [descend-λ] instruction adds a 0 offset to the renaming environment.

When the control string is a variable n, the binding for n is accessed from the continuation stack by accessing the $(n + R(n) + 1)$-th frame in the stack. The [lookup-arg] instruction moves the argument that is bound to the variable into the control string register. The `op` frame on top of the stack is updated to store all the frames inside the binding λ, in the same order that they appear in the stack. Using this strategy, the machine can "jump" back to this context after it is done evaluating the argument. For a term $(\lambda.E[n])\ M$, this is equivalent to evaluating M while saving E and then returning to the location of n after the argument M has been evaluated. Note that the [lookup-arg] transition does not perform substitution. The argument has been copied into the control string register, but it has also been removed from the continuation stack register.

When the frame on top of the stack is an `op`, it means the current control string is an argument in an application term. When that argument is a value, then a redex has been found and the value should be substituted for the variable that represents it. The [resume] rule is the only rule in figure 3 that performs a reduction in the sense of the by-need calculus. It is the implementation of the *deref* notion of reduction from the calculus. Specifically, the [resume] rule realizes this substitution by restoring the frames in the `op` frame back into the continuation stack as well as copying the value into a new `bind` frame. The result is nearly equivalent to the left hand side of the [lookup-arg] rule except that the argument has been evaluated and has been substituted for the variable.

Since the [resume] rule performs substitution, it must also update the renaming environment. Hence, the distance between V and its binding frame is added to every offset in the renaming environment R, as indicated by $R \oplus \text{len}(\bar{K})$. In other words, each offset in the environment is being incremented by the number of `bind` continuations that are added to the control stack.

In summary, the four rules of figure 3 represent intermediate partitions of the program into a subterm and an evaluation context before a partitioning of the program into an evaluation context and a *deref* redex is found. As a result, the CK+ machine does not need to repartition the entire program on every machine step and is therefore more efficient than standard reduction. To complete the machine now, we must make it deal with answers.

4.7   Dealing with Answers

The CK+ machine described so far has no mechanism to identify whether a control string represents an answer. The by-need calculus, however, assumes that it is possible to distinguish answers from terms on several occasions, one of which is the completion of evaluation. To efficiently identify answers, the CK+ machine uses a fourth "answer" register. The CK+ machine identifies answers by searching the continuation stack for frames that are answer contexts. To distinguish answer contexts from evaluation contexts, we characterize answer contexts in figure 4. A final machine state has the form $\langle V, R, \| \, \| , \bar{A} \rangle$.

$$S, T ::= \langle C, R, \bar{K} \rangle \mid \langle V, R, \| F, \, \ldots, \, K, \, \ldots \| , \bar{A} \rangle \qquad \text{machine states}$$
$$F ::= (\texttt{bind } M \ R \ \texttt{mt}) \qquad \text{answer (complete) frame}$$
$$\bar{A} ::= \| \texttt{mt}, \ F, \, \ldots \| \qquad \text{answer stacks}$$

Fig. 4. CK+ machine answer states

When the control string is a value V and $\texttt{mt}$ is the topmost stack frame, then some subterm in the program is an answer. In this situation, the $\texttt{mt}$ frame in the stack is followed by an arbitrary number of F frames. The machine searches for the answer by shifting $\texttt{mt}$ and F frames from the continuation stack register to the answer register. The machine continues searching until either a K frame is seen or the end of the continuation stack is reached. If the end of the continuation stack is reached, the entire term is an answer and evaluation is complete.

The presence of a K frame means an *assoc-L* or an *assoc-R* redex has been found. In order to implement these shifts, the CK+ machine requires four additional rules for handling answers, as shown in figure 5. The [ans-search1] rule shifts the $\texttt{mt}$ frame to the answer register. The [ans-search2] rule shifts F frames to the answer register. The [assoc-L] rule and the [assoc-R] rule roughly correspond to the *assoc-L* and *assoc-R* notions of reduction in the calculus, respectively. The rules are optimized versions of corresponding notions of reduction in the calculus because the transition after the reduction is always known. The [assoc-L] machine rule performs the equivalent of an *assoc-L* reduction in the calculus, followed by a [descend-λ] machine transition. The [assoc-R] machine rule performs the equivalent of an *assoc-R* reduction in the calculus, followed by a [resume] machine transition.

In figure 5, the function $\oplus$ has been extended to a family of functions defined over renaming environments, continuation stacks, and stack frames: $R \oplus x$ increments every offset in the renaming environment R by x and the function $\bar{K} \oplus x$ increments every offset in every renaming environment in every frame in

---

$$\longmapsto_{ck+}$$

[ans-search1]

$\langle V, R, \|\texttt{mt}, K, \ldots \| \rangle$ $\langle V, R, \| K, \ldots \|, \|\texttt{mt}\| \rangle$

[ans-search2]

$\langle V, R, \| F', K, \ldots \|, \|\texttt{mt}, F, \ldots \| \rangle$ $\langle V, R, \| K, \ldots \|, \|\texttt{mt}, F, \ldots, F' \| \rangle$

[assoc-L]

$\langle \lambda.M', R, \| (\texttt{bind } M \ R' \ (\texttt{arg } N \ R'' \ k)), K, \ldots \|, \|\texttt{mt}, F, \ldots \| \rangle$

$$\langle M', 0{:}R, \|\texttt{mt}, (\texttt{bind } N \ R''' \ \texttt{mt}), F, \ldots, (\texttt{bind } M \ R' \ k), K, \ldots \| \rangle$$
$$\text{where } R''' = R'' \oplus \texttt{len}(\| F, \ldots \|) + 1$$

[assoc-R]

$\langle V, R, \| (\texttt{bind } M \ R' \ (\texttt{op } \bar{K} \ k)), K, \ldots \|, \|\texttt{mt}, F, \ldots \| \rangle$

$$\langle V, R'', \bar{K}' {+}{+} \| (\texttt{bind } V \ R \ \texttt{mt}), F, \ldots \ (\texttt{bind } M \ R' \ k), K, \ldots \| \rangle$$
$$\text{where } \bar{K}' = \bar{K} \oplus \texttt{len}(\| F, \ldots \|) + 1, \text{ and } R'' = R \oplus \texttt{len}(\bar{K}')$$

Fig. 5. Transitions of the CK+ machine that handle answer terms

$\bar{K}$ by x. The function $\texttt{len}(\| F, \ldots \|)$ returns the number of frames in $\| F, \ldots \|$. Maintaining the offsets in this manner is equivalent to obeying Garcia et al.'s "well-formedness" condition on machine states.

4.8 Correctness

Correctness means that the standard reduction machine and the CK+ machine define the same evaluator functions. Let us start with an appropriate definition for the CK+ machine:

$$\texttt{eval}_{ck+}(M) = \begin{cases} a, & \text{if } \langle M, (\,), \|\texttt{mt}\| \rangle \longmapsto_{ck+} \langle V, R, \| \ \|, \bar{A} \rangle, \\ & \text{where } a = \varphi(\langle V, R, \| \ \|, \bar{A} \rangle) \\ \bot, & \text{if for all } \langle M, (\,), \|\texttt{mt}\| \rangle \longmapsto_{ck+} S, S \longmapsto_{ck+} T \end{cases}$$

Recall that the function φ converts CK+ machine states to λ-calculus terms (figure 2). Here, φ has been extended to handle "answer" machine states:

$$\varphi(\langle M, R, \bar{K}, \bar{A} \rangle) = \bar{K}[\bar{A}[M \Leftarrow R]]$$

The desired theorem says that the two $\texttt{eval}$ functions are equal.

Theorem 1. $eval_{need} = eval_{ck+}$.

To prove the theorem, we first establish some auxiliary lemmas on the totality of $eval_{ck+}$ and the relation between CK+ transitions and standard reduction transitions.

Lemma 2. $eval_{ck+}$ is a total function.

Proof. The lemma is proved via a subject reduction argument. □

The central lemma uses φ to relate CK+ machine transitions to reductions.

Lemma 3. *For all CK+ machine states S and T, if $S \longmapsto_{ck+} T$, then either $\varphi(S) \longmapsto_{need} \varphi(T)$ or $\varphi(S) = \varphi(T)$.*

Proof. We proceed by case analysis on each machine transition, starting with [resume]. Assume

$$\langle V, R, \|(\text{op } \bar{K} \ k), \ K, \ \dots\|\rangle \longmapsto_{ck+}$$
$$\langle V, R \oplus \text{len}(\bar{K}), \bar{K}{+}{+}\|(\text{bind } V \ R \ k), \ K, \ \dots\|\rangle \ ,$$

then let

$$M_1 = \varphi(\langle V, R, \|(\text{op } \bar{K} \ k), \ K, \ \dots\|\rangle)$$
$$= \|K, \ \dots\| \ [k[(\lambda.\bar{K}[\text{len}(\bar{K}) - 1]) \ (V{\Leftarrow}R)]]$$
$$M_2 = \varphi(\langle V, R \oplus \text{len}(\bar{K}), \bar{K}{+}{+}\|(\text{bind } V \ R \ k), \ K, \ \dots\|\rangle)$$
$$= \|K, \ \dots\| \ [k[(\lambda.\bar{K}[V{\Leftarrow}(R \oplus \text{len}(\bar{K}))]) \ (V{\Leftarrow}R)]] \ .$$

Since M_1 is a standard *deref* redex, we have:

$$\|K, \ \dots\| \ [k[(\lambda.\bar{K}[\text{len}(\bar{K}) - 1]) \ (V{\Leftarrow}R)]] \longmapsto_{need}$$
$$\|K, \ \dots\| \ [k[(\lambda.\bar{K}[(V{\Leftarrow}R){\uparrow}_0^{\text{len}(\bar{K})}]) \ (V{\Leftarrow}R)]]$$

To conclude that $M_1 \longmapsto_{need} M_2$ by the *deref* notion of reduction, we need to show:
$$(V{\Leftarrow}R){\uparrow}_0^{\text{len}(\bar{K})} = V{\Leftarrow}(R \oplus \text{len}(\bar{K}))$$

Lemma 4 proves the general case for this requirement. Therefore, we can conclude that $M_1 \longmapsto_{need} M_2$. The proofs for [assoc-L] and [assoc-R] are similar.

As for the remaining instructions, they only shift subterms/contexts back and forth between registers, so the proof is a straightforward calculation. □

Lemma 4. $\forall R, R_1, R_2$, *where $R = R_1{+}{+}R_2$ and $m = len(R_1)$:*

$$(M{\Leftarrow}R){\uparrow}_m^x = M{\Leftarrow}(R_1{+}{+}(R_2 \oplus x))$$

Proof. By structural induction on M. □

Using lemma 3, the argument to prove our main theorem is straightforward.

Proof (of Theorem 1). We show $\text{eval}_{ck+}(M) = a \iff \text{eval}_{\text{need}}(M) = a$.

The left-to-right direction follows from the observation that for all CK+ machine starting states S and final machine states S_{final}, if $S \longmapsto\!\!\!\twoheadrightarrow_{ck+} S_{final}$, then $M \longmapsto\!\!\!\twoheadrightarrow_{\text{need}} a$, where $\varphi(S_{final}) = a$. This is proved using lemma 3 and induction on the length of the $\longmapsto\!\!\!\twoheadrightarrow_{ck+}$ sequence.

The other direction is proved by contradiction. Assume $\text{eval}_{\text{need}}(M) = a \neq \bot$ and $\text{eval}_{ck+}(M) \neq a$. Since eval_{ck+} is a total function, either:

1. $\langle M, (\ ), \|\text{mt}\| \rangle \longmapsto\!\!\!\twoheadrightarrow_{ck+} S_{final}$, where $\varphi(S_{final}) \neq a$, or
2. the reduction of $\langle M, (\ ), \|\text{mt}\| \rangle$ diverges.

It follows from the left-to-right direction of the theorem that, in the first case, $\text{eval}_{\text{need}}(M) = \varphi(S_{final}) \neq a$, and in the second case, $\text{eval}_{\text{need}}(M) = \bot$. However, $\text{eval}_{\text{need}}(M) = a$ was assumed and $\text{eval}_{\text{need}}$ is a total function, so a contradiction has been reached in both cases. Since none of the cases are possible, we conclude that if $\text{eval}_{\text{need}}(M) = a$, then $\text{eval}_{ck+}(M) = a$.   □

5   Stack Compacting

Because the by-need λ-calculus does not substitute the argument of a function call for all occurrences of the parameter at once, applications are never removed. In the CK+ machine, arguments accumulate on the stack and remain there forever. For a finite machine, an ever-growing stack is a problem. In this section, we explain how to compact the stack.

To implement a stack compaction algorithm in the CK+ machine, we introduce a separate SC machine which removes all unused stack bindings from a CK+ machine state. Based on the SC machine, the CK+ machine can be equipped with a non-deterministic [sc] transition:

$$\langle M, R, \bar{K} \rangle \longmapsto_{ck+} \langle M, R', \bar{K}' \rangle \qquad \text{[sc]}$$
$$\text{where } \langle (\text{FV } M\ R\ 0), (M, R), \bar{K}, \|\ \|\rangle \longmapsto\!\!\!\twoheadrightarrow_{sc} \langle \mathcal{F}, (M, R'), \|\ \|, \bar{K}' \rangle$$

Figure 6 presents the SC machine. In this figure, **FV** refers to a family of functions that extracts the set of free variables from terms, stack frames, and continuation stacks. The function **FV** takes a term M, a renaming environment R and a variable m, and extracts free variables from M, where a free variable is defined to be all n such that $n + R(n) \geq m$. The function **FV** is similarly defined for stack frames and continuation stacks. In addition, $\mathcal{F}-\!-$ denotes the set obtained by decrementing every element in $\mathcal{F}$ by one. Finally, $\bar{K}@k$ represents a frame merged appropriately into a continuation stack. For example, $\|k', K, \ldots, (\text{bind } M\ R\ k'')\| @k = \|k', K, \ldots, (\text{bind } M\ R\ k'')@k\|$, where $(\text{bind } M\ R\ k'')@k = (\text{bind } M\ R\ k''@k)$, and so on, until finally $\text{mt}@k = k$.

Also in figure 6, $\uparrow\uparrow$ denotes a family of functions that adjusts the offsets in renaming environments to account for the fact that a λ has been removed from the term. If a variable n refers to a **bind** stack frame that is deeper in the stack than the frame that is removed, then the offset for that variable needs to

$$S_{sc} ::= \langle \mathcal{F}, (M, R), \bar{\mathcal{K}}, \bar{\mathcal{K}} \rangle \qquad \text{machine states}$$
$$\mathcal{F} ::= \{n, \ldots\} \qquad \text{set of free variables}$$
$$\bar{\mathcal{K}} ::= \|k,\ K,\ \ldots\| \ \mid \ \|K,\ \ldots\| \qquad \text{partial stacks}$$

$$\longmapsto_{sc}$$

[shift-partial-frame]
$$\langle \mathcal{F}, (M, R), \|k,\ K,\ \ldots\|, \| \ \| \rangle \qquad \langle \mathcal{F} \cup (\mathbf{FV}\ k\ 0), (M, R), \|K,\ \ldots\|, \|k\| \rangle$$

[shift-complete-frame]
$$\langle \mathcal{F}, (M, R), \|K',\ K,\ \ldots\|, \|k,\ K'',\ \ldots\| \rangle \quad \langle \mathcal{F}', (M, R), \|K,\ \ldots\|, \|k,\ K'',\ \ldots,\ K'\| \rangle$$
$$0 \in \mathcal{F} \qquad\qquad\qquad \text{where } \mathcal{F}' = (\mathcal{F}\text{--}) \cup (\mathbf{FV}\ K'\ 0)$$

[pop-frame]
$$\langle \mathcal{F}, (M, R), \|(\mathtt{bind}\ M\ R\ k),\ K,\ \ldots\|, \bar{K} \rangle \qquad \langle \mathcal{F}\text{--}, (M, R'), \|K,\ \ldots\|, \bar{K}'@k \rangle$$
$$0 \notin \mathcal{F} \qquad\qquad\qquad \text{where } R' = (M, R){\uparrow}{\uparrow}^{-1}_{\mathtt{len}(\bar{K})-1}$$
$$\text{and } \bar{K}' = \bar{K}{\uparrow}{\uparrow}^{-1}_{\mathtt{len}(\bar{K})-1}$$

Fig. 6. The SC machine

be decremented by one. A variable n refers to a $\mathtt{bind}$ that is deeper than the removed frame if $n + R(n)$ is greater than the depth of the removed frame. The ${\uparrow}{\uparrow}$ function can be applied to renaming environments directly or to continuation stacks or stack frames that contain renaming environments. We use the notation $(M, R){\uparrow}{\uparrow}^x_\ell$ to mean that the offsets in R are incremented by x for all variables n in M where $n + R(n) > \ell$. The result of $(M, R){\uparrow}{\uparrow}^x_\ell$ is a new renaming environment with the adjusted offsets. The notation $\bar{K}{\uparrow}{\uparrow}^x_\ell$ means that the offsets for all M and R pairs in the continuation stack $\bar{K}$ are adjusted. $\bar{K}{\uparrow}{\uparrow}^x_\ell$ evaluates to a new continuation stack that contains the adjusted renaming environments.

6   Related Work and Conclusion

The call-by-need calculus is due to Ariola et al. [2,7,8]. Garcia et al. [3] derive an abstract machine for Ariola and Felleisen's calculus and, in the process, uncover a correspondence between the by-need calculus and delimited control operations. Danvy et al. [9] derive a machine similar to Garcia et al. by applying "off-the-shelf" transformations to the by-need calculus. Danvy and Zerny's def-use chains also share similarities with our control stack structure [10].

Our paper has focused on the binding structure of call-by-need programs implied by Ariola and Felleisen's calculus. We have presented the CK+ machine, which restructures the control stack of Garcia et al.'s machine, and we have shown that lexical addresses can be used to directly access binding sites for variables in this dynamic control stack, a first in the history of programming languages. The use of lexical addresses has also simplified hygiene maintenance by eliminating the need for the set of "active variables" that is present in Garcia et al.'s machine states. In addition, we show how using indices in place of variables allows for simple maintenance of Garcia et al.'s "well-formed" machine states. Finally, we have presented a stack compaction algorithm, which is used in the CK+ machine to prevent stack overflow. The compaction algorithm used in this paper is a restriction of the more general garbage collection notion of reduction of Felleisen and Hieb [11] and is also reminiscent of Kelsey's work [12].

Acknowledgments. Thanks to the anonymous reviewers for their feedback and to Daniel Brown for inspiring discussions.

References

1. Plotkin, G.D.: Call-by-name, call-by-value and the λ-calculus. Theoretical Computer Science 1, 125–159 (1975)
2. Ariola, Z.M., Felleisen, M.: The call-by-need lambda calculus. Journal of Functional Programming 7, 265–301 (1997)
3. Garcia, R., Lumsdaine, A., Sabry, A.: Lazy evaluation and delimited control. In: Proceedings of the 36th Annual Symposium on Principles of Programming Languages, pp. 153–164. ACM, New York (2009)
4. Barendregt, H.P.: The Lambda Calculus: Its Syntax and Semantics. North Holland, Amsterdam (1981)
5. De Bruijn, N.G.: Lambda calculus notation with nameless dummies, a tool for automatic formula manipulation, with application to the Church-Rosser theorem. Indagationes Mathematicae, 381–392 (1972)
6. Felleisen, M., Findler, R.B., Flatt, M.: Semantics Engineering with PLT Redex. MIT Press, Cambridge (2009)
7. Ariola, Z.M., Felleisen, M., Maraist, J., Odersky, M., Wadler, P.: The call-by-need lambda calculus. In: Proceedings of the 22nd Annual Symposium on Principles on Programming Languages, pp. 233–246 (1995)
8. Maraist, J., Odersky, M., Wadler, P.: The call-by-need lambda calculus. Journal of Functional Programming 8, 275–317 (1998)
9. Danvy, O., Millikin, K., Munk, J., Zerny, I.: Defunctionalized interpreters for call-by-need evaluation. In: Blume, M., Kobayashi, N., Vidal, G. (eds.) FLOPS 2010. LNCS, vol. 6009, pp. 240–256. Springer, Heidelberg (2010)
10. Danvy, O., Zerny, I.: Three syntactic theories for combinatory graph reduction. In: Alpuente, M. (ed.) 20th International Symposium on Logic-Based Program Synthesis and Transformation (2010) (invited talk)
11. Felleisen, M., Hieb, R.: The revised report on the syntactic theories of sequential control and state. Theoretical Computer Science 103, 235–271 (1992)
12. Kelsey, R.: Tail-recursive stack disciplines for an interpreter. Technical Report NU-CCS-93-03, Northeastern University (1993)

Typing Coroutines

Konrad Anton and Peter Thiemann

Institut für Informatik, Universität Freiburg, Germany
{anton,thiemann}@informatik.uni-freiburg.de

Abstract. A coroutine is a programming construct between function
and thread. It behaves like a function that can suspend itself arbitrarily
often to yield intermediate results and to get new inputs before returning a result. This facility makes coroutines suitable for implementing
generator abstractions.

Languages that support coroutines are often untyped or they use
trivial types for coroutines. This work supplies the first type system
with dedicated support for coroutines. The type system is based on the
simply-typed lambda calculus extended with effects that describe control
transfers between coroutines.

1 Introduction

A coroutine is a programming construct between function and thread. It can be
invoked like a function, but before it returns a value (if ever) it may suspend
itself arbitrarily often to return intermediate results and then be resumed with
new inputs. Unlike with preemptive threading, a coroutine does not run concur-
rently with the rest of the program, but rather takes control until it voluntarily
suspends to either return control to its caller or to pass control to another coroutine. Coroutines are closely related to cooperative threading, but they add value
because they are capable of passing values into and out of the coroutine and
they permit explicit switching of control.

Coroutines were invented in the 1960s as a means for structuring a compiler
[4]. They have received a lot of attention in the programming community and
have been integrated into a number of programming languages, for instance in
Simula 67 [5], BETA, CLU [11], Modula-2 [19], Python [17], and Lua [15], and
Knuth finds them convenient in the description of algorithms [8]. Coroutines are
also straightforward to implement in languages that offer first-class continuations
(e.g., Scheme [7]) or direct manipulation of the execution stack (e.g., assembly
language, Smalltalk).

The main uses of coroutines are the implementation of compositions of state
machines as in Conway's seminal paper [4] and the implementation of generators. A generator enumerates a potentially infinite set of values with successive
invocations. The latter use has led to renewed interest in coroutines and to
their inclusion in mainstream languages like C# [13], albeit in restricted form as
generators.

R. Page, Z. Horváth, and V. Zsók (Eds.): TFP 2010, LNCS 6546, pp. 16–30, 2011.

Despite the renewed interest in the programming construct per se, the typing aspects of coroutines have not received much attention. Indeed, the supporting languages are either untyped (e.g., Lua, Scheme, Python), the typing for coroutines is trivialized, or coroutines are restricted so that a very simple typing is sufficient. For instance, in Modula-2, coroutines are created from parameterless procedures so that all communication between coroutines must take place through global variables. Also, for describing generators, a simple function type seems sufficient.

Contribution. We propose a static type system for first-class, stackful coroutines that may be used in both, symmetric and asymmetric ways.[1] Moreover, we permit passing arguments to a coroutine at each start and resume operation, and we permit returning results on each suspend and on termination of the coroutine (and we distinguish between these two events). Our type system is based on the simply-typed lambda calculus. It includes an effect system that describes the way the coroutine operations are used. We present a small-step operational semantics for the language and prove type soundness.

Outline. Sec. 2 describes the language CorDuroy. It starts with some examples (Sec. 2.1) before delving into operational semantics (Sec. 2.2) and the type system (Sec. 2.3). Sec. 3 proves type soundness by establishing preservation and progress properties following the syntactic approach [20]. Sec. 4 discusses related work, and Sec. 5 concludes and outlines directions of further research.

2   CorDuroy

The language CorDuroy is a simply typed lambda calculus with recursive functions and operations for handling coroutines. Fig. 1 specifies the syntax; labels ℓ only occur at run time. We define λ-abstraction as sugar for the fixpoint operator: $\lambda x.e := \text{fix } \lambda\_.\lambda x.e$.

Coroutines in CorDuroy are run-time entities identified by a label ℓ. The only way to create them is by applying the **create** operator to a function. Once a coroutine has been created, it can be executed. Unlike threads in a multi-threaded language, only one coroutine is active at any given time.

To activate a coroutine, there is a symmetric (**transfer**) and an asymmetric (**resume**) operator. The symmetric operator **transfer** suspends the currently executing coroutine and executes another[2]. The asymmetric operator **resume** builds

---

[1] This terminology is due to De Moura and Ierusalemschy [14]. A coroutine is *stackful*, if it can suspend inside nested function calls. Coroutines are *asymmetric* if coroutine activity is organized in a tree-like manner: each coroutine invocation or resumption always returns and yields to its caller. In contrast, *symmetric* coroutines can transfer control among each others without restrictions.

[2] We use the keywords established by De Moura and Ierusalemschy [14]. In Simula [5], transfer corresponds to the system procedure RESUME, whereas "asymmetric", yield and resume correspond to "semi-symmetric", DETACH and CALL, respectively.

$$v ::= k^0 \mid \text{fix } \lambda f.\lambda x.e \mid \ell$$

$$B ::= \text{Bool} \mid \text{Unit} \mid \ldots$$

$$e ::= k^n\, e_1 \ldots e_n \mid \text{fix } \lambda f.\lambda x.e$$

$$k^0 ::= \text{true} \mid \text{false} \mid \text{unit} \mid \ldots$$

$$\mid x \mid e\, e \mid \text{if } e \text{ then } e \text{ else } e$$

$$k^1 ::= \neg \mid \ldots$$

$$\mid \text{create } x.e \mid \text{yield } e$$

$$k^2 ::= \wedge \mid \ldots$$

$$\mid \text{resume } e\, e\, e\, e \mid \text{transfer } e\, e$$

$$\ell, \ell', \ldots \in \text{Labels}$$

$$\mid \ell$$

$$x, y, f, \ldots \in \text{Var}$$

$$\varphi ::= \bot \mid \tau \overset{\cdot}{\leadsto} \tau / \tau \mid \top$$

$$\tau ::= B \mid \tau \xrightarrow{\varphi} \tau \mid \top \mid \bot \mid \tau \leadsto \tau / \tau$$

Fig. 1. Syntax

a caller-callee relationship: if a coroutine resumes another coroutine, they become caller and callee. The yield operator inside the callee suspends the coroutine and returns control to the caller. Each of the three operators passes a value. In the remaining paper, we understand "activate" to mean either transfer or resume, but not yield.

The caller-callee relationship is also used when a coroutine finally returns a value, as the value is then passed to the caller. Activating a coroutine after it has returned causes a run-time error; hence, the caller needs to know whether the callee coroutine has terminated. resume requires therefore as its third and fourth parameter two *result functions*, one to call with yielded values and one to call with the returned value[3].

The language includes a countable set of primitive functions k^n, having each an arity $n \geq 0$. Partial application of primitive functions is not allowed.

2.1 Examples

This section contains short examples of CorDuroy programs. We assume that integers and strings are among the basic types B and that there are constants k^n for arithmetic operations, comparison, and printing. We also use the common let $\cdot = \cdot$ in $\cdot$ sugar for readability.

Divisors. Generators can be used to compute sequences one element at a time. Fig. 2(a) shows a coroutine which generates the divisors of a number, and a consumer which iterates over the divisors until the generator returns (and the second result function of resume is called).

Mutable references. Coroutines are the only stateful construct in CorDuroy. In Fig. 2(b), a mutable reference is simulated by a coroutine which keeps an integer value in a local variable. Whenever it is resumed with a function Int → Int, it

---

[3] Alternatively, the λ-calculus could be extended with variant types in order to tag the result of resume with how it was obtained. We chose the two-continuation resume for simplicity.

```
 1  let divisors_of = λn.
 2    create _.λ_.
 3      ((fix λloop.λk.
 4        if (> k n) then unit
 5        else let rem = (mod n k) in
 6          let _= (if (= rem 0)
 7            then yield k else unit)
 8          in loop (+ k 1 )) 1)
 9  in let g = divisors_of 24 in
10    ((fix λf. λ_.
11      resume g unit
12        (λn. let _ = (print_int n)
13          in (f unit) )
14        (λ_. (print_str "finito")))
15      unit)
16  // output: 1 2 3 4 6 8 12 24 finito
          (a) Compute all divisors.
```

```
 1  let makeref = λx0.
 2    let main = fix λloop.λx.λupd.
 3      let x' = upd x in
 4      let upd' = yield x' in
 5        loop x' upd'
 6    in create _. main x0
 7  in let undef = fix λf.λx.(f x)
 8  in let write = λr.λv.
 9    resume r (λ_.v)
10      (λ_.unit) (λ_.unit)
11  in let read = λ r.
12    resume r (λx.x) (λx.x) undef
13  in
14    let r = makeref 1 in
15    let _ = print_int (read r) in
16    let _ = write r 2 in
17    print_int (read r)
18  // output: 1 2
          (b) Mutable references.
```

Fig. 2. Code examples

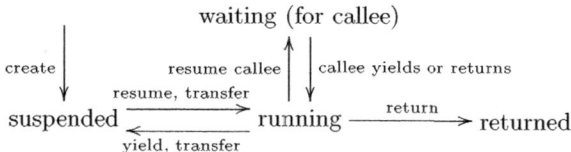

Fig. 3. Life cycle of coroutines

lets the function update the value and returns the new value. The example also shows how fix can be used to create a diverging function with any desired return type in the read function[4].

2.2 Operational Semantics

This section presents a small-step operational semantics for CorDuroy, starting with a life-cycle based view on coroutines to motivate the stack-based representation used in the reduction rules in Fig. 5.

The life cycle of a coroutine consists of the states *suspended*, *running*, *waiting* and *returned*, as shown in Fig. 3. At any moment, there is only one running coroutine.

The running coroutine can apply create to a function, creating a new coroutine which starts life in the suspended state (E-CREATE). It can also resume a

---

[4] The language could alternatively be extended with a special variant of the resume operator for coroutines which never return.

$$C ::= \Box \mid k^n \, v_1 \dots v_{i-1} \, C \, e_{i+1} \dots e_n \quad (1 \le i \le n)$$
$$\mid e \, C \mid C \, v \mid \text{if } C \text{ then } e \text{ else } e$$
$$\mid \text{resume } C \, e \, e \mid \text{resume } v \, C \, e \mid \text{resume } v \, v \, C \, e \mid \text{resume } v \, v \, v \, C$$
$$\mid \text{yield } C \mid \text{transfer } C \, e \mid \text{transfer } v \, C$$

$$S ::= \ell @ e; S^? \qquad \qquad \text{labels}(\ell @ e; S^?) = \{\ell\} \cup \text{labels}(S^?)$$
$$S^? ::= \epsilon \mid S \qquad \qquad \text{labels}(\epsilon) = \emptyset$$

Fig. 4. Evaluation contexts and stacks

$$\frac{n > 0}{\left\langle \ell @ C[k^n \, v_1 \dots v_n]; S^? \mid \mu \right\rangle \to \left\langle \ell @ C[[\![k^n]\!] \, (v_1, \dots, v_n)]; S^? \mid \mu \right\rangle} \text{ E-Const}$$

$$\left\langle \ell @ C[(\text{fix } \lambda f.\lambda x.e) \, v]; S^? \mid \mu \right\rangle \to \left\langle \ell @ C[e[f \mapsto \text{fix } \lambda f.\lambda x.e] \, [x \mapsto v]]; S^? \mid \mu \right\rangle \text{ E-Fix}$$

$$\left\langle \ell @ C[\text{if true then } e_t \text{ else } e_f]; S^? \mid \mu \right\rangle \to \left\langle \ell @ C[e_t]; S^? \mid \mu \right\rangle \text{ E-IfT}$$

$$\left\langle \ell @ C[\text{if false then } e_t \text{ else } e_f]; S^? \mid \mu \right\rangle \to \left\langle \ell @ C[e_f]; S^? \mid \mu \right\rangle \text{ E-IfF}$$

$$\frac{\begin{array}{c} x^* \notin \text{free}(e) \cup \{x\} \qquad \ell^* \notin \text{dom}(\mu) \cup \text{labels}(S^?) \cup \{\ell\} \\ v^* = \lambda x^*.((\lambda x.e \, x^*) \, \ell^*) \qquad \mu' = \mu \cup \{(\ell^*, v^*)\} \end{array}}{\left\langle \ell @ C[\text{create } x.e]; S^? \mid \mu \right\rangle \to \left\langle \ell @ C[\ell^*]; S^? \mid \mu' \right\rangle} \text{ E-Create}$$

$$\frac{\ell' \in \text{dom}(\mu) \qquad e = \text{resume } \ell' \, v_a \, v_s \, v_n}{\left\langle \ell @ C[e]; S^? \mid \mu \right\rangle \to \left\langle \ell' @ (\mu(\ell') \, v_a); \ell @ C[e]; S^? \mid \mu \setminus \ell' \right\rangle} \text{ E-Res}$$

$$\frac{x^* \text{ fresh} \qquad e_2 = \text{resume } \ell \, v_a \, v_s \, v_n}{\left\langle \ell_1 @ C_1[\text{yield } v_y]; \ell_2 @ C_2[e_2]; S^? \mid \mu \right\rangle \to \left\langle \ell_2 @ C_2[v_s \, v_y]; S^? \mid \mu[\ell_1 \mapsto \lambda x^*.C_1[x^*]] \right\rangle} \text{ E-Yie}$$

$$\left\langle \ell_1 @ v_r; \ell_2 @ C_2[\text{resume } \ell \, v_a \, v_s \, v_n]; S^? \mid \mu \right\rangle \to \left\langle \ell_2 @ C_2[v_n \, v_r]; S^? \mid \mu \right\rangle \text{ E-CoRet}$$

$$\left\langle \ell @ C[\text{transfer } \ell \, v_a]; S^? \mid \mu \right\rangle \to \left\langle \ell @ C[v_a]; S^? \mid \mu \right\rangle \text{ E-TraSelf}$$

$$\frac{\ell' \in \text{dom}(\mu) \qquad x^* \text{ fresh}}{\left\langle \ell @ C[\text{transfer } \ell' \, v]; S^? \mid \mu \right\rangle \to \left\langle \ell' @ (\mu(\ell') \, v); S^? \mid (\mu \setminus \ell') \cup \{(\ell, \lambda x^*.C[x^*])\} \right\rangle} \text{ E-Tra}$$

E-TraErr
$$\frac{\ell' \notin \text{dom}(\mu)}{\left\langle \ell @ C[\text{transfer } \ell' \, v_a] \mid \mu \right\rangle \to \text{Error}}$$

E-ResErr
$$\frac{\ell' \notin \text{dom}(\mu)}{\left\langle \ell @ C[\text{resume } \ell' \, v_a \, v_s \, v_n] \mid \mu \right\rangle \to \text{Error}}$$

Fig. 5. Small-step operational semantics rules

suspended coroutine (the *callee*), becoming its *caller* (E-RES). In doing so, it enters the *waiting* state, and the callee becomes *running*.

A running coroutine can also yield, after which it is *suspended* and the caller *running* (E-YIE). If a running coroutine reduces to a value, it is said to *return* that value. The returning coroutine enters its terminal state, and the value is then passed to the caller if there is one (E-CORET) or becomes the final result of the program.

Alternatively, the running coroutine can transfer control to a suspended coroutine, suspending itself. In this case, the successor coroutine not only enters the running state, but it also becomes the (only) callee of the predecessor's caller (E-TRA).

In the rules, the state of a program being evaluated is represented as a pair $\langle S \mid \mu \rangle$ of stack and store. The stack S contains, from left to right, the running coroutine, its caller, its caller's caller and so on, each in the form of labeled contexts $\ell @ e$ (see Fig. 4). As the running coroutine is the top of the stack, the reduction rules must never pop the last labeled context off the stack.

All suspended coroutines[5] are kept in the store μ, a function from labels ℓ to values v. The values in the store are the continuations of the yield and transfer expressions which caused the coroutine to be suspended, or, in the case of newly created coroutines, functions which are constructed to be applied likewise.

Coroutines in the returned state are neither in the stack nor in the store because they play no further role in the execution. The waiting and suspended states resemble each other in that neither state permits β-reductions.

The coroutine-related rules all maintain the invariant that a coroutine never rests in the stack and in the store simultaneously. Rule E-CREATE sets up a continuation v^* which makes the new label ℓ^* known under the name x inside the body expression e and passes the first input value to e. E-RES removes the stored continuation of the given coroutine from the store and applies it to the argument in a new labeled context on top of the stack. In the now-waiting coroutine, the resume expression remains, awaiting a result from the coroutine above. The third and fourth resume parameters are the result functions to be called later with yielded and returned values, respectively.

E-YIE and E-TRA put the continuation of the running coroutine into the store. While E-YIE passes the argument to the first of the two result functions of the caller, E-TRA sets up a new stack top in which the continuation from the store is applied to the argument, just like in E-RES. E-CORET passes the return value to the other result function in the caller and discards the callee. Of the resume expression in E-YIE and E-CORET, only the two result functions are used; the old label ℓ need not match the returning or yielding coroutine because the stack top may have been replaced in a transfer action.

If a coroutine attempts to activate another coroutine which is not in the store (i.e., not suspended), execution aborts with a run-time error (E-RESERR,

---

[5] An implementation would keep the coroutines within the store all the time and annotate them with their state instead; however, the notion of putting coroutines into the store and taking them out again makes the rules easier to read.

E-TraErr)[6]. As an exception to this rule, a coroutine may safely transfer to itself, e.g. in a multitasking system with just one ready task (E-TraSelf).

Rule E-Yie is only enabled if the stack contains a suitable waiting coroutine below; fortunately, the type system rejects all programs in which a yield expression could appear as a redex in the lowest labeled context.

There is no distinguished main program; the initial expression is also treated as a coroutine, except that it starts in the running state. In order to evaluate a CorDuroy program e, it is wrapped in an initial state with the fixed label ℓ_0:

$$\text{initState}(e) = \langle S_0 \mid \emptyset \rangle \quad S_0 = \ell_0 @ e; \epsilon \tag{1}$$

The function $\llbracket \cdot \rrbracket$ in E-Const maps primitive function symbols $k^n, n > 0$ to partial functions of the same arity. The notation $e[x \mapsto f]$ stands for standard capture-avoiding substitution which replaces all free occurrences of x in e by f. The set of free variables in e is free(e).

2.3   Type System

The type system ensures that values passed to and from coroutines do not cause type errors at run time, and that coroutine operations within the same coroutine body are compatible with each other. It is based on the simply-typed λ-calculus, with an effect system describing which coroutine actions may occur during the evaluation of an expression.

Effects. The effect part of the type and effect system summarizes the yield and transfer expressions which may be evaluated during the evaluation of an expression. The propagation of effects through function application permits a called function to yield and transfer on behalf of the running coroutine in a type-safe way.

If an expression has the effect $\tau_i \overset{\cdots}{\leadsto} \tau_o / \tau_r$, then its execution may yield a value of type τ_o to the calling coroutine and expect a value of type τ_i when it is activated again. It may also transfer execution to a coroutine which yields values of type τ_o or returns a value of type τ_r.

Effects φ form a lattice with bottom element $\bot$ and top element $\top$ (see Fig. 6). $\bot$ means that the expression will under no circumstance ever yield. Effect $\top$ means that yield expressions with different types are possible and nothing can be said about the values.

Types. The type system features basic types B, function types, coroutine types as well as top and bottom types.

---

[6] This class of runtime errors can be eliminated if E-Res and E-Tra leave the coroutine in the store. Then, activating a terminated or waiting coroutine would invoke (a copy of) the last stored continuation, similar to multi-shot continuations. We chose the error-rules because they are more similar to how Lua and Python handle these situations, and they do not need a facility to copy continuations.

$$\bot \sqcup \varphi = \varphi \sqcup \bot = \varphi$$
$$\top \sqcup \varphi = \varphi \sqcup \top = \top$$

$$\top \sqcup \tau = \tau \sqcup \top = \top$$
$$\bot \sqcap \tau = \tau \sqcap \bot = \bot$$
$$\bot \sqcup \tau = \tau \sqcup \bot = \top \sqcap \tau = \tau \sqcap \top = \tau$$

$$(\tau_i \overset{\bot}{\rightsquigarrow} \tau_o / \tau_r) \sqcup (\tau_i' \overset{\bot}{\rightsquigarrow} \tau_o' / \tau_r')$$
$$= (\tau_i \sqcap \tau_i') \overset{\bot}{\rightsquigarrow} (\tau_o \sqcup \tau_o') / (\tau_r \sqcup \tau_r')$$

$$\tau_1^+ \sqcup \tau_2^+ = \begin{cases} \tau_1^+ & \tau_1^+ = \tau_2^+ \\ \top & \text{otherwise} \end{cases}$$

$$\varphi_1 \sqsubseteq \varphi_2 \quad \text{iff} \quad \exists \varphi_1'. \varphi_1 \sqcup \varphi_1' = \varphi_2$$

$$\tau_1^+ \sqcap \tau_2^+ = \begin{cases} \tau_1^+ & \tau_1^+ = \tau_2^+ \\ \bot & \text{otherwise} \end{cases}$$

(a) Effects.   (b) Types.

Fig. 6. Join and meet

Function arrows are annotated with the effect which may occur during the function's evaluation. We write $\tau_1 \to \tau_2$ for $\tau_1 \overset{\bot}{\to} \tau_2$.

A value of type $\tau_i \rightsquigarrow \tau_o / \tau_r$ corresponds to a coroutine which can be resumed with values of input type τ_i and yields values of output type τ_o or returns a value of return type τ_r.

Types form a flat lattice with bottom $\bot$ and top $\top$. For simplicity, subtyping is not allowed, and subeffecting is only allowed in create and fix expressions. Join and meet on types are defined in figure 6, where τ^+ represent types except for $\top$ and $\bot$.

Typing rules. The rules are given in Fig. 7. The type environment Γ maps variables to their types. The store typing

$$\Sigma \subseteq \text{Labels} \times \{\tau_i \rightsquigarrow \tau_o / \tau_r | \tau_{i,o,r} \neq \top, \tau_i \neq \bot\} \tag{DefΣ}$$

maps labels to the types of the corresponding coroutines at run time. The exclusion of $\top$ and $\bot$ serves to avoid subtyping. Note that type rules do not extend Σ; expressions are type-checked against a fixed Σ, and preservation (Sec. 3.1) guarantees that some Σ can be found after each evaluation step.

The type function $\text{basty}_k(k^n)$ maps constants to their types of the form $B_1 \to B_2 \to \ldots \to B_{n+1}$. We assume that $\text{basty}_k(k^n)$ agrees with the primitive denotation $[\![k^n]\!]$. We also assume that true and false are the only k^0 of type Bool, and that only unit inhabits Unit.

Most type rules compute the effect of their expression by joining the effects of the subexpressions. The only exceptions are T-FIX and T-CREATE, in which the effect of the body expression is moved onto the function arrow or into the coroutine type.

The create expression creates a coroutine from a function. In doing so, it binds a variable to the freshly created coroutine label.

yield and transfer contribute an effect with its input type τ_i. Both suspend the current coroutine and expect a value of type τ_i the next time it is activated. The output and return types in the effect of yield describe that yield certainly causes the coroutine to yield a value of that type, but never causes a return. transfer, however, transfers control *and the relationship to the caller* to a coroutine which, in turn, may yield and return. Therefore, T-TRA puts the other coroutine's output and return types into the effect in order to force the surrounding yield and return expressions to match.

Rule T-PROG defines when an entire program is well-typed. The input type Unit is an arbitrary choice, but since the initial label ℓ_0 is not lexically accessible in the program, the input type is of little importance anyway[7]. The output type is bounded to $\bot$ so that an expression which yields can never be the bottom-most expression in a stack (and yield with $e : \bot$, while allowed, will diverge instead of yielding).

The initial store typing for a program e with $\vdash_{\text{prog}} e : \tau$ is defined as follows:

$$\Sigma_0^\tau = \{(\ell_0, \text{Unit} \rightsquigarrow \bot/\tau)\} \tag{2}$$

3   Soundness

This section contains the soundness proof [8]. In Sec. 3.1, we prove that reduction steps preserve typing. Sec. 3.2 contains the progress proof, stating that all well-typed execution states are reducible or have finished.

3.1   Preservation

This section states and proves the preservation theorem (Theorem 1). We define the notion of a well-typed execution state before we formulate some lemmas in preparation for the main proof.

Fig. 8 contains the definition of an execution state $\langle S \mid \mu \rangle$ being well-typed, T-STATE. Apart from requiring that the types of store and stack members correspond to the store typing Σ, which is defined in T-STORE and T-STACKN, it poses a constraint $\Sigma \vdash_w S$ about the waiting coroutines in the stack: the redex of waiting callers must be a resume expression whose result functions are compatible with the output and return types of the callee.

Lemma 1. *If $\emptyset | \Sigma \vdash C[e] : \tau \& \varphi$, then $\emptyset | \Sigma \vdash e : \tau' \& \varphi'$ for some τ', $\varphi' \sqsubseteq \varphi$, and free$(e) = \emptyset$*

Lemma 2. *If $\Gamma | \Sigma \vdash v : \tau \& \varphi$, then $\varphi = \bot$ and $\tau \neq \bot$.*

Lemma 3. *If $\Gamma, x : \tau' | \Sigma \vdash e : \tau \& \varphi$ and $\emptyset | \Sigma \vdash v : \tau' \& \bot$, then $\Gamma | \Sigma \vdash e[x \mapsto v] : \tau \& \varphi$.*

---

[7] If the program's design features multiple coroutines transferring to each other, there is still the possibility of having the initial program create one or more such coroutines, each of which knows its label, and transferring control to one of them.

[8] For space reasons, we have omitted most proofs. They are contained in the extended version of this paper, available from
http://proglang.informatik.uni-freiburg.de/projects/coroutines/

T-Const
$$\text{basty}_k\,(k^n) = B_1 \rightarrow \ldots \rightarrow B_{n+1} \qquad \forall i = 1 \ldots n.\ \Gamma|\Sigma \vdash e_i : B_i \& \varphi_i$$

$$\Gamma|\Sigma \vdash k^n\,e_1 \ldots e_n : B_{n+1} \& \bigsqcup_{i=1\ldots n} \varphi_i$$

T-Var
$$\frac{\Gamma(x) = \tau}{\Gamma|\Sigma \vdash x : \tau \& \bot}$$

T-App
$$\frac{\Gamma|\Sigma \vdash e_1 : \tau_2 \xrightarrow{\varphi_3} \tau_1 \& \varphi_1 \qquad \Gamma|\Sigma \vdash e_2 : \tau_2 \& \varphi_2}{\Gamma|\Sigma \vdash e_1\,e_2 : \tau_1 \& \varphi_1 \sqcup \varphi_2 \sqcup \varphi_3}$$

T-If
$$\frac{\Gamma|\Sigma \vdash e_c : \text{Bool}\,\&\varphi_c \qquad \Gamma|\Sigma \vdash e_t : \tau \& \varphi_t \qquad \Gamma|\Sigma \vdash e_{\bar{f}} : \tau \& \varphi_f}{\Gamma|\Sigma \vdash \text{if}\,e_c\,\text{then}\,e_t\,\text{else}\,e_f : \tau \& \varphi_c \sqcup \varphi_t \sqcup \varphi_f}$$

T-Fix
$$\frac{\Gamma, f : \tau_1 \xrightarrow{\varphi} \tau_2, x : \tau_1 | \Sigma \vdash e : \tau_2 \& \varphi' \qquad \varphi' \sqsubseteq \varphi}{\Gamma|\Sigma \vdash \text{fix}\,\lambda f.\lambda x.e : (\tau_1 \xrightarrow{\varphi} \tau_2) \& \bot}$$

T-Label
$$\frac{\Sigma(\ell) = \tau_i \rightsquigarrow \tau_o / \tau_r}{\Gamma|\Sigma \vdash \ell : \tau_i \rightsquigarrow \tau_o / \tau_r \& \bot}$$

T-Create
$$\frac{\Gamma, x : \tau_i \rightsquigarrow \tau_o / \tau_r | \Sigma \vdash e : \tau_i \xrightarrow{\varphi} \tau_r \& \varphi' \qquad \varphi, \varphi' \sqsubseteq \tau_i \overset{\cdots}{\rightsquigarrow} \tau_o / \tau_r \qquad \tau_{i,o,r} \neq \top, \tau_i \neq \bot}{\Gamma|\Sigma \vdash \text{create}\,x.e : \tau_i \rightsquigarrow \tau_o / \tau_r \& \bot}$$

T-Res
$$\Gamma|\Sigma \vdash e_c : \tau_i \rightsquigarrow \tau_o / \tau_r \& \varphi_1$$
$$\frac{\Gamma|\Sigma \vdash e_a : \tau_i \& \varphi_2 \qquad \Gamma|\Sigma \vdash e_s : \tau_o \xrightarrow{\varphi_3} \tau_q \& \varphi_4 \qquad \Gamma|\Sigma \vdash e_n : \tau_r \xrightarrow{\varphi_5} \tau_q \& \varphi_6}{\Gamma|\Sigma \vdash \text{resume}\,e_c\,e_a\,e_s\,e_n : \tau_q \& \bigsqcup_{i=1\ldots 6} \varphi_i}$$

T-Yie
$$\frac{\Gamma|\Sigma \vdash e : \tau_o \& \varphi_1 \qquad \tau_i \neq \top}{\Gamma|\Sigma \vdash \text{yield}\,e : \tau_i \& (\tau_i \overset{\cdots}{\rightsquigarrow} \tau_o / \bot) \sqcup \varphi_1}$$

T-Tra
$$\frac{\Gamma|\Sigma \vdash e_c : \tau_a \rightsquigarrow \tau_o / \tau_r \& \varphi_1 \qquad \Gamma|\Sigma \vdash e_a : \tau_a \& \varphi_2}{\Gamma|\Sigma \vdash \text{transfer}\,e_c\,e_a : \tau_i \& (\tau_i \overset{\cdots}{\rightsquigarrow} \tau_o / \tau_r) \sqcup (\varphi_1 \sqcup \varphi_2)}$$

T-Prog
$$\frac{\emptyset|\emptyset \vdash e : \tau \& \varphi \qquad \varphi \sqsubseteq \text{Unit} \overset{\cdots}{\rightsquigarrow} \bot / \tau}{\vdash_{\text{prog}} e : \tau}$$

Fig. 7. Typing rules

Definition 1. *Given Γ, Σ, we write $\Gamma|\Sigma \vdash e_1 \leq e_2$, if $\Gamma|\Sigma \vdash e_1 : \tau \& \varphi_1$ and $\Gamma|\Sigma \vdash e_2 : \tau \& \varphi_2$ with $\varphi_1 \sqsubseteq \varphi_2$. $\Sigma \vdash e_1 \leq e_2$ is an abbreviation for $\emptyset|\Sigma \vdash e_1 \leq e_2$.*

Lemma 4 (Contexts are effect-monotone). *If $\Gamma|\Sigma \vdash e' \leq e$ and for some τ, φ, $\Gamma|\Sigma \vdash C[e] : \tau \& \varphi$, then $\Gamma|\Sigma \vdash C[e'] : \tau \& \varphi'$ for some $\varphi' \sqsubseteq \varphi$, and $\Gamma|\Sigma \vdash C[e'] \leq C[e]$.*

Lemma 5. *Let $S = \ell @ C[e]\,; S^?$, $S' = \ell @ C[e']\,; S^?$ such that $\Sigma \vdash e' \leq e$. Then $\Sigma \vdash_{le*} S \Rightarrow \Sigma \vdash_{le*} S'$ and $\Sigma \vdash_w S \Rightarrow \Sigma \vdash_w S'$ hold.*

Lemma 6. *Let $S = \ell_1 @ e_1; \ell_2 @ C[\text{resume}\,\ell'\,v_p\,v_s\,v_n]\,; S^?$ such that $\Sigma \vdash_{le*} S$ and $\Sigma \vdash_w S$. Let $\tau_i \rightsquigarrow \tau_s / \tau_n = \Sigma(\ell_1)$. Let v be a value with $\emptyset|\Sigma \vdash v : \tau_\alpha \& \bot$ for an $\alpha \in \{s, n\}$. Then, $S' = \ell_2 @ C[v_\alpha\,v]\,; S^?$ satisfies $\Sigma \vdash_{le*} S'$ and $\Sigma \vdash_w S'$.*

T-State
$$\Sigma \vdash_{\text{sto*}} \mu \qquad \Sigma \vdash_{\text{le*}} S \qquad \Sigma \vdash_{\text{w}} S \qquad \text{labels}(S) \cap \text{dom}\,(\mu) = \emptyset$$
$$\Sigma \vdash \langle S \mid \mu \rangle$$

T-Stack0
$$\frac{}{\Sigma \vdash_{\text{le*}} \epsilon}$$

T-StackN
$$\frac{\ell \notin \text{labels}(S^?) \qquad \Sigma \vdash_{\text{le}} \ell@e \qquad \Sigma \vdash_{\text{le*}} S^?}{\Sigma \vdash_{\text{le*}} S} \quad \text{where } S = \ell@e; S^?$$

T-StackE
$$\frac{\Sigma(\ell) = \tau_i \leadsto \tau_o/\tau_r \qquad \emptyset|\Sigma \vdash e : \tau_r \& \varphi \qquad \varphi \sqsubseteq \tau_i \overset{\leadsto}{\leadsto} \tau_o/\tau_r}{\Sigma \vdash_{\text{le}} \ell@e}$$

T-WaitN
$$\frac{S = \ell_1@e_1; S' \quad \tau_i \leadsto \tau_o/\tau_r = \Sigma(\ell_1) \quad S' = \ell_2@e_2; S^? \quad e_2 = C[\text{resume}\,\ell\,v_a\,v_s\,v_n]}{\emptyset|\Sigma \vdash v_s : \tau_o \overset{\varphi_s}{\longrightarrow} \tau \& \bot \qquad \emptyset|\Sigma \vdash v_n : \tau_r \overset{\varphi_n}{\longrightarrow} \tau \& \bot \qquad \Sigma \vdash_{\text{w}} S'}{\Sigma \vdash_{\text{w}} S}$$

T-Wait1
$$\frac{S = \ell@e; \epsilon \qquad \Sigma(\ell) = \tau_i \leadsto \bot/\tau_r}{\Sigma \vdash_{\text{w}} S}$$

T-Store
$$\frac{\mu \text{ is function} \qquad \forall (\ell, v) \in \mu : \Sigma \vdash_{\text{sto}} (\ell, v)}{\Sigma \vdash_{\text{sto*}} \mu}$$

T-StoreE
$$\frac{\Sigma(\ell) = \tau_i \leadsto \tau_o/\tau_r \qquad \emptyset|\Sigma \vdash v : \tau_i \overset{\varphi}{\longrightarrow} \tau_r \& \bot \qquad \varphi \sqsubseteq \tau_i \overset{\leadsto}{\leadsto} \tau_o/\tau_r}{\Sigma \vdash_{\text{sto}} (\ell, v)}$$

Fig. 8. Well-typed execution states, stacks, stores

Lemma 7. *If $\tau_i \overset{\leadsto}{\leadsto} \tau_o/\tau_r \sqsubseteq \tau_i' \overset{\leadsto}{\leadsto} \tau_o'/\tau_r'$, then all of the following hold:*

- $\tau_i = \tau_i'$ or $\tau_i = \top$ or $\tau_i' = \bot$
- $\tau_o = \tau_o'$ or $\tau_o = \bot$ or $\tau_o' = \top$
- $\tau_r = \tau_r'$ or $\tau_r = \bot$ or $\tau_r' = \top$

Lemma 8 (Well-typed initial states). *Let e be an expression with $\vdash_{prog} e : \tau$, and $\langle S \mid \mu \rangle = \text{initState}(e)$. Then $\Sigma_0^\tau \vdash \langle S \mid \mu \rangle$.*

Theorem 1 (Preservation). *If $\Sigma \vdash \langle S \mid \mu \rangle$ and $\langle S \mid \mu \rangle \to \langle S' \mid \mu' \rangle$, then $\Sigma' \vdash \langle S' \mid \mu' \rangle$ for some $\Sigma' \supseteq \Sigma$.*

Proof. We focus on the main cases (see the extended version for the remainder). *Case distinction* on the evaluation rule.

- *Case* E-Create: So $S = \ell@C[\text{create}\,x.e]; S^?$, $S' = \ell@C[\ell^*]; S^?$, and $\mu' = \mu \cup \{(\ell^*, v^*)\}$ with $v^* = \lambda x^*.((\lambda x.e\,x^*)\,\ell^*)$. From the assumed $\Sigma \vdash_{\text{le*}} S$, Lemma 1 yields $\emptyset|\Sigma \vdash \text{create}\,x.e : \tau_c \& \varphi_c$ for some τ_c, φ_c. The only rule to derive this is T-Create, from which we can conclude that $\varphi_c = \bot$ and $\tau_c = \tau_i \leadsto \tau_o/\tau_r$. Furthermore, the same rule requires that

$$x{:}\tau_c|\Sigma \vdash e : \tau_i \overset{\varphi}{\longrightarrow} \tau_r \& \varphi' \tag{3}$$

for some $\varphi, \varphi' \sqsubseteq \tau_i \overset{\leadsto}{\leadsto} \tau_o/\tau_r$. Choose $\Sigma' = \Sigma \cup \{(\ell^*, \tau_c)\}$, which still is a function due to freshness condition on ℓ^*. Also, the constraints on occurrences of $\top$ and $\bot$ in $\tau_{i,o,r}$, as demanded in (DefΣ), are satisfied by the precondition in T-CREATE. Then $\emptyset|\Sigma' \vdash \ell^* : \tau_c \& \bot$ holds, and $\Sigma' \vdash_{le^*} S'$ follows by Lemma 5. $\Sigma' \vdash_w S'$ follows from $\Sigma \vdash_w S$ (using that $\vdash_w$ is obviously montone in Σ).

$\Sigma' \vdash_{sto^*} \mu'$ requires that μ' is a function (true due to the freshness of ℓ^*), and that v^* has the right type: $\emptyset|\Sigma' \vdash v^* : \tau_i \xrightarrow{\varphi^*} \tau_r \& \bot$ for some $\varphi^* \sqsubseteq \tau_i \rightsquigarrow \tau_o / \tau_r$. This follows from (3) by T-APP and T-FIX, observing that all type derivations using Σ also work with its superset Σ'. ✓

- *Case* E-YIE: Then $S = \ell_1 @ e_1; \ell_2 @ e_2; S^?$ and $S' = \ell_2 @ e_2'; S^?$ with $e_1 = C_1[\text{yield } v_y]$, $e_2 = C_2[\text{resume } \ell\, v_a\, v_s\, v_n]$, $e_2' = C_2[v_s\, v_y]$. Also $\mu' = \mu \cup \{(\ell_1, e_1')\}$ with $e_1' = \lambda x^*.C_1[x^*]$.

  We choose $\Sigma' = \Sigma$. Due to $\Sigma \vdash_{le^*} S$, Σ must contain entries for ℓ_1, ℓ_2 of the form $\Sigma(\ell_k) = \tau_i^k \rightsquigarrow \tau_o^k / \tau_r^k$ for $k = 1, 2$. Furthermore, by T-STACKN, $\emptyset|\Sigma \vdash e_1 : \tau_r^1 \& \varphi_e^1$ and $\emptyset|\Sigma \vdash e_2 : \tau_r^2 \& \varphi_e^2$ must hold for some $\varphi_e^1 \sqsubseteq \varphi^1, \varphi_e^2 \sqsubseteq \varphi^2$ (where $\varphi^k = \tau_i^k \rightsquigarrow \tau_o^k / \tau_r^k$).

  To prove $\Sigma' \vdash_{le^*} S'$ and $\Sigma' \vdash_w S'$ using Lemma 6, we need to show $\emptyset|\Sigma \vdash v_y : \tau_o^1 \& \bot$ (the rest follows immediately from the assumptions and $\Sigma' = \Sigma$). Let τ_y, τ_i^* be the types assigned to v_y and yield v_y, respectively, in the type derivation for the assumed $\Sigma \vdash_{le} \ell_1 @ e_1$. By T-YIE and Lemma 1, we get

$$\tau_i^* \rightsquigarrow \tau_y / \bot \sqsubseteq \tau_i^1 \rightsquigarrow \tau_o^1 / \tau_r^1 \tag{4}$$

By Lemma 7, $\tau_y = \bot$ (impossible: Lemma 2), or $\tau_o^1 = \top$ (contradicting (DefΣ)), or $\tau_y = \tau_o^1$. ✓

  To prove $\Sigma \vdash_{sto^*} \mu'$, it remains to prove that μ' is still a function (by T-STATE, $\ell_1 \notin \text{dom}(\mu)$, so adding ℓ_1 preserves the function property of μ), and that $\emptyset|\Sigma \vdash \mu'(\ell_1) : \tau_i^1 \xrightarrow{\varphi} \tau_r^1 \& \bot$ with some $\varphi \sqsubseteq \varphi_1$. Applying Lemma 7 to (4), we know that $\tau_i^1 = \tau_i^*$ (T-YIE forbids $\tau_i^* = \top$, (DefΣ) forbids $\tau_i^1 = \bot$). Setting $\Gamma := x^* : \tau_i$, we immediately get $\Gamma|\Sigma \vdash x^* \leq \text{yield } v_y$, and by Lemma 4, $\Gamma|\Sigma \vdash C_1[x^*] \leq e_1$. Hence, by T-FIX, $\emptyset|\Sigma \vdash \lambda x^*.C_1[x^*] : \tau_i^1 \xrightarrow{\varphi'} \tau_r^1 \& \bot$ for some $\varphi' \sqsubseteq \varphi_1$. ✓

- *Case* E-RES: So $S = \ell_2 @ C[\text{resume } \ell_1\, v_a\, v_s\, v_n]; S^?$, and $S' = \ell_1 @ (v_1\, v_a); S$ with $v_1 = \mu(\ell_1), \mu' = \mu \setminus \ell_1$. Furthermore, we know that $\Sigma(\ell_1) = \tau_i \rightsquigarrow \tau_o / \tau_r$ for some τ_i, τ_o, τ_r because $\Sigma \vdash_{le^*} S$ holds.

  We choose $\Sigma' = \Sigma$. For $\Sigma' \vdash \langle S' \mid \mu' \rangle$, we need to prove: (a) $\Sigma \vdash_{sto^*} \mu'$, (b) $\Sigma \vdash_{le} \ell_1 @ v_1\, v_a$, (c) $\ell_1 \notin \text{labels}(S^?)$ (which yields $\Sigma' \vdash_{le^*} S'$ together with (b)), (d) $\Sigma \vdash_w S'$, and (e) $\text{labels}(S') \cap \text{dom}(\mu') = \emptyset$.

  Proposition (a) follows immediately from μ' being a subset of μ and the assumption $\Sigma \vdash_{sto^*} \mu$. ✓ Proposition (c) is clear from $\Sigma \vdash \langle S \mid \mu \rangle$. ✓ Proposition (e) is clear because moving ℓ_1 between sets preserves disjointness. ✓

  Proposition (b): prove $\emptyset|\Sigma \vdash v_1\, v_a : \tau_r \& \varphi_1$ for some $\varphi_1 \sqsubseteq \tau_i \rightsquigarrow \tau_o / \tau_r$. By assumption $\Sigma \vdash_{sto^*} \mu$, we know about v_1 that $\emptyset|\Sigma \vdash v_1 : \tau_i \xrightarrow{\varphi_1'} \tau_r \& \bot$ holds with $\varphi_1' \sqsubseteq \tau_i \rightsquigarrow \tau_o / \tau_r$. With Lemma 1, Lemma 2 and T-RES, we conclude that $\emptyset|\Sigma \vdash v_a : \tau_i \& \bot$, which yields the desired result using T-APP.

$$R ::= k^n \, v_1 \ldots v_n \mid (\text{fix}\, \lambda f.\lambda x.e) \, v$$
$$\mid \text{if true then } e_1 \text{ else } e_2 \mid \text{if false then } e_1 \text{ else } e_2$$
$$\mid \text{create}\, x.e \mid \text{yield}\, v \mid \text{resume}\, \ell\, v\, v\, v \mid \text{transfer}\, \ell\, v$$

Fig. 9. The language of redexes

Proposition (d): By Lemma 1, Lemma 2 and T-RES, we know that $\emptyset|\Sigma \vdash v_s : \tau_o \xrightarrow{\varphi_s} \tau_q \& \bot$ and $\emptyset|\Sigma \vdash v_n : \tau_r \xrightarrow{\varphi_n} \tau_q \& \bot$, which matches the precondition of T-WAITN about v_s and v_n. The other preconditions follow directly from the assumptions. ✓

End case distinction on the evaluation rule. ∎

3.2   Progress

In this section, we state the progress property. First, we define a language of redexes in Fig. 9, then we show in Lemma 10 that well-typed expressions are either values or redexes embedded in evaluation contexts, which facilitates the main progress theorem, Theorem 2.

Lemma 9 (Canonical forms)

1. *If $\Gamma|\Sigma \vdash v : \tau \xrightarrow{\varphi} \tau' \& \varphi'$, then $v = \text{fix}\,\lambda f.\lambda x.e$ for some f, x, e.*
2. *If $\Gamma|\Sigma \vdash v : \text{Bool}\&\varphi'$, then $v = \text{true}$ or $v = \text{false}$.*
3. *If $\Gamma|\Sigma \vdash v : \text{Unit}\&\varphi'$, then $v = \text{unit}$.*
4. *If $\Gamma|\Sigma \vdash v : \tau_i \rightsquigarrow \tau_o/\tau_r \& \varphi'$, then $v = \ell$ for some $\ell \in \text{dom}(\Sigma)$.*

Lemma 10 ($C[R]$-decomposition). *Let $\emptyset|\Sigma \vdash e : \tau\&\varphi$ for some e, Σ, τ, φ. Then e is a value, or $e = C[R]$ for some C, R.*

Theorem 2 (Progress). *Let $\langle S \mid \mu \rangle$ be an evaluation state and Σ a store typing so that $\Sigma \vdash \langle S \mid \mu \rangle$. Then $S = \ell@v; \epsilon$ for some v, ℓ, or $\langle S \mid \mu \rangle \rightarrow \langle S' \mid \mu' \rangle$ for some S', μ', or $\langle S \mid \mu \rangle \rightarrow \text{Error}$.*

4   Related Work

Formalizations of coroutines. De Moura and Ierusalemschy [14] formally define coroutines in an untyped λ-calculus with mutable variables as a model for Lua coroutines. Their interexpressibility results (e.g. transfer in terms of resume/yield) make heavy use of untyped mutable variables; it is yet unclear which of the transformations can be adapted to a statically-typed setting. Their work contains a comprehensive overview of the state of the art in coroutines and related techniques.

Wang and Dahl [18] formalize the control-flow aspects of idealized Simula coroutines. The operational semantics of Belsnes and Østvold [1] also focuses on the control-flow aspects but includes threads and thread-coroutine interaction. Laird [10] presents a process calculus in which the coroutine is the basic building block. Berdine and coworkers [2] define coroutines in their process calculus.

Language design. Languages with parameterless coroutines include Simula [5], Modula-2 [19], and BETA [9]. However, the type systems of these languages need not treat coroutines with much sophistication because the coroutine operations do not pass values.

Some mainstream dynamically-typed languages like Python [17] and Lua [15] pass values to and from coroutines, but without a static type system. C# [13] has static typing and generators (asymmetric coroutines with parameters only for yield), but as the yield-equivalent may only be used lexically inside the generator's body, the type system avoids the complexity involved with stackful coroutines.

Marlin's ACL [12] is a (statically typed) coroutine extension of Pascal in which coroutines can accept parameters. In analogy to the separation between procedures and functions in Pascal, it features separate syntax for symmetric and asymmetric coroutines. The problem of procedures performing coroutine operations on behalf of the enclosing coroutine is solved by referring to the static block structure, which simplifies the type system at the expense of flexibility.

Haynes and coworkers [7] express coroutines using continuations in Scheme; Harper and colleagues [6] in turn describe a type system for continuations.

Lazy languages like Haskell [16] get asymmetric coroutines for free: a coroutine can be viewed as a transformer of a stream of input values to a stream of output values, which is straightforward to implement using lazy lists. Blazevic [3] produced a more sophisticated monad-based implementation of symmetric coroutines.

5 Conclusion

We presented CorDuroy, a language with type-safe stackful asymmetric and symmetric first-class coroutines, and proved its soundness. CorDuroy constitutes the first provably sound type system for an eager-evaluated language that supports realistic and expressive facilities for coroutines.

One obvious direction of further research is the addition of polymorphism. For subtype polymorphism, (a subset of) C# would be a promising candidate since it already has generators. Parametric polymorphism would likely bring challenges similar to those caused by mutable references.

As this work was inspired by De Moura and Ierusalemschy's paper [14] in which they present translations between various styles of coroutines, continuations and threads in an untyped setting with mutable variables, it would be interesting to see if the corresponding typed equivalences also hold.

Currently, the operational semantics contains failure rules. Instead, linearity could be introduced to prevent the activation of returned coroutines by keeping track of the coroutine state.

References

1. Belsnes, D., Østvold, B.M.: Mixing threads and coroutines (2005), submitted to FOSSACS 2005, bjarte@nr.no
2. Berdine, J., O'Hearn, P., Reddy, U., Thielecke, H.: Linear continuation-passing. Higher-Order and Symbolic Computation 15(2-3), 181–208 (2002)

3. Blazevic, M.: monad-coroutine: Coroutine monad transformer for suspending and resuming monadic computations (2010),
http://hackage.haskell.org/package/monad-coroutine
4. Conway, M.E.: Design of a separable transition-diagram compiler. Comm. ACM 6(7), 396–408 (1963)
5. Dahl, O.J., Myrhaug, B., Nygaard, K.: SIMULA 67 Common Base Language. Norwegian Computing Center, Oslo (1970) (revised version 1984)
6. Harper, R., Duba, B.F., MacQueen, D.: Typing first-class continuations in ML. In: Proc. 1991 ACM Symp. POPL. ACM Press, Orlando (1991)
7. Haynes, C.T., Friedman, D.P., Wand, M.: Obtaining coroutines with continuations. Computer Languages 11(3), 143–153 (1986)
8. Knuth, D.E.: Fundamental Algorithms, The Art of Computer Programming, 2nd edn., vol. 1. Addison-Wesley, Reading (1968)
9. Kristensen, B.B., Pedersen, B.M., Madsen, O.L., Nygaard, K.: Coroutine sequencing in BETA. In: Proc. of 21st Annual Hawaii International Conference on Software Track, pp. 396–405. IEEE Computer Society Press, Los Alamitos (1988)
10. Laird, J.: A calculus of coroutines. In: Díaz, J., Karhumäki, J., Lepistö, A., Sannella, D. (eds.) ICALP 2004. LNCS, vol. 3142, pp. 882–893. Springer, Heidelberg (2004)
11. Liskov, B.: CLU reference manual. LNCS, vol. 114. Springer, Heidelberg (1981)
12. Marlin, C.D.: Coroutines: a programming methodology, a language design and an implementation. Springer, Heidelberg (1980)
13. Microsoft Corp.: C# Version 2.0 Specification (2005),
http://msdn.microsoft.com/en-US/library/618ayhy6(v=VS.80).aspx
14. de Moura, A.L., Ierusalimschy, R.: Revisiting coroutines. ACM Trans. Program. Lang. Syst. 31(2), 1–31 (2009)
15. de Moura, A.L., Rodriguez, N., Ierusalimschy, R.: Coroutines in Lua. Journal of Universal Computer Science 10, 925 (2004)
16. Peyton Jones, S. (ed.): Haskell 98 Language and Libraries, The Revised Report. Cambridge University Press, Cambridge (2003)
17. Van Rossum, G., Eby, P.: PEP 342 – coroutines via enhanced generators (2005),
http://www.python.org/dev/peps/pep-0342/
18. Wang, A., Dahl, O.J.: Coroutine sequencing in a block structured environment. BIT Numerical Mathematics 11(4), 425–449 (1971),
http://www.springerlink.com/content/g870vkxx22861w50
19. Wirth, N.: Programming in Modula-2. Springer, Heidelberg (1982)
20. Wright, A., Felleisen, M.: A syntactic approach to type soundness. Information and Computation 115(1), 38–94 (1994)

An Expression Processor:
A Case Study in Refactoring Haskell Programs

Christopher Brown[1], Huiqing Li[2], and Simon Thompson[2]

[1] School of Computer Science, University of St. Andrews, UK
`chrisb@cs.st-andrews.ac.uk`
[2] School of Computing, University of Kent, UK
`{H.Li,S.J.Thompson}@kent.ac.uk`

Abstract. Refactoring is the process of changing the structure of a program while preserving its behaviour in order to increase code quality, programming productivity and code reuse. With the advent of refactoring tools, refactoring can be performed semi-automatically, allowing refactorings to be performed (and undone) easily.

In this paper, we briefly describe a number of new refactorings for Haskell 98 programs implemented in the Haskell Refactorer, HaRe. In particular, a number of new structural and data-type refactorings are presented. We also implement a simple expression processor, clearly demonstrating how the refactorings and the HaRe tool can aid programmers in developing Haskell software. We conclude the paper with a discussion of the benefits of refactoring Haskell programs, together with their implementation and design limitations.

1 Introduction

Often programmers write a first version of a program without paying full attention to programming style or design principles [1]. Having written a program, the programmer will realise that a different approach would have been much better, or that the context of the problem has changed. Refactoring tools provide software support for modifying the design of a program without changing its functionality: often this is precisely what is needed in order to begin adapting or extending it.

The term 'refactoring' was first introduced by Opdyke in his PhD thesis in 1992 [2] and the concept goes at least as far back as the fold/unfold system proposed by Burstall and Darlington in 1977 [3], although, arguably, the fold/unfold system was more about algorithm change than structural changes. A key aspect of refactoring — illustrated by the 'rename function' operation — is that its effect is across a code base, rather than being focussed on a single definition: renaming a function will have an effect on all the modules that call that function, for instance.

The Haskell Refactorer, HaRe, is a product of the *Refactoring Functional Programs* project at the University of Kent [4] [5] by Li, Reinke, Thompson and Brown. HaRe provides refactorings for programs written in the full Haskell 98

R. Page, Z. Horváth, and V. Zsók (Eds.): TFP 2010, LNCS 6546, pp. 31–49, 2011.
© Springer-Verlag Berlin Heidelberg 2011

standard language [6], and is integrated with the two most popular development environments for Haskell programs [7], namely Vim [8] and (X)Emacs [9]. HaRe refactorings can be applied to both single- and multi-module projects.

HaRe is itself implemented in Haskell, and is built upon the Programatica [10] compiler front-end, and the Strafunski [11] library for generic tree traversal. The HaRe programmers' application programming interface (API) provides the user with an abstract syntax tree (AST) for the program together with utility functions (for example, tree traversal and tree transforming functions) to assist in the implementation of refactorings.

In this paper, we describe briefly a number of new refactorings for HaRe and demonstrate their use by applying them to an expression processing example. Using Haskell as the implementation language allows us to explore the usability of Haskell for implementing transformation and analysis tools.

We are also able to reflect on how refactoring functional programs – and in particular programs in Haskell – is different from refactoring within the OO paradigm. Pure functional languages such as Haskell make some refactorings substantially more straightforward: consider the example in which a function definition is *generalised* by selecting a sub-expression to pass as an argument, as in the transformation of the following program on selection of the sub-expression 1 within the definition of addOne,

```
addOne [] = []
addOne (x:xs) = x+1 : addOne xs

fun xs = sum (addOne xs)
```

where for good measure we also rename the function appropriately:

```
addNum n [] = []
addNum n (x:xs) = x+n : addNum n xs

fun xs = sum (addNum 1 xs)
```

We note three aspects of this transformation.

- In performing a generalisation over an arbitrary sub-expression we can be sure that the expression has no side-effects, and so it can be passed as an argument without changing the order in which these effects take place.
- Because Haskell is evaluated lazily, we know that the argument will only be evaluated if it is used, and so we will not change the strictness of the function by generalising in this way; this would not be the case in a strict language.
- Finally, if we choose as a sub-expression something of functional type then because functions are 'first-class citizens' in Haskell the generalisation can take place: the use of arbitrary closures in (e.g.) object-oriented languages would make this generalisation awkward or indeed impossible.

If we were to introduce side-effects in a measured way – as in Haskell monads or in Erlang's communication primitives – it is possible to detect where side-effects may take place, and indeed to 'wrap' the effects in a function closure when generalising, if that is required.

In general refactorings for Haskell can be more far-reaching because of the purity of the language, but some features – especially overloading by means of type classes – can lead to some difficulties in implementation; for example in generalisation two or more sub-expressions may be similar, but have potentially different types.

To date HaRe has a number of refactorings implemented, each refactoring falls into one of two categories: structural or data-type based. Structural refactorings affect the expression level of a program, including function definitions; whereas data-type based refactorings affect the type definitions of a program, or affect the expressions of the program taking into account a type constraint. The refactorings were jointly implemented by Li [12] and Brown [13] in their PhD theses. Here we attempt to declare the authorship and category of all the existing refactorings for HaRe.

- **Structural**
  Renaming, demote/promote a definition, unfold a definition, introduce/ delete a definition, generalise a definition, add/remove an argument and duplicate a function [12].
  Folding, generative folding, folding/unfolding as-patterns, converting between let and where and case analysis simplification [13].
- **Data-Type**
  From concrete to abstract data type [12].
  Add/remove a constructor, add/remove a field and *introduce pattern matching* [13].
- **Miscellaneous.** Duplicate code elimination [14] and program slicing, including: dead code elimination, splitting and *merging* [13].

We note that removing a constructor and removing a field are *pseudo refactorings*; that is, they are refactorings if performed directly after their inverse which adds the construct, but they may change behaviour if used in other situations. The particular contributions presented here are:

- **Structural and Data-Type Refactorings.** The design and implementation of a new set of structural and data-type refactorings, taken from Brown [13]. These refactorings are introduced in Section 2, and are italicised in the list of refactorings above.
- **Refactoring Case Study.** A case study for refactoring Haskell programs. In particular we apply the refactorings described in this paper to an expression processing example. The example is used to demonstrate the capacity of the refactorings from this paper in a simple, but still useful, context. This case study is presented in Section 3.

We conclude the paper with a discussion of the general benefits for the Haskell programmer of refactoring, and a discussion of some of the difficulties of implementing the various refactorings; we conclude by reviewing our agenda for future work.

2   Structural and Data-Type Refactorings

This section describes some new structural and data-type refactorings that have
been defined and implemented in HaRe by Brown [13]. In this paper we chose
to select the refactorings that would appear most useful to the Haskell programmer. The refactorings presented here follow on from the refactoring work by Li
[12], and use the refactoring catalogue [15] maintained by Thompson as a basis. In particular, the following refactorings are described in this section: folding
(Section 2.1); merging (Section 2.2); adding a constructor (Section 2.3); removing a constructor (Section 2.4); adding and removing a data type field (Section
2.5); and introducing pattern matching (Section 2.6).

We note that the refactorings are only very briefly described here. For a much
more detailed overview of the transformation rules and side conditions for each
refactoring described in this section, we refer the reader to Brown's PhD thesis
[13].

2.1   Folding

Folding replaces instances of the right hand side of a definition by the corresponding left-hand-side. This refactoring is designed to be the complement of
unfolding which is described in Li's PhD thesis [12]. Folding can be used to
eliminate some duplicate expressions within a program; it can also be used to
create a name for a common abstraction occurring within the program by ab-
stracting away from a common sub-expression, as long as there is a definition
to fold against. This is achieved by first extracting the common definition using
the *introduce new definition* refactoring [12], and then folding against this newly
introduced definition.

Example. An example of folding an instance of the right hand side of a definition, `table`, is shown in Figure 1. In the figure, two definitions are given:

Before: After:

```
showAll = (concat . format) . (map show)   showAll = table . map show
table  = concat . format                   table   = concat . format
```

Fig. 1. Folding (`concat . format`) against the definition of `table` is shown from left
to right. The inverse of this (*unfolding* `table` within `showAll`) is shown from right to
left.

`showAll` and `table`. The right hand side of `table`, as can be seen, also appears as a sub-expression on the right hand side of `showAll`. Folding allows the
definition `table` to be selected and all occurrences of its right hand side (occurrences within different entities in the same scope as `table`, except those that
appear on the right hand side of `table`) are replaced with a call to `table`. The
top row of the example shows that the sub-expression, (`concat . format`) has
been replaced with a call to `table`, passing in (`map show`) as an argument; this
therefore eliminates some duplicated code within the program.

Before:

```
splitAt_1 :: Int -> [a] -> [a]
splitAt_1 0 _ = []
splitAt_1 _ []= []
splitAt_1 n (x:xs)
    = x : splitAt_1 (n-1) xs

splitAt_2 :: Int -> [a] -> [a]
splitAt_2 0 xs = xs
splitAt_2 _ [] = []
splitAt_2 n (x:xs)
    = splitAt_2 (n-1) xs
```

After:

```
splitAt :: Int -> [a] -> ([a], [a])
splitAt 0 xs = ([],xs)
splitAt _ [] = ([],[])
splitAt n (x:xs) = (x:ys,zs)
    where
        (ys,zs) = splitAt (n-1) xs
```

Fig. 2. Merging a pair of definitions is shown from left to right; the merged definition is recursive and introduces a shared list traversal

2.2 Merging

Merging takes a number of selected definitions and creates a new, *generative*, definition that returns a tuple. Each component of the tuple returned by the merged definition encapsulates the behaviour of the selected entities. The merged definition is generative in the sense that it is recursive, and removes duplicate parts of the function by introducing code sharing. Merging is the inverse of splitting, as defined in [13].

Merging is actually known as *tupling* in the field of program transformation, and was originally proposed by Pettorossi [16], as a strategy for composing efficient computations by avoiding repeated evaluations of recursive functions.

Example. An example of merging the functions splitAt_1 and splitAt_2 is shown, from left to right, in Figure 2. In order to perform the merge, the user must first select each function splitAt_1 and splitAt_2 in turn and add them to a merging *cache*, so that HaRe can perform the refactoring over the selected entities. The newly introduced definition, splitAt, uses only one list traversal, rather than a separate traversal for each of splitAt_1 and splitAt_2.

2.3 Adding a Constructor to a Data Type

Adding a constructor to a defined data type. The introduced constructor is added immediately after a selected constructor definition in a data type. New pattern matching is introduced for all functions defined over the modified data type.

Example. An example of adding a constructor Var to a data type Expr is shown in Figure 3. In the example, we select the constructor Minus and choose to add a new constructor immediately after (the result is shown in the right column). We add the new constructor Var with an argument Int. This is done by HaRe prompting the user for the constructor name and the types of its fields

Before:

```
data Expr = Plus Expr Expr
          | Minus Expr Expr

eval :: Expr -> Int
eval (Plus e1 e2)
    = (eval e1) + (eval e2)
eval (Minus e1 e2)
    = (eval e1) - (eval e2)
```

After:

```
data Expr = Plus Expr Expr
          | Minus Expr Expr
          | Var Int

addedVar = error "added Var Int to Expr"
eval :: Expr -> Int
eval (Plus e1 e2)
    = (eval e1) + (eval e2)
eval (Minus e1 e2)
    = (eval e1) - (eval e2)
eval (Var a) = addedVar
```

Fig. 3. Adding a constructor `Var` with the field `Int` is shown from left to right. Removing the constructor and its field is shown from right to left.

when the refactoring is selected from the menu. The function `eval` is updated automatically to include pattern matching for the newly added constructor.

2.4   Removing a Constructor from a Data Type

Removing a constructor is defined as the inverse of adding a constructor. Removing is not a refactoring in the sense that it eliminates equations from the program space; this therefore may change the behaviour. However, removing a constructor is a *pseudo refactoring* if it is performed directly after adding a constructor, but this does not apply generally to the transformation. Removing a constructor allows a constructor to be identified and all clauses that involve pattern matching over the constructor are commented out. All occurrences of the constructor in an expression are replaced with calls to `error`.

Example. An example of removing a constructor `Var` from a data type `Expr` is defined in Figure 3 read from right to left. `Var` is selected for removal and the refactoring removes the value from its defining definition, `Expr` and comments out all equations referring to the value `Var` in a pattern. When used on the right hand side `Var` is replaced with a call to `error`. The equation `eval (Var a) =` `addedVar` is also commented out, although this is not shown in the figure.

2.5   Adding or Removing a Field to or from a Constructor

Adding a field to a constructor allows a new field to be added to an identified data type constructor. The new field is always added to the beginning of the type to allow for partial applications of the constructor in the program. The reason for this is to complement the *add a new parameter* refactoring, which also adds arguments to the beginning of the argument list of a function.

Removing a field is defined as the inverse of adding a field. All references to the removed field in pattern matches or sub-expressions are commented out of

Before:

```
data Data1 a = C1 a Int Char
             | C2 Int
             | C3 Float

f :: Data1 a -> Int
f (C1 a b c) = b
f (C2 a) = a
f (C3 a) = 42

g (C1 (C1 x y z) b c) = y

h :: Data1 a
h = C2 42
```

After:

```
data Data1 b a = C1 a Int Char
               | C2 Int
               | C3 b Float

f :: (Data1 b a) -> Int
f (C1 a b c) = b
f (C2 a) = a
f (C3 c3_1 a) = 42

g (C1 (C1 x y z) b c) = y

h :: Data1 b a
h = C2 42
```

Fig. 4. Adding and removing a field b to the constructor C3 shown from left to right. Removing the field is shown from right to left.

the program. Similarly, if the removed field was referred to in the program then the sub-expression will be commented out after the removal process. Removing a field is a destructive transformation rather than a refactoring, as it changes behaviour. Removing a field is also a *pseudo refactoring* if performed directly after adding a field.

Example. Figure 4, read from left to right, shows an example of a new field being added to a data type. The new field, of the polymorphic type b, generalises the data type further. b is added to the left hand side of the type definition, and also to all type signatures which involve the type Data1 in the program.

Conversely, Figure 4, read from right to left, shows an example of a field being destructively removed from a data type. The field in question, of the polymorphic type b, is removed from the left hand side of the type definition, and also from all type signatures involving Data1.

2.6   Introduce Pattern Matching over an Argument Position

This refactoring introduces pattern matches for a function with a variable in a particular argument position. Pattern matching is introduced in all its defining equations by replacing the variable with an exhaustive set of patterns for the type of the variable.

Example. An example of introducing pattern matches is given in Figure 5 from left to right. In the example, the new pattern matches are added to the definition of f and the introduced patterns for x are placed within an as pattern. The right hand side is copied into the new equations and any new pattern variables that are introduced are given new, distinct, names so that no binding conflicts can occur. In the example, the pattern variables y and ys are introduced.

Before:

```
f :: [Int] -> Int
f x = head x + head (tail x)
```

After:

```
f :: [Int] -> Int
f x@[] = head x + head (tail x)
f x@(y:ys) = head x + head (tail x)
```

Fig. 5. Introducing pattern matches for the pattern x is shown from left to right

3 Refactoring an Expression Processor

In this section we present a simple example illustrating how the majority of the refactorings described in this paper could be used in practical program development. In the example, we design a very simple language; we then write a parser, evaluator and pretty printer for that language. As the application is being implemented, there are cases where the use of a refactoring tool greatly increases the productivity of the programmer, and improves the design of the program, making the succeeding implementation steps easier to perform. In addition to the previously mentioned techniques, we also make use of the following refactorings from Li's thesis [12]: *renaming*; *generalising*; *introducing a new definition*; and *adding an argument to a definition*.

The example starts with the very basics of implementing a language, parser and evaluator. The code for this is shown below; the grammar for the language is described in the `data` type on Line 1 in Figure 6. So far, the language only has the capacity to handle `Integer` literals and applications of `Plus`. The function `parseExpr` is the parser for the language, taking a `String` and converting it into a tuple: the first element being the Abstract Syntax Tree for `Expr`, and the second the unconsumed input. To show this in practice, the following shows how the parser and evaluator can be invoked from the GHCi command line:

```
Prelude Parser> parseExpr "+ 1 2"
(Plus (Literal 1) (Literal 2),"")

Prelude Parser> eval $ fst $ parseExpr "+ 1 2"
3
```

For reasons of simplicity, the language does not include parentheses (although this could easily be integrated into future versions) and + is not applied as an infix function, also the expressions only take unsigned (positive) integers. For the purpose of this example the expressions are given in a prefix format. The complete implementation, for each stage of the case study, can be found at [17]; at each stage we have also attempted to motivate how we have proceeded with choosing which refactorings to perform.

3.1 Stage 1: Initial Implementation

With the basics of the parser and evaluator set up, the first step is to start integrating other constructs into the language. Therefore, we add the constructor `Mul` to `Expr` in order to represent the application of * in our programs. We do

```
1      data Expr = Literal Int | Plus Expr Expr
2                     deriving Show
3
4      parseExpr :: String -> (Expr, String)
5      parseExpr (' ':xs) = parseExpr xs
6      parseExpr ('+':xs) = (Plus parse1 parse2, rest2)
7                          where
8                             (parse1, rest1) = parseExpr xs
9                             (parse2, rest2) = parseExpr rest1
10     parseExpr (x:xs)
11        | isNumber x = (Literal (read (x:lit)::Int), drop (length lit) xs)
12              where
13                 lit = parseInt xs
14                 parseInt :: String -> String
15                 parseInt [] = []
16                 parseInt (x:xs) | isNumber x = x : parseInt xs
17                                 | otherwise  = []
18     parseExpr xs = error "Parse Error!"
19
20     eval :: Expr -> Int
21     eval (Literal x) = x
22     eval (Plus x y) = (eval x) + (eval y)
```

Fig. 6. The basic language and parser with prefix `Plus` expressions and `Int` literals

this by using the refactoring *add a constructor* (described in Section 2.3). The refactoring asks us for the name of the constructor and any arguments. We enter `Mul Expr Expr` and select the constructor `Plus`. The refactoring always adds the new constructor immediately after the highlighted constructor. In this case the refactoring adds the new constructor to the end of the definition of `Expr` and also generates additional pattern matching clauses to `eval` (we use italics to show code introduced by the refactorer):

```
data Expr = Literal Int | Plus Expr Expr | Mul Expr Expr
addedMul = error "Added Mul Expr Expr to Expr"
...
eval :: Expr -> Int
eval (Literal x) = x
eval (Plus x y) = (eval x) + (eval y)
eval (Mul p_1 p_2) = addedMul
```

The refactoring has also inserted a call to the (automatically created) definition of `addedMul` which is easily replaced with actual functionality in the succeeding steps.

3.2   Stage 2: Introduce Binary Operators

It is anticipated that the language should be able to handle any number of mathematical binary operators. In order to handle this design decision, we implement a new data type `Bin_Op` to handle binary operators, and a new constructor to

Expr to handle this abstraction. In order to achieve this, we first *remove* the constructors Plus and Mul (using the *remove a constructor* refactoring, defined in Section 2.3). The refactoring then automatically removes both constructors and their pattern matching:

```
data Expr = Literal Int
...
parseExpr ('+':xs) = (error "Plus removed from Expr"
                           {-Plus parse1 parse2, rest2-})
                     where
                           (parse1, rest1) = parseExpr xs
                           (parse2, rest2) = parseExpr rest1
...
eval :: Expr -> Int
eval (Literal x) = x
{- eval (Plus x y) = (eval x) + (eval y) -}
{- eval (Mul p_1 p_2) = (eval x) * (eval y) -}
```

The Bin_Op data type is then created with the constructors, Mul and Plus. This operation of removing constructors and introducing a new, generalised, type, may be implemented as refactoring, and is known as *introduce layered data type* in the catalogue of refactorings, maintained by Thompson [15].

A new function, called eval_op is then introduced, with a skeleton implementation, as follows:

```
eval_op :: (Num a) => Bin_Op -> (a -> a -> a)
eval_op x = error "Undefined Operation"
```

We then proceed to define the implementation for eval_op: by choosing *introduce pattern matching* (described in Section 2.6 on Page 37) from HaRe and selecting the argument x within eval_op, the refactoring produces the following:

```
eval_op :: (Num a) => Bin_Op -> (a -> a -> a)
eval_op p_1@(Mul) = error "Undefined Operation"
eval_op p_1@(Plus) = error "Undefined Operation"
eval_op _ = error "Undefined Operation"
```

All that is left to do for this stage is to replace the right hand sides of eval_op with (*) and (+) respectively.

The next stage is to do some tidying of our newly introduced type, Bin_Op. In particular, we need to define a constructor within Expr and modify the evaluator to call eval_op for the Bin_Op case.

To start, we *add a constructor* to Expr where HaRe also automatically adds a new pattern clause to eval:

```
data Expr = Literal Int | Bin Bin_Op Expr Expr
addedBin = error "Added Bin Bin_Op Expr Expr to Expr"
...
eval :: Expr -> Int
eval (Literal x) = x
eval (Bin p_1 p_2 p_3) = addedBin
```

The call to `error` on the right hand side of `parseExpr` for the `'+'` case is then
replaced with `Bin Plus parse1 parse2`. The next step is also to *rename* (using
the *rename* refactoring in HaRe) the variables in the introduced pattern match
to something more meaningful:

```
eval :: Expr -> Int
eval (Literal x) = x
eval (Bin op e1 e2) = eval_op op (eval e1) (eval e2)
```

Multiplication is then introduced in the parser, by copying the `'+'` case into a
`'*'` case, and substituting `Plus` for `Mul` on the right hand side.

```
1   parseExpr :: String -> (Expr, String)
2   parseExpr (' ':xs) = parseExpr xs
3   parseExpr ('*':xs) = (Bin Mul parse1 parse2, rest2)
4                        where
5                          (parse1, rest1) = parseExpr xs
6                          (parse2, rest2) = parseExpr rest1
7   parseExpr ('+':xs) = (Bin Plus parse1 parse2, rest2)
8                        where
9                          (parse1, rest1) = parseExpr xs
10                         (parse2, rest2) = parseExpr rest1
11  parseExpr (x:xs)
12    | isNumber x = (Literal (read (x:lit)::Int), drop (length lit) xs)
13            where
14              lit = parseInt xs
15              parseInt :: String -> String
16              parseInt [] = []
17              parseInt (x:xs) | isNumber x = x : parseInt xs
18                              | otherwise  = []
19  parseExpr xs = error "Parse Error!"
```

Fig. 7. The parser implementation with plus and multiplication

3.3   Stage 3: Generalisation

In stage 3, we observe that there are occurrences of (near) duplicated expressions
in the program. Typically, refactoring can remove duplicated expressions by
introducing one of the instances of the duplicated expressions at the top level of
the program, and then *generalising* it so that all other instances can be *folded*
against the new definition. As can be seen from Figure 7, two equations of
`parseExpr` contain some duplicated code (this is highlighted in the figure). We
eliminate this duplicate code, by first *introducing a new definition* (using the
introduce new definition refactoring in HaRe) by highlighting the code on lines
7 - 10 from Figure 7. We enter `parseBin` as the name for the new expression,
and HaRe introduces the following code:

```
. . .
parseExpr ('+':xs) = parseBin xs
. . .
parseBin xs = (Bin Plus parse1 parse2, rest2)
                where
                    (parse1, rest1) = parseExpr xs
                    (parse2, rest2) = parseExpr rest1
```

The code highlighted in italics show how the refactoring has replaced the right
hand side of the equation `parseExpr` with a call to `parseBin`. Obviously, the
function `parseBin` should now be generalised so that the constructors `Plus` and
`Mul` can be passed in as formal arguments. This will also allow us to *fold* (using
folding as described in Section 2.1) the equation `parseExpr` defined in Figure 7
against the new definition `parseBin`. The following code illustrates this:

```
parseExpr :: String -> (Expr, String)
parseExpr (' ':xs) = parseExpr xs
parseExpr ('*':xs) = parseBin Mul xs
parseExpr ('+':xs) = parseBin Plus xs
parseExpr (x:xs)
   | isNumber x = ...
parseExpr xs = error "Parse Error!"

parseBin p_1 xs = (Bin p_1 parse1 parse2, rest2)
                  where
                      (parse1, rest1) = parseExpr xs
                      (parse2, rest2) = parseExpr rest1
```

This refactoring has allowed to keep the implementation simple: there is now
a separate evaluator for binary operators (defined in Section 3.2) as well as
a separate parser for binary operators; this allows for the code to be easily
maintained in future versions.

3.4   Stage 4: Introduce Variables

We now add variables to the language by defining the `let` expression. In order
to do this, the `Let` and `Var` constructs need to be added to the language, taking
a variable name to be a `String`. The parser is then extended to handle the new
constructs, with the input `let x=4 in 1+x` giving the AST

`Let "x" (Literal 4) (Bin Plus (Literal 1) (Var "x"))`

Having variables in the language means that bindings of variables to values need
to be stored in an environment, and that environment variable needs to be passed
into the evaluator as an extra argument: when a variable is evaluated `lookup` is
used to find its value in the environment.

　　To perform this extension to the language, first we perform two *add construc-*
tor refactorings to the definition of `Expr`, adding `LetExp String Expr Expr`
and then `Variable String` as arguments to the refactoring. The refactorings
introduce new pattern matches for `eval`, thus:

```
1    eval :: Environment -> Expr -> (String, Int)
2    eval env (Literal x) = (show x, x)
3    eval env (Bin op e1 e2) = ((fst (eval_op op)) ++ " "
4                               ++ (fst $ eval env e1) ++ " "
5                               ++ (fst $ eval env e2),
6                               (snd $ eval_op op) (snd $ eval env e1)
7                               (snd $ eval env e2))
8                      where
9                        eval_op :: (Num a) => Bin_Op -> (String, (a -> a -> a))
10                       eval_op p_1@(Mul) = ("*", (*))
11                       eval_op p_1@(Plus) = ("+",(+))
12                       eval_op _ = error "Undefined Operation"
13   eval env (LetExp n e e_2) = ("let " ++ n ++ " = " ++ (fst $ eval env e)
14                               ++ " in " ++ (fst $ eval env e_2),
15                               snd $ eval (addEnv n e env) e_2)
16   eval env (Var n) = (n, snd $ eval env (lookUp n env))
```

Fig. 8. The evaluator implementation with the generality of binary operators expressed

```
data Expr = ... | LetExp String Expr | Var String
  ...
addedLetExp = error "Added LetExp String Expr Expr to Expr"
addedVar = error "Added Var String to Expr"
  ...
eval :: Expr -> Int
  ...
eval (LetExp p_1 p_2 p_3) = addedLetExp
eval (Var p_1) = addedVar
```

The Environment type, addEnv and lookup functions are now defined (not part of the refactoring sequence). Finally the definition of eval needs to be modified to take a new argument, namely the Environment. This can be added using an "add argument" refactoring, but the definition needs then to be edited by hand to thread the environment through the computation, giving

```
eval :: Environment -> Expr -> Int
eval env (Literal x) = x
eval env (Bin op e1 e2) = eval_op op (eval env e1) (eval env e2)
eval env (LetExp p_1 p_2 p_3) = eval (addEnv p_1 p_2 env) p_3
eval env (Var p_1) = lookup p_1 env
```

3.5   Stage 5: Merging

Finally, the last stage requires us to implement a pretty printer for our language. We do this by defining a function prettyPrint over the type Expr with a type signature. Initially prettyPrint is defined with the equation prettyPrint x = error "Unable to pretty print!". We choose the *introduce pattern matching* from HaRe, which produces the following:

```
prettyPrint :: Expr -> String
prettyPrint x@(Literal x) = error "Unable to pretty print!"
prettyPrint x@(Bin op e1 e2) = error "Unable to pretty print!"
prettyPrint x@(LetExp n e e_2) = error "Unable to pretty print!"
prettyPrint x@(Var n) = error "Unable to pretty print!"
prettyPrint x = error "Unable to pretty print!"
```

The implementation for `prettyPrint` is completed, and the same procedure is repeated for a function `prettyBinOp` (including *introduce pattern matching*) in order to represent the pretty printing of binary operators. This gives us the following definitions:

```
prettyPrint :: Expr -> String
prettyPrint x@(Literal y) = show y
prettyPrint x@(Bin op e1 e2) = prettyPrintBinOp op
            ++ " " ++ (prettyPrint e1) ++ " " ++ (prettyPrint e2)
prettyPrint x@(LetExp n e e_2) = "let " ++ n ++ " = "
            ++ (prettyPrint e) ++ " in " ++ (prettyPrint e_2)
prettyPrint x@(Var n) = n
prettyPrint x = error "Unable to pretty print!"

prettyPrintBinOp :: Bin_Op -> String
prettyPrintBinOp x@(Mul) = "*"
prettyPrintBinOp x@(Plus) = "+"
prettyPrintBinOp x = error "Unable to pretty print binary operator"
```

To show how the pretty printer and parser work in practice, the following shows an example from the GHCi prompt:

```
Prelude Parser> parseExpr "let x + 1 1 x"
(LetExp "x" (Bin Plus (Literal 1) (Literal 1)) (Var "x"),"")

Prelude Parser> prettyPrint (LetExp "x" (Bin Plus (Literal 1)
                (Literal 1)) (Var "x"))
"let x = + 1 1 in x"

Prelude Parser> eval [] (LetExp "x" (Bin Plus (Literal 1)
                (Literal 1)) (Var "x"))
2
```

As can be seen, both `eval` and `prettyPrint` take an Expr as an argument. It would be nice to merge the two functions together so that it may be possible to pretty print and evaluate an abstract syntax tree simultaneously. This may lead to a function that parses an input, and pretty prints and evaluates the output, as follows:

```
Prelude Parser> parse "let x + 1 1 x"
"The value of let x = + 1 1 in x is 2"
```

In order to implement this feature, we first *merge* the definitions of `prettyPrint` and `eval` together (the *merge* refactoring is defined in Section 2.2). We also move the definitions of `eval_op` and `prettyPrintBinOp` to a `where` clause of the newly merged `eval` function.

Conclusions for the case study are discussed in Section 5.

4   Related Work

Program transformation for functional programs has a long history, with early work in the field being described by Partsch and Steinbruggen in 1983 [18]. Other work in program transformation for functional languages is described by Hudak in his survey [19]. For an extensive survey of refactoring tools and techniques, Mens produced a refactoring survey in 2004 detailing the most common refactoring tools and practices [20].

The University of Kent and Eötvös Loránd University are now in the process of building refactoring tools for Erlang programs [21]. However, different techniques have been used to represent and manipulate the program under refactoring. The Kent approach uses the *Annotated Abstract Syntax Tree* (AAST) as the internal representation of an Erlang program, and program analyses and transformations manipulate the AAST directly. The Eötvös Loránd university approach uses the Erlang-based database Mnesia [22] to store both syntactic and semantic information of the Erlang program under refactoring; therefore, program analyses and transformations are carried out by manipulating the information stored in the database.

The fold/unfold system of Burstall and Darlington [3] was intended to transform recursively defined functions. The overall aim of the fold/unfold system was to help programmers to write correct programs which are easy to modify. There are six basic transformation rules that the system is based on: unfolding; folding; instantiation; abstraction; definition and laws. The advantage of using this methodology is that it is simple and very effective at a wide range of program transformations which aim to develop more efficient definitions; the disadvantage is that the use of the *fold* rule may result in non-terminating definitions. Indeed, the fold refactorings implemented for HaRe also suffer from the same termination problems.

The Haskell Equational Reasoning Assistant, HERA [23] is a system that provides both a GUI level and a batch level Haskell rewrite engine inside a single tool. HERA shares the basic properties of HaRe. It is important to notice a difference however, HaRe works purely at the source level of a program, and applies well-understood software engineering patterns. HERA handles large-scale rewrites in a different way, using only a series of small steps performed in a strict bottom up manner. It is possible to implement particular refactorings from HaRe in HERA such as renaming and generalisation. However, the HERA tool doesn't provide an advanced API for program transformation and so refactorings would have to be described in terms of small transformations, which in some respects would make it more difficult to scale to large-scale transformations.

5   Conclusions and Future Work

This paper presented a number of refactorings implemented for the Haskell refactorer, HaRe, together with a case study in transforming programs written in Haskell. Specifically, the contributions of this paper are as follows:

- In Section 2, we briefly described a number of structural and data-type refactorings from Brown's PhD thesis [13]; these include: folding, merging, adding/removing a constructor, adding/removing a field and introduce pattern matching.
- In Section 3, we demonstrated a case study for refactoring Haskell programs. The case study serves not only as a basic demonstration of the refactorings discussed in Section 2, but also as a tutorial on how to refactor Haskell programs.

The case study presented in Section 3 resulted in some interesting conclusions. It seems that the simpler, more atomic, refactorings are more useful in refactoring large-scale programs than the larger more complex ones. It seems natural, therefore, to create larger refactorings by gluing together lots of smaller atomic refactorings. The most commonly used refactorings were *introduce new definition, generalise definition* and *folding*; these three refactorings exploit the idea of higher-order polymorphism resulting in code reuse by abstraction [24]. Some specific conclusions that came from the case study are:

- A refactoring tool aids the process of improving programs, by lowering the cost of making the changes. For example, in Sections 3.1 and 3.2 we add and remove constructors. This may be performed using a search and replace facility in an editor, but with extreme care. A refactoring tool, on the other hand, lowers the overall cost of making these changes, especially across large projects. In addition to this, HaRe also has an undo feature, allowing the user to try a particular refactoring without committing to the changes.
- Refactoring encourages code reuse. For example, in Section 3.3 it is possible to eliminate some duplicated code by *introducing* a top level definition from a selected expression, *generalising* over the definition and then *folding* against the new definition. This process also helps to encourage code understanding: by introducing a new name for an abstraction, for example.
- Pure, lazy, languages can appear to offer more opportunities for refactoring than strict, impure ones. *Generalisation*, as discussed in Section 1, is an example of a refactoring that could not be performed in a language with side-effects such as C or Java. Furthermore, the merging process as shown in Section 3.5 introduces a *shared computation*: a concept that is implicitly built into the Haskell language.

5.1   Implementation and Design Difficulties

Haskell is a very complex language, and its model of type signatures, pattern matching, guards, where clauses, recursive modules and type classes, makes it a difficult language to refactor due its richness of expression; for many of the refactorings presented in this paper, there have been occasions where it was not clear precisely how a particular refactoring should be defined, and indeed in a number of cases it makes sense to implement more than one version. For example, in the case of unfolding, there was a design choice to be made when guards are converted into an `if..then..else` clause. This can lead to problems where the guards may not have an `otherwise` clause defined, or the programmer was intending for the pattern matching to drop to the next equation in the definition. In this situation, we made the decision to introduce a default `else` clause that introduces an `error` if the guards cannot be converted directly. Consider unfolding the definition of f in the body of g:

```
f x
   | x == 1 = 10
   | x == 2 = 20
g y = f y
```

Unfolding f gives us:

```
f x
   | x == 1 = 10
   | x == 2 = 20
g y = if y == 1 then 10
            else if y == 2 then 20
                    else error "Unmatched Pattern"
```

Another choice we made was in the introduction of a field to a constructor. Because partial application of constructors is possible in Haskell – they are, after all, constructor *functions* – we chose to add the field in the first position, since this allows the field to be added in a straightforward way to any partial application. Although it is possible to implement the refactoring to allow the user to add the field to any position of the constructor, in practice it is more difficult, as it requires the refactorer to check for partial applications, and to perform the appropriate 'plumbing' to pass this extra argument in. We also observe that this same choice was made (for the same reasons) in the implementation of function generalisation, where the 'new' argument appears in the first position. We refer the reader to the PhD theses by Li [12] and Brown [13] for much more descriptive and technical discussions of the limitations of refactoring in general, and also with implementing a refactoring tool for Haskell programs.

5.2 Future Work

The work presented in this paper can still be carried forward in a number of directions.

- Adding more refactorings to HaRe. The number of refactorings for HaRe has increased, but there are still a number of refactorings listed in the catalogue [15] that are still awaiting implementation.
- Make more use of type information with the current refactorings in HaRe. For instance, when generalising a function definition that has a type signature declared, the type of the identified expression needs to be inferred, and added to the type signature as the type of the function's first argument.

- We hope to extend HaRe to allow refactorings to be scripted. Scripting refactorings allows elementary —or atomic— refactorings to be stitched together, creating the effect of a complete refactoring process. Indeed, the commonly occurring sequence of refactorings steps (such as introducing, generalising and folding) can be seen as generalised refactoring patterns, and could be abstracted away by the scripting process.
- Finally, we wish to port HaRe to GHC Haskell —the *de facto* standard of Haskell— and use the GHC API instead of Programatica for implementing refactorings.

The authors would like to thank Dave Harrison for his editorial advice, and the anonymous reviewers for their comments. We would also like to acknowledge EPSRC for supporting the original development of HaRe.

References

1. Brooks, F.P.: The Mythical Man-Month: After 20 Years. IEEE Software 12(5), 57–60 (1995)
2. Opdyke, W.F.: Refactoring Object-Oriented Frameworks. PhD thesis, Department of Computer Science, University of Illinois at Urbana-Champaign, Champaign, IL, USA (1992)
3. Burstall, R.M., Darlington, J.: A Transformation System for Developing Recursive Programs. J. ACM 24(1), 44–67 (1977)
4. Li, H., Thompson, S., Reinke, C.: The Haskell Refactorer, HaRe, and its API. Electronic Notes in Theoretical Computer Science 141(4), 29–34 (2005); Proceedings of the Fifth Workshop on Language Descriptions, Tools, and Applications (LDTA 2005)
5. Li, H., Reinke, C., Thompson, S.: Tool Support for Refactoring Functional Programs. In: ACM SIGPLAN 2003 Haskell Workshop, Association for Computing Machinery, pp. 27–38 (August 2003)
6. Peyton Jones, S., Hammond, K.: Haskell 98 Language and Libraries, the Revised Report. Cambridge University Press, Cambridge (2003)
7. Refactor-fp Group, T.: The Haskell Editing Survey (2004), http://www.cs.kent.ac.uk/projects/refactor-fp/surveys/haskell-editors-July-2002.txt
8. Oualine, S.: Vim (Vi Improved). Sams (April 2001)
9. Cameron, D., Elliott, J., Loy, M.: Learning GNU Emacs. O'Reilly, Sebastopol (2004)
10. Hallgren, T.: Haskell Tools from the Programatica Project. In: Haskell 2003: Proceedings of the 2003 ACM SIGPLAN Workshop on Haskell, pp. 103–106. ACM Press, New York (2003)
11. Lämmel, R., Visser, J.: A Strafunski Application Letter. In: Dahl, V. (ed.) PADL 2003. LNCS, vol. 2562, pp. 357–375. Springer, Heidelberg (2002)
12. Li, H.: Refactoring Haskell Programs. PhD thesis, School of Computing, University of Kent, Canterbury, Kent, UK (September 2006)
13. Brown, C.: Tool Support for Refactoring Haskell Programs. PhD thesis, School of Computing, University of Kent, Canterbury, Kent, UK (September 2008), http://www.cs.kent.ac.uk/projects/refactor-fp/publications/ChrisThesis.pdf

14. Brown, C., Thompson, S.: Clone Detection and Elimination for Haskell. In: Gallagher, J., Voigtlander, J. (eds.) PEPM 2010: Proceedings of the 2010 ACM SIGPLAN Workshop on Partial Evaluation and Program Manipulation, pp. 111–120. ACM Press, New York (2010)
15. Refactor-fp Group, T.: Refactoring Functional Programs (2008), http://www.cs.kent.ac.uk/projects/refactor-fp
16. Pettorossi, A.: A Powerful Strategy for Deriving Efficient Programs by Transformation. In: LFP 1984: Proceedings of the 1984 ACM Symposium on LISP and Functional Programming, pp. 273–281. ACM, New York (1984)
17. Brown, C., Thompson, S.: Expression processor example code (2010), http://www.cs.st-and.ac.uk/~chrisb/tfp2010.html
18. Partsch, H., Steinbruggen, R.: Program Transformation Systems. ACM Comput. Surv. 15(3), 199–236 (1983)
19. Hudak, P.: Conception, Evolution, and Application of Functional Programming Languages. ACM Computing Survey 21(3), 359–411 (1989)
20. Mens, T., Tourwé, T.: A Survey of Software Refactoring. IEEE Trans. Softw. Eng. 30(2), 126–139 (2004)
21. Kozsik, T., Csörnyei, Z., Horváth, Z., Király, R., Kitlei, R., Lövei, L., Nagy, T., Tóth, M., Víg, A.: Use cases for refactoring in erlang. In: Horváth, Z., Plasmeijer, R., Soós, A., Zsók, V. (eds.) Central European Functional Programming School. LNCS, vol. 5161, pp. 250–285. Springer, Heidelberg (2008)
22. Mattsson, H., Nilsson, H., Wikström, C., Ericsson Telecom Ab: Mnesia – A distributed robust DBMS for telecommunications applications. In: Gupta, G. (ed.) PADL 1999. LNCS, vol. 1551, pp. 152–163. Springer, Heidelberg (1999)
23. Gill, A.: Introducing the Haskell Equational Reasoning Assistant. In: Proceedings of the 2006 ACM SIGPLAN Workshop on Haskell, pp. 108–109. ACM Press, New York (2006)
24. Thompson, S.: Higher-order + Polymorphic = Reusable (May 1997)

Static Balance Checking for First-Class Modular Systems of Equations

John Capper and Henrik Nilsson

Functional Programming Laboratory,
School of Computer Science,
University of Nottingham,
United Kingdom
{jjc,nhn}@cs.nott.ac.uk

Abstract. Characterising a problem in terms of a system of equations is common to many branches of science and engineering. Due to their size, such systems are often described in a modular fashion by composition of individual equation system fragments. Checking the balance between the number of variables (unknowns) and equations is a common approach to early detection of mistakes that might render such a system unsolvable. However, current approaches to modular balance checking have a number of limitations. This paper investigates a more flexible approach that in particular makes it possible to treat equation system fragments as true first-class entities. The central idea is to record balance information in the type of an equation fragment. This information can then be used to determine if individual fragments are well formed, and if composing fragments preserves this property. The type system presented in this paper is developed in the context of Functional Hybrid Modelling (FHM). However, the key ideas are in no way specific to FHM, but should be applicable to any language featuring a notion of modular systems of equations.

Keywords: Systems of equations, equation-based, non-causal modelling, first-class components, equation-variable balance, structural analysis, linear constraints, refinement types.

1 Introduction

Systems of equations [3], also known as simultaneous equations, are abundant in science and engineering. Applications include modelling, simulation, optimisation, and more. Such systems of equations are often parametrised, describing not just a specific problem instance, but a set of problems. The size and nature of the systems frequently necessitates numerical methods and computers for solving them. The equations thus need to be turned into programs that can be used to solve for various problem instances. Such programs can be written manually, but a more expedient route is to transcribe the equations into a high-level language, e.g. a modelling language, thus making it possible to automatically translate the equations into a program that attempts to compute a solution given specific

R. Page, Z. Horváth, and V. Zsók (Eds.): TFP 2010, LNCS 6546, pp. 50–65, 2011.

values for any parameters. Due to the size of the equation systems, some form of abstraction mechanism that supports a *modular* formulation by composition of individual equation system fragments, *components*, is often a practical necessity.

Of course, as with any large and complex task, there is always a risk of mistakes being made. In this case, mistakes may render the system of equations unsolvable. In a modular development, an error in a component might not manifest itself until an attempt is made to use that component. In the worst case, problems might not become apparent until much later when the final program is run. In some applications, the system of equations may even evolve dynamically, say *during* a simulation run, meaning that it may take a long time indeed to discover certain errors. Static checks that catch mistakes early, preferably applicable to individual components in isolation, can thus be very helpful.

One might hope to statically impose sufficient constraints to guarantee that a system of equations has a solution. Unfortunately, the question of whether such a system has a solution or not can in general only be answered by studying complete systems with full knowledge of all coefficients, ruling out checking of components in isolation as well as parametrisation. Moreover, without actually attempting solving, the question can only be answered for relatively simple systems (e.g. linear systems of equations). In other words, if the setting is reasonably general, we *cannot* hope to develop e.g. a type system that guarantees that a well-typed equation system or fragments thereof are solvable.

However, there are simple criteria that if violated are *indicative* of problems, or that may even imply that an attempt to solve a system by a specific method (e.g. as embodied by a tool that translates equations to a program for solving them) will necessarily fail. One such criterion is that the number of variables, or *unknowns*, must equal the number of equations. A more refined criterion is that there should exist a bijective mapping between variables and equations. Some of these kinds of criteria *can* be enforced statically, e.g. through a type system.

Enforcing the balance of systems of equations is considered very useful in practise. For example, the state-of-the-art, equation-based modelling and simulation language Modelica insists that complete models are balanced [9, pp.40–46]. Indeed, translation to simulation code will fail if systems are unbalanced. Broman et al. propose a similar but more refined approach [1].

These criteria stem from the fact that a *linear* system of equations has a unique solution if and only if the equations are linearly independent and the number of equations and unknowns agree. However, they are useful heuristic criteria more generally, intuitively because each equation commonly can be used to solve for one variable occurring in it. For a (very) simple example, consider:

$$x^2 + y = 0 \tag{1}$$
$$3x = 10 \tag{2}$$

Here (2) can be used to solve for x, and the value of x can then be substituted into (1), enabling it to be used to solve for y. Note that both the variable-equation balance criterion and the pairing criterion are satisfied.

On the other hand, it is easy to see that neither criterion is sufficient to guarantee solvability. Consider:

$$x^2 + y = 0 \tag{3}$$

$$cx = 10 \tag{4}$$

Note that the system is now parametrised on a coefficient c. The two criteria are still satisfied, but whether the system has a unique solution or not depends on the value of c: for $c = 0$ there is no unique solution. Conversely, violation of the criteria does not necessarily mean a system is unsolvable; for example, consider adding an extra copy of (2) to the first system. The resulting system can of course still be solved, despite both criteria now being formally violated.

The existing approaches to balance checking have weaknesses. For example, in Modelica, a component either has to be balanced, or it is explicitly declared to be possibly unbalanced, in which case no balance checking is performed for that component. See Sect. 4 for a more in-depth discussion. In this paper we develop an approach that is both more flexible and capable of catching more problems:

- The type of a component is refined by adding a balance variable to it, reflecting the number of equations the component contributes to the overall system. This is a refinement type system [4] in that erasure of the extra type information recovers a term that is well-typed in the original system.
- Parametrised components may also have a parametrised balance.
- Balance information can be inferred for components in isolation, even when parametrised on other components and without any explicit declaration of balance information for such parameters.
- Additional structural constraints beside the balance are exploited for a more refined analysis. For example, in certain cases, it can be established that a component necessarily would render a system imbalanced whenever it is used, which thus can be reported as an error.

The upshot of this is that if a complete system is assembled modularly from components that are well-typed in the refined sense, and if the assembled system is balanced overall, then the "flat" system that results by unfolding all definitions will also be balanced.

Our immediate motivation comes from Functional Hybrid Modelling (FHM) [11,12,5] where it is desired to treat components as true first-class entities, including the possibility to modify the overall system of equations *during* simulation, at "run-time", as alluded to earlier. Static checks that help prevent accidentally changing a system from one that can be simulated (solved) to one that cannot are thus of particular interest. We do not explicitly consider structurally dynamic systems of equations here, but our type system can be easily extended to that setting thanks to the first-class notion of components.

However, it should be noted that the essence of the ideas presented in this paper are not at all specific to FHM: in principle, it should be relatively straightforward to adapt them to other equation-based modelling languages, like Modelica, or to any language featuring a notion of modular system of equations.

The structure of the remainder of this paper is as follows. Sect. 2 explains the idea of modular systems of equations in more depth. Sect. 3 describes the type system developed. Sect. 4 gives a comparative review of the related work. Sect. 5 looks at possible avenues for expansion of the type system. Finally, Sect. 6 provides some concluding remarks.

2   Modular Systems of Equations

This section introduces the idea of modular systems of equations in more detail. As FHM provided the immediate motivation for this work, we will draw on FHM for examples and we will adopt a concrete syntax derived from Hydra, an FHM language currently being developed. We will only explain FHM and Hydra to the extent needed for this paper; for further details, please consult Nilsson et al. [11,12] or Giorgidze & Nilsson [5].

Hydra, like Modelica, is concerned with modelling of dynamic, physical systems using Differential Algebraic Equations (DAE). The solution to such a system of equations is a set of time-varying reals, i.e. real-valued functions of time. In practise, it is usually the case that only approximate solution through numerical simulation is feasible. However, for our formal type system development, the domain of the variables and the exact form of the equations is of no consequence: all that matters is which variables occur in each equation. This is reflected in the precise syntax of terms for which our type system is defined (see Fig. 3.2 in Sect. 3.2), where equations are only considered in the abstract as a set of occurring variables.

2.1   Equation System Basics

A *system of equations* is a set of equations over a set of *variables* or *unknowns*. It has a solution if every variable in the system can be instantiated with a value such that all the equations are simultaneously satisfied. Again, for the type system developed in this paper, the domain of the variables is not important. However, in our examples, the domain is either the reals, $\mathbb{R}$, or time-varying reals.

A *linear* system of equations has a unique solution if all equations are independent and there are equally many equations and variables. If there are more independent equations than variables, the system is *over-constrained*. Such a system has no solution as there are too many constraints, some of which will be in conflict. If there are fewer independent equations than variables, the system is *under-constrained*. Such a system has infinitely many solutions.

The *equation-variable balance* of a system of equations is the difference between the number of equations and variables. Note that this is strictly a structural property: the details of exactly what the equations look like is of no consequence. This is true in general in our development: we only consider structural properties, i.e. equations in the abstract, as we cannot assume that all details are known. By analogy, we refer to a system with positive equation-variable balance as over-constrained, and one with negative balance as under-constrained, regardless of whether the equations actually are independent or even linear.

2.2   Abstraction over Systems of Equations

The equation systems needed to describe real-world problems are usually large and complicated. On the other hand, there tends to be a lot of repetitive structure making it beneficial to describe the systems in terms of reusable equation system fragments. For example, consider an electrical circuit comprising resistors, capacitors, and inductors. Each component can be described by a small equation system, and the entire circuit can then be described *modularly* by composition of *instances* of these for specific values of the components.

While the exact syntactic details vary between languages, the idea, in essence, is to encapsulate a set of equations as a component with a well-defined interface. Let us illustrate with an example, temporarily borrowing the syntax of the λ-calculus for the abstraction mechanism:

$$r \quad \equiv \quad \lambda(x, y) \rightarrow \begin{array}{c} x + y + z = 0 \\ x - z = 1 \end{array}$$

This makes r a *relation* that constrain the possible values of the two *interface variables* x and y according to the encapsulated equations. The variable z is *local*, not visible from the outside.

The relation r can now be used as a building block by *instantiating* it: substituting expressions for the interface variables and renaming local variables as necessary to avoid name clashes. We express this as application, denoted by $\diamond$:

$$u + v + w = 10$$
$$r \diamond (u, v)$$
$$r \diamond (v, w + 7)$$

After unfolding and renaming, a process we refer to as *flattening*, we get:

$$u + v + w = 10$$
$$u + v + z_1 = 0$$
$$u - z_1 = 1$$
$$v + (w + 7) + z_2 = 0$$
$$v - z_2 = 1$$

Note that each application of r effectively *contributes* one equation to the overall system as one of the instances of the encapsulated equations in each case must be used to solve for the corresponding instance of the local variable, z_1 and z_2.

2.3   FHM and Hydra

In this section, we introduce the FHM framework as embodied by the language Hydra [11,12,5]. We use this as the setting for the rest of the paper. The central idea of FHM is to embed an abstraction mechanism over equations as described in Sect. 2.2 into a pure functional language, allowing equation system abstractions to be *first-class entities* at the functional level. The equations are Differential Algebraic Equations (DAE), meaning that the domain of the variables is time-varying reals, or *signals*. An abstraction over an equation is therefore referred to as a *signal relation*. In the case of Hydra, the host language is Haskell [6].

In Hydra, the type of a signal relation is written $SR\ \alpha$. A signal relation can be thought of as a predicate on a signal:

$$SR\ \alpha \approx Signal\ \alpha \rightarrow Bool$$

where $Signal\ \alpha$ is a time-varying value of type α. As a product of signals is isomorphic to a signal of products, unary signal relations suffice to represent n-ary relations. For example, given a binary predicate $\equiv$ on $\mathbb{R}$:

$(\equiv_{sr}) :: SR\ (\mathbb{R}, \mathbb{R})$
$(\equiv_{sr})\ s = \forall\ (t :: Time).\quad fst\ (s\ t) \equiv snd\ (s\ t)$

First-class signal relations are constructed as follows:

sigrel *pattern* **where** *equations*

The pattern introduces *interface variables* that scope over the equations. The latter may refer to additional, implicitly declared, *local variables*. Together, these two kinds of variables are referred to as *signal variables* as they stand for time-varying quantities. There are two forms of equations:

$$e_1 = e_2 \tag{5}$$
$$sr \diamond e_3 \tag{6}$$

where sr is a *time-invariant* expression (*free* signal variables must not occur in it[1]) denoting a signal relation, and $\diamond$ denotes signal relation application, similarly to Sect. 2.2. Functional level objects can be used as time-invariant entities inside signal relations. In particular, functional-level variables can be used as coefficients in equations, thus allowing the equations to be parametrised: see the *resistor* example below for an example. On the other hand, time-varying signal-level entities are not permitted to escape to the functional level.

Signal variables scope over the time-varying, top-level equations of a signal relation. Since only time-invariant expressions may appear to the left of an application, nested signal relations are not permitted.

To illustrate, consider a component *twoPin*, encapsulating equations common to all electrical components with two pins, and a component *resistor*, defined as an extension of *twoPin* by adding an equation that describes the behaviour of a resistor:

---

[1] However, a manifest signal relation expression is fine as it binds *all* signal variables occurring in it. That is, signal relations can be "nested", but the signal variable scope is flat.

type $Pin = (\mathbb{R}, \mathbb{R})$

$twoPin :: SR\ (Pin, Pin, Voltage)$
$twoPin = \textbf{sigrel}\ (p, n, u)\ \textbf{where}$
  $fst\ p - fst\ n\ \ \ = u$
  $snd\ p + snd\ n = 0$

$resistor :: Resistance \rightarrow SR\ (Pin, Pin)$
$resistor\ r = \textbf{sigrel}\ (p, n)\ \textbf{where}$
  $twoPin \diamond (p, n, u)$
  $r * snd\ p = u$

Note that the resistor is modelled by a function that maps a resistance to a signal relation. In the definition of *resistor*, r is thus a time-invariant value, not an unknown. Note also that u is local. Flattening the signal relation that results from the *function* application *resistor* 220 yields the flat equation system:

  $fst\ p - fst\ n\ \ \ = u$
  $snd\ p + snd\ n = 0$
  $220 * snd\ p\ \ \ = u$

3   The Type System

The type system is presented as an embedding of an equation-based language into the simply-typed λ-calculus. An embedding into the λ-calculus reflects the two-level approach taken by FHM, from which much of the expressivity of the language is gained. The type system has been implemented in the dependently typed programming language Agda [13], giving us assurances that the algorithm is both total and terminating.

Description	Symbol	Description	Symbol
λ-bound variables	x, y	Equations	q
Expressions (λ-terms)	$e \in \Lambda$	Simple types	τ
Signal-variables	z	Type schemes	σ
Balance type-variables	$n, m, o \in \mathbb{Z}$	Typing environments	Γ
Signal level expressions	s	Constraint sets	C

Fig. 1. Notational Conventions

The notation $\overline{\chi}$ is used to denote a sequence $\chi_1, \ldots, \chi_n$ without repetition of elements. We will also allow ourselves to treat $\overline{\chi}$ as sets equipped with the usual set-theoretic operations. One should also note that x (and y) and z are *meta-variables*, ranging over the names of concrete function-level and signal-level variables, respectively.

3.1   Overview

As signal relations are first-class entities, it cannot be assumed that components can be flattened in order to determine the equation-variable balance. The only reasonable assumption is that all that is known statically is the *type* of a relation.

To track the equation-variable balance, the type of a signal relation is refined by annotating it with the number of equations it is able to contribute to a system. The contribution of a signal relation may also depend on the contribution of the parameters to the signal relation. Hence, signal relations can behave in a polymorphic fashion, contributing varying numbers of equations depending on the context in which the relation is used. See Sect. 4 for a comparative review of alternative type system designs.

Since the structural information required to determine a precise contribution may not always be available, the context in which a signal relation is applied is used to generate *balance constraints* (from now on, simply constraints). These constraints restrict the balance of a component to an interval.

Note that a representation of integers and linear inequalities has been introduced at the type level. This extension may appear to be a restricted form of dependent types [8]. However, these type level representations, whilst determined by the structure of terms, are not value level terms themselves. As such, we do not consider our system to be dependently typed.

Constraints may mention the contributions of several components, and hence are not directly associated with a single signal relation. As a result, the type of a signal relation is restricted to being annotated by a *balance variable* which is then further refined using constraints. The type checking algorithm generates a fresh balance variable for each signal relation, with type equality defined up to alpha equivalence of balance variables. As an example, the refined type for *resistor* from Sect. 2.3 is:

$$resistor :: (n = 2) \Rightarrow Resistance \rightarrow SR\,(Pin, Pin)\,n$$

Haskell's type class constraint syntax has been adopted to express that the balance type variable n is constrained to the value 2. This can be verified by first flattening the signal relation applications to obtain a set of 3 equations over 5 variables (note that each *Pin* contains two variables), then removing one equation which must be used to solve for the local variable u, giving a net contribution of two equations.

3.2   Generating Constraints

In this section we address the issue of what constraints should be generated. It is conceivable that different application domains could generate constraints specific to that domain. This is not a problem, as the system developed is independent of the constraints generated. For the purposes of this paper, 4 criteria for generating constraints have been chosen. Before introducing the criteria, a number of definitions are required.

Fig. 2 and 3 give the syntax of terms and types from which the type checking algorithm will be developed. A number of simplifications have been made to the FHM framework in order to keep the presentation of the type system concise. Note that all simplifications are superficial and do not fundamentally change the nature of the problem.

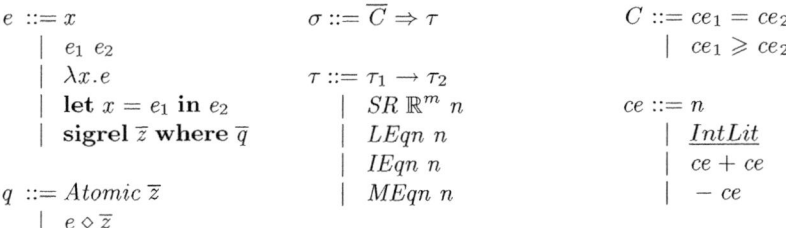

Fig. 2. Syntax of terms, types, and constraints

We consider the simply-typed λ-calculus, given by e, augmented with first-class signal relation constructs. Signal relations abstract over sets of signal variables, denoted $\overline{z}$, and embed a new syntactic category of *equations* into the calculus, given by q.

Signal relations range over sets of equations, which may take one of two forms. An atomic equation of the form $s_1 = s_2$ is abstracted to just the set of distinct signal variables occurring in the signal expressions s_1 and s_2. Similarly, an equation of the form $e \diamond \overline{s}$ is abstracted to the expression denoting the applied signal relation and the set of signal variables that occur on the right-hand-side of the application. More detailed comments on theses syntactic categories are given in Sect. 3.3.

An equation q is said to *mention* a signal variable z if and only if $z \in vars\ (q)$. The function *total* returns the raw number of atomic equations contributed by an equation. Whereas $|\overline{q}|$ denotes the cardinality of the set of *modular* equations. Both *vars* and *total* are also overloaded for sets of equations.

$$
\begin{aligned}
vars\ (Atomic\ \overline{z}) &= \overline{z} & total\ (Atomic\ \_) &= 1 \\
vars\ (\_ \diamond \overline{z}) &= \overline{z} & total\ (e : SR\ \_\ n \diamond \_) &= n \\
vars\ (\overline{q}) &= & total\ (\overline{q}) &= \\
\bigcup \{\, vars\ (q) \mid q \in \overline{q}\,\} & & \sum \{\, total\ (q) \mid q \in \overline{q}\,\}
\end{aligned}
$$

Given a signal relation **sigrel** $\overline{z}$ **where** $\overline{q}$, the set of interface variables is defined $I_Z = \overline{z}$, and the set of local variables $L_Z = vars\ (\overline{q}) \backslash \overline{z}$. The set of equations $\overline{q}$ can be partitioned into the disjoint subsets of interface equations I_Q, local equations L_Q, and mixed equations M_Q, where I_Q is the set of equations mentioning only interface variables, L_Q is the set of equations mentioning only local variables, and $M_Q = (\overline{q} \backslash I_Q) \backslash L_Q$. Finally, the balance of a signal relation, written $bal\ (sr)$, is given as $bal\ (\textbf{sigrel}\ \overline{z}\ \textbf{where}\ \overline{q}) = total\ (\overline{q}) - |L_Q|$. Intuitively, balance is an aggregate of the equations in the body of a signal relation, excluding sufficiently many equations to solve for the local variables.

1. $|L_Q| + |M_Q| \geqslant |L_Z|$. The local variables are not under-constrained.
2. $|L_Q| \leqslant |L_Z|$. The local variables are not over-constrained.
3. $|I_Q| \leqslant |I_Z|$. The interface variables are not over-constrained.
4. $0 \leqslant bal\ (sr) \leqslant |I_Z|$. A signal relation must contribute equations only for its interface variables. It should not be capable of removing equations from other components (negative balance), or adding equations for variables not present in its interface.

The above criteria produce constraints that give adequate assurances for detecting structural anomalies. There is potential to further refine these criteria. However, for the purposes of this paper, these criteria are sufficient to demonstrate the value of the type system.

To illustrate the application of the above five criteria, consider the Hydra example *par* that connects two circuit components in parallel. The operational details of this example are not important; the only important aspect is that of equations *mentioning* variables. The type signature gives the type of *par* under the simply typed approach. The reader may wish to refer back to Sect. 2.3 at this point for clarification on **sigrel** terms.

$par :: SR\ (Pin, Pin) \rightarrow SR\ (Pin, Pin) \rightarrow SR\ (Pin, Pin)$
$par\ sr_1\ sr_2 =$
    sigrel $((pi, pv), (ni, nv))$ **where**
        $sr_1 \diamond ((p1i, p1v), (n1i, n1v))$
        $sr_2 \diamond ((p2i, p2v), (n2i, n2v))$
        $pi + p1i + p2i = 0$
        $ni + n1i + n2i = 0$
        $pv = p1v = p2v$
        $nv = n1v = n2v$

Under the new type system, the signal relations in *par* are annotated by balance variables, which are then constrained by the criteria producing the following refined type:

$$par :: \{m = n + o - 2, 6 \geqslant n + o \geqslant 2, 0 \leqslant m \leqslant 4, 0 \leqslant n \leqslant 4, 0 \leqslant o \leqslant 4\} \Rightarrow$$
$$SR\ (Pin, Pin)\ n \rightarrow SR\ (Pin, Pin)\ o \rightarrow SR\ (Pin, Pin)\ m$$

While this type may appear daunting at first, all balance variables and constraints can be inferred without requiring the programmer to annotate the terms explicitly. It is also useful to see an example of a program that fails to type check under the new type system – a program that previously would have been accepted, despite being faulty.

$broken\ sr = $ **sigrel** (a, b) **where**
    $sr \diamond (w + x, y + z)$
    $sr \diamond (a, b)$
    $x + z = 0$

The above function *broken* is flawed in that there is no relation to which it can be safely applied. The relation *sr* is required to provide at least 3 equations for local variables, but must not exceed a contribution of 2 variables as dictated by the second relation application. As expected, our type system catches this error by attempting to impose the following inconsistent set of constraints:

$$broken :: (m = n + n - 3, 0 \leqslant m \leqslant 2, 0 \leqslant n \leqslant 2, 4 \leqslant n + 1 \leqslant 4)$$
$$\Rightarrow SR\ (\mathbb{R}, \mathbb{R})\ n \rightarrow SR\ (\mathbb{R}, \mathbb{R})\ m$$

During type checking, the Fourier-Motzkin elimination method is used to check the consistency of constraint sets [7]. The method allows one to check not only if a set of linear inequalities is satisfiable, but also finds a continuous interval for each bound variable. It is expected that this will be useful when reporting type errors to the programmer.

The elimination algorithm has worst case exponential time complexity in the number of balance variables. However, as shown by Pugh [15], the modified variant that searches for integer solutions is capable of solving most common problem sets in low-order polynomial time. Furthermore, systems typically involve only a handful of balance variables, making most exponential cases still feasible to check.

3.3   Formalising the Type System

Fig. 3 presents a small-step semantics for our calculus by way of a flattening for a system of equations. Values in our system are closed lambda-terms of the form $\lambda x.e$, signal relations encapsulating atomic equations, and atomic equations.

The notation $\{\overline{z_1}/\overline{z_2}\}$ denotes the substitution that occurs when reducing signal relation application. Our abstract treatment of equations allows us to read this notation as substituting every variable in $\overline{z_1}$ for all variables in $\overline{z_2}$, a simplification of the substitution discussed in Sect. 2.2. The symbol *fresh* denotes a fresh sequence of signal variables, used in S-SigApp2 to rename local variables to prevent name clashes during flattening (again, see Sect. 2.2).

The simplification of substitution discussed above has introduced a slight disparity between our abstract formalisation and the concrete system. In the FHM system, applying a signal relation contributing n equations to a mixed set of variables results in n mixed equations. However, during evaluation, it may be discovered that some of the equations within the signal relation do not mention both local and interface variables. Hence, the number of mixed, local, and interface equations may be refined as a result of evaluation.

This problem is avoided in our semantics by the simplification to substitution mentioned above. However, this should not pose a real problem in the concrete system either. The preservation problem is reminiscent of the record subtyping problem addressed in Peirce [14], pages 259–260. It should be possible to adapt the technique of *stupid casts* used in Pierce to solve the preservation problems that would be present in a more concrete semantics. To be more precise, one could allow a *stupid cast* of local and interface equations back into mixed equations, thus retaining the same contribution and maintaining the same constraints. We

$$\frac{e_1 \rightsquigarrow e_2}{e_1\ e_3 \rightsquigarrow e_2\ e_3} \quad \text{(S-App1)} \qquad \qquad \frac{}{(\lambda x.e_1)\ e_2 \rightsquigarrow [x \mapsto e_2]\ e_1} \quad \text{(S-App2)}$$

$$\frac{}{\textbf{let } x = e_1 \textbf{ in } e_2 \rightsquigarrow [x \mapsto e_1]\ e_2} \quad \text{(S-Let)} \qquad \frac{e_1 \rightsquigarrow e_2}{e_1 \diamond \overline{z} \rightsquigarrow e_2 \diamond \overline{z}} \quad \text{(S-SigApp1)}$$

$$\frac{\exists q_1 \in \overline{q}.\ q_1 \rightsquigarrow q_2}{\textbf{sigrel } \overline{z} \textbf{ where } \overline{q} \rightsquigarrow \textbf{sigrel } \overline{z} \textbf{ where } [q_1 \mapsto q_2]\ \overline{q}} \quad \text{(S-SigRel)}$$

$$\frac{\overline{q_2} = \{(vars(\overline{q}) \backslash \overline{z_1})/fresh\}\ \overline{q_1}}{(\textbf{sigrel } \overline{z_1} \textbf{ where } \overline{q_1}) \diamond \overline{z_2} \rightsquigarrow \{\overline{z_1}/\overline{z_2}\}\ \overline{q_2}} \quad \text{(S-SigApp2)}$$

Fig. 3. Small-step semantics

leave this alteration as future work, as the current semantics are sufficient for the purposes of this paper.

The syntax of types is similar to that of the simply-typed λ-calculus. Simple types consist of functions, signal relations, and equation types specified by $\rightarrow$, SR, and $I/M/LEqn$ respectively. The three varieties of equation types give distinct representations for interface, mixed, and local equations. Signal relation types and equation types are parametrised with a balance variable that denotes the number of equations a system is capable of contributing. Simple types are then parametrised by a constraint set that refines the possible interval of balance variables.

Fig. 4 gives the typing judgements for terms in our language. The rules for λ-terms, T-Var, T-Abs, and T-App are similar to those of the simply-typed λ-calculus, with the addition of constraint sets. Operations that render a constraint sets inconsistent indicate that a term is ill-typed; e.g, a judgement that involves taking the union of two consistent sets of constraints is only valid when the resulting constraint set is also consistent.

The T-Atomic judgement assigns equation types to atomic equations by examining the variables that occur in the equation. The helper function *eqkind* checks how the variables in an equation coincide with the interface variables to determine whether the equation is local, interface, or mixed.

The T-RelApp judgement assigns an equation type to a relation application. The preconditions for this judgement state that the type of the expression e appearing to the left of the application must be a signal relation. Additionally, the contribution of such a signal relation must not exceed the number of interface variables to which it is being applied. T-RelApp and T-Atomic depend on the read-only environment I which stores the set of interface variables the equations range over.

The final judgement assigns signal relation types to **sigrel** constructs and calculates constraints on the fresh balance variable of that signal relation. The first precondition defines the set of variables local to the relation. The second precondition is a pointwise judgement over the set of equations. The third

$$\frac{\Gamma(x) = C \Rightarrow \tau}{\Gamma \vdash x : C \Rightarrow \tau} \quad \text{(T--Var)} \qquad \frac{\Gamma, x : C_1 \Rightarrow \tau_1 \vdash e : C_2 \Rightarrow \tau_2}{\Gamma \vdash \lambda x.e : C_1 \cup C_2 \Rightarrow \tau_1 \rightarrow \tau_2} \quad \text{(T--Abs)}$$

$$\frac{\Gamma \vdash e_1 : C_1 \Rightarrow \tau_2 \rightarrow \tau_1 \qquad \Gamma \vdash e_2 : C_2 \Rightarrow \tau_2}{\Gamma \vdash e_1\ e_2 : C_1 \cup C_2 \Rightarrow \tau_1} \quad \text{(T--App)}$$

$$\frac{\Gamma \vdash e_1 : C_1 \Rightarrow \tau_2 \qquad \Gamma, x : C_2 \Rightarrow \tau_2 \vdash e_2 : C_1 \Rightarrow \tau_1}{\Gamma \vdash \textbf{let } x = e_1 \textbf{ in } e_2 : C_1 \cup C_2 \Rightarrow \tau_1} \quad \text{(T--Let)}$$

$$\frac{}{I \cdot \Gamma \vdash Atomic\ \overline{z} : \emptyset \Rightarrow eqkind_I(\overline{z}, 1)} \quad \text{(T--Atomic)}$$

$$\frac{\Gamma \vdash e : C \Rightarrow SR\ \mathbb{R}^m\ n \qquad |\overline{z}| \geqslant n}{I \cdot \Gamma \vdash e \diamond \overline{z} : C \Rightarrow eqkind_I(\overline{z}, n)} \quad \text{(T--RelApp)}$$

$$\frac{L = vars(\overline{q}) \setminus \overline{z} \qquad \overline{z} \cdot \Gamma \vdash \overline{q} : \overline{C} \Rightarrow \overline{\tau} \qquad n_X = \Sigma\{\ b \mid XEqn\ b \in \overline{\tau}\ \}}{\Gamma \vdash \textbf{sigrel } \overline{z} \textbf{ where } \overline{q} : \bigcup \overline{C} \cup C \Rightarrow SR\ \mathbb{R}^{|\overline{z}|}\ n}$$

$$C = \{n = n_I + n_L + n_M - |L|, 0 \leqslant n \leqslant |\overline{z}|, n_I \leqslant |\overline{z}|, n_L \leqslant |L|, n_L + n_M \geqslant |L|\}$$

$$eqkind_I(Z, n) = \begin{cases} IEqn\ n & \text{if } \emptyset \subset Z \subseteq I \\ LEqn\ n & \text{if } Z \cap I = \emptyset \\ MEqn\ n & \text{otherwise} \end{cases}$$

Fig. 4. Typing rules

precondition sums the number of equations of a given form in $\overline{q}$ specified by the parameter X, where $X \in \{I, L, M\}$. Finally, using the previous three conditions, a set of constraints is generated for the balance variables occurring in the type.

We have identified two key properties of soundness for our type system with respect to the semantics. Firstly, the preservation of types under evaluation for **sigrel** constructs ensures that flattening a modular system of equations does not alter the contribution of the system. Formally, if **sigrel** $\overline{z}$ **where** $\overline{q_1} \leadsto$ **sigrel** $\overline{z}$ **where** $\overline{q_2}$, and **sigrel** $\overline{z}$ **where** $\overline{q_1}$ $: C \Rightarrow SR\ \mathbb{R}^{|\overline{z}|}\ n$, where C is a consistent set of constraints, then **sigrel** $\overline{z}$ **where** $\overline{q_2}$ $: C \Rightarrow SR\ \mathbb{R}^{|\overline{z}|}\ n$. Hence, the contribution of the sets of equations q_1 and q_2 is equal under the same set of interface variables $\overline{z}$.

Secondly, a system can only be completely reduced to a simple set of equations if the top-level **sigrel** construct abstracts over an empty set of signal variables. In these circumstances, a fully assembled system should contribute no equations as no more signal variables will be introduced. Formally, if **sigrel** $\emptyset$ **where** $\overline{q}$ $: C \Rightarrow SR\ ()\ n$, and C is consistent, then C should resolve the interval of n to $[0, 0]$.

At this point, it is interesting to note the equational embedding effectively operates as a form of heterogeneous meta-programming; a modular system of equations is first evaluated to flat set of equations which is then transformed into a program that is used to solve for the unknowns of the original system. Hence, the balance and structure of a system of equations are really properties of the flattened system of equations that rule out (a class of) *second stage* runtime/simulation-time problems. Hence, a soundness statement regarding balance and structure falls to the meta-theory of a type system at the second stage. In summary, attempting to capture these properties during the initial phase make the soundness properties of our system quite unusual. As such, we leave the investigation of soundness of other structural properties as future work.

The type checking algorithm has been implemented in the dependently typed programming language Agda [13]. The source code can be found on the primary authors website at `http://cs.nott.ac.uk/~jjc`. The implementation guarantees that the algorithm is both total and termination. It should be noted that the function for computing the most general unifier of two types is postulated. We have yet to implement the semantics and prove that these are sound with respect to the typing judgements, this is left as future work.

4   Related Work

4.1   Modelica

Modelica, as of version 3.0 [9], requires that models be locally balanced. This is much more restrictive than our approach as components that are individually unbalanced may still be combined to produce a balanced system. When unbalanced components are needed, the current Modelica approach is to declare them as such, turning of all balance checking for that component. Moreover, models are not first-class entities in Modelica which simplifies the static checking.

4.2   Bunus and Fritzon

Bunus and Fritzon [2] describe an analysis technique for pinpointing problems with systems of equations developed in equation-based modelling languages such as Modelica. They look at structural properties, as we do, but, to allow fine-grained localisation, in much more detail by considering incidence matrices (which variables occur in which equations). This is only possible by analysing fully assembled systems, meaning the technique is primarily suitable for debugging. It could even be used *during* simulation to catch problems with structurally dynamic systems. Thus, this work is in many ways complementary to ours.

4.3   Structural Constraint Delta

Broman et al. [1] have developed a type system called structural constraint delta (C_Δ). The type system is developed for a simplified version of Modelica: Featherweight Modelica. The C_Δ represents the difference between the number of unknowns and the number of equations in an instance of a component. Hence,

C_Δ improves upon the Modelica approach by allowing models to be unbalanced, provided that a fully assembled system is balanced. As the type (class) of a constituent component is always manifest, and as the rules for subtyping are such that a replaceable component can only be replaced by one having the same C_Δ, component balances can always be computed in a bottom-up fashion.

In contrast, the type system presented in this paper does not rely on manifest type information. Furthermore, it supports a more flexible notion of balance as, if there are more than one component parameter, what matters is the collective number of contributed equations, not the numbers contributed individually.

To our knowledge, the idea of incorporating balance checking into the type system of a non-causal modelling language was suggested independently by Nilsson et al. [11] and Broman, with the latter giving the first detailed account.

4.4   Structural Types

Nilsson [10] outlines an approach to static checking that safeguards against a much wider class of errors than what is possible by just considering the balance. This is done by making an approximation of the incidence matrix part of the type of an equation system fragment, allowing structural singularities to be detected in many cases and thus approaching the capabilities of Bunus and Fritzon's technique, while retaining the capability of checking fragments in isolation.

While Nilsson presents the work within the context of FHM, he forgoes the consideration of first-class models, concentrating on the handling of static models. In contrast, the type system presented here handles first-class models, but cannot find as many problems.

5   Future Work

The type system presented in this paper captures the essence of the idea of balance checking in a setting with first-class equation system fragments. The system is abstract, but as such a suitable starting point for a type system for any such language. There are two imminent avenues for developing this work further. One is to elaborate the system so as to bring it closer to a system suitable for a concrete language like FHM. Handling of compound signal variables such as matrices should also be considered, as the size of matrices can affect the balance if equations between matrices is supported. The other avenue is to formalise the system and the dynamic semantics to prove soundness.

6   Conclusion

In this paper, we presented a type system for modular systems of equations capable of detecting classes of errors related to the equation-variable balance. Components can be analysed in isolation, rather than requiring assembly into a complete system of equations first, thus allowing over- and under-constrained systems to be detected early, aiding error localisation. First-class equation system fragments are supported. Our system thus lays down the foundations for a practical yet strong type system. The context of this work is equation-based, non-causal modelling, but the ideas should be readily adaptable to other settings.

Acknowledgments. The authors would like to thank David Broman, Neil Sculthorpe, and the anonymous reviewers for helpful and constructive feedback.

References

1. Broman, D., Nyström, K., Fritzson, P.: Determining Over- and Under-Constrained Systems of Equations using Structural Constraint Delta. In: GPCE. ACM, New York (2006)
2. Bunus, P., Fritzson, P.: A debugging scheme for declarative equation based modeling languages. In: Adsul, B., Ramakrishnan, C.R. (eds.) PADL 2002. LNCS, vol. 2257, p. 280. Springer, Heidelberg (2002)
3. Conkwright, N.B.: Introduction to the Theory of Equations. Ginn, Boston (1957)
4. Freeman, T., Pfenning, F.: Refinement Types for ML. In: PLDI (1991)
5. Giorgidze, G., Nilsson, H.: Higher-Order Non-Causal Modelling and Simulation of Structurally Dynamic Systems. In: Casella, F. (ed.) Proceedings of the 7th International Modelica Conference. Linköping Electronic Conference Proceedings (2009)
6. Jones, S.: Haskell 98 Language and Libraries: the Revised Report (2003)
7. Kuhn, H.: Solvability and Consistency for Linear Equations and Inequalities. American Mathematical Monthly 63 (1956)
8. McKinna, J., Altenkirch, T., McBride, C.: Why Dependent Types Matter. ACM SIGPLAN Notices 41(1) (2006)
9. The Modelica Association. Modelica – A Unified Object-Oriented Language for Physical Systems Modeling: Language Specification Version 3.2 (2010)
10. Nilsson, H.: Type-Based Structural Analysis for Modular Systems of Equations. In: Proceedings of the 2nd International Workshop on Equation-Based Object-Oriented Languages and Tools. Linköping Electronic Conference Proceedings (2008)
11. Nilsson, H., Peterson, J., Hudak, P.: Functional hybrid modeling. In: Dahl, V. (ed.) PADL 2003. LNCS, vol. 2562, pp. 376–390. Springer, Heidelberg (2002)
12. Nilsson, H., Peterson, J., Hudak, P.: Functional Hybrid Modeling from an Object-Oriented Perspective. In: Simulation News Europe (2007)
13. Norell, U.: Towards a Practical Programming Language Based on Dependent Type Theory. PhD thesis, Department of Computer Science and Engineering, Chalmers University of Technology, Göteborg, Sweden (2007)
14. Pierce, B.: Types and Programming Languages. The MIT Press, Cambridge (2002)
15. Pugh, W.: The Omega Test: a Fast and Practical Integer Programming Algorithm for Dependence Analysis. In: Supercomputing 1991 (1991)

Graphical and Incremental Type Inference: A Graph Transformation Approach

Silvia Clerici, Cristina Zoltan, and Guillermo Prestigiacomo

Dept. Llenguatges i Sistemes Informàtics
Universitat Politècnica de Catalunya
Barcelona, Spain

Abstract. We present a graph grammar based type inference system for a totally graphic development language. NiMo (Nets in Motion) can be seen as a graphic equivalent to Haskell that acts as an on-line tracer and debugger. Programs are process networks that evolve giving total visibility of the execution state, and can be interactively completed, changed or stored at any step. In such a context, type inference must be incremental. During the net construction or modification only type safe connections are allowed. The user visualizes the type information evolution and, in case of conflict, can easily identify the causes. Though based on the same ideas, the type inference system has significant differences with its analogues in functional languages. Process types are a non-trivial generalization of functional types to handle multiple outputs, partial application in any order, and curried-uncurried coercion. Here we present the elements to model graphical inference, the notion of structural and non-structural equivalence of type graphs, and a graph unification and composition calculus for typing nets in an incremental way.

Keywords: type inference, graphical language, process networks, type visualization.

1 Introduction

The data flow view of lazy functional programs as process networks was first introduced in [1]. The graphical representation of functions as processes and infinite lists as non-bounded channels helps to understand the program overall behaviour. The net architecture shows bi-dimensionally the chains of function compositions, exhibits implicit parallelism, and back arrows give an insight into the recurrence relations between the new results and those already calculated. The graphic execution model that the net animation suggests was the outset of the NiMo language design, whose initial version was presented in [2]. It was completely defined with graph grammars and implemented in the graph transformation system AGG [3]. This first prototype NiMoAGG showed the feasibility of a graphical equivalent for Miranda or Haskell, also fully graphically executable. A small set of graphic elements allows dealing with higher order, partial application, non-strict evaluation, and type inference with parametric polymorphism.

R. Page, Z. Horváth, and V. Zsók (Eds.): TFP 2010, LNCS 6546, pp. 66–83, 2011.

As the net represents the code and its computation graph at the same time, users have total visibility of the execution internals in a comprehensible model. Partially defined nets can be executed, dynamically completed or modified and stored at any step, enabling incremental development on the fly. Execution steps can also be undone, acting as an on line tracer and debugger where everything can be dynamically modified, even the evaluation policy. In the current version, five modes of increasing activity can be globally or locally assigned to each process, thus allowing to increase parallelism, reduce channel size (number of elements) and synchronize subnets. Symbolic execution is also admitted. The execution model is defined in [4].

In this context, where incompleteness does not inhibit execution, editing a program is a discontinuous process with execution intervals where code evolves up to the next interaction; hence type inference is by necessity incremental. On the other hand, in NiMo there is no textual code at all. Programs are graphs whose nodes are interfaces of processes or data. Interfaces are graphic tokens with typed in/out ports. Net construction equates to building a bi-dimensional term, where sub-expressions are like puzzle pieces that can be pairwise connected in any order if their shapes fit (both port types unify), thus ensuring type safeness by construction. In the first version, static inference was partial in presence of polymorphism. Now the full type information of each interface port is carried up by means of a second kind of graphs, and updated with each connection. Users can visualize the type information evolution and realize why a connection is rejected. Though based on the same principles, the inference system has significant differences with its functional analogues. Besides being graphical and incremental, the data flow ingredient imposes coping with multiple-output processes and curried-uncurried interpretation of multiple inputs, partial application in any order and partial disconnection for multiple outputs. In the current version this is admitted even in HO parameters. Hence, a process type is a non-trivial generalization of a functional type. The current inference system was also firstly defined with graph grammars [5] and implemented in AGG, since the graph transformation approach is the natural framework to formalize actions in NiMo. They are all subnet transformations, and so is the type inference process as well.

Here we present the type inference system of NiMoToons; the NiMo environment (overviewed in [6]). Graphical typing and incremental inference are described using a textual denotation for type graphs. A type graph unifier operator and a net typing calculus are intended to bridge the gap with the underlying formalism in terms of graph transformation rules. The paper is organized as follows: the next section introduces the syntax and main constructions of NiMo[1]. Section 3 presents the graphical representation of types, their interpretation in a textual notation, and the differences between process and function types. Section 4 defines the notion of structural and non-structural equivalence of type descriptors and unification in both cases. Section 5 covers net typing. A set of port connection and composition operators is the basis for the incremental component type

---

[1] It does not cover evaluation aspects because they are not relevant to the issue of types and can be found in the papers mentioned above.

calculus. All along the paper the topics are illustrated with screen-shot examples. The last section discusses some related work and summarizes our contributions.

2   NiMo Language Elements

NiMo programs are directed graphs with two kinds of nodes: processes and data items. Horizontal arrows represent channels of flowing data streams, and vertical arrows entering a process are non-channel parameters, which can also be processes. Processes can have any number of inputs and outputs, making the use of tuples unnecessary. There are neither patterns nor specific graphical syntax for conditionals. The tokens are: *rounded rectangles* for processes, *circles* (or ovals) for constant values, *black-dots* for duplicators, *hexagons* for data elements, and

green-arrows for non productive outputs (◀–) or delayed arguments (↧).Circles are labelled with their value for atomic types or with their names for symbolic constants of any type, even polymorphic. Hexagon labels are I, R, B ,L and F for integers, reals, booleans, lists, and functional processes. Polymorphic data are labelled with ?. In the current version neither user defined types nor Haskell type classes are supported. Ad-hoc polymorphism for functions like > is handled as in Miranda. There are two different processes for real and integer operators. The NiMo syntax makes intensive use of colour. In hexagons and circles it indicates their type, in process names it denotes the evaluation mode, and edges have a state shown as a colored *diamond* to indicate process activation or data evaluation degree. Some program examples can be seen in [7].

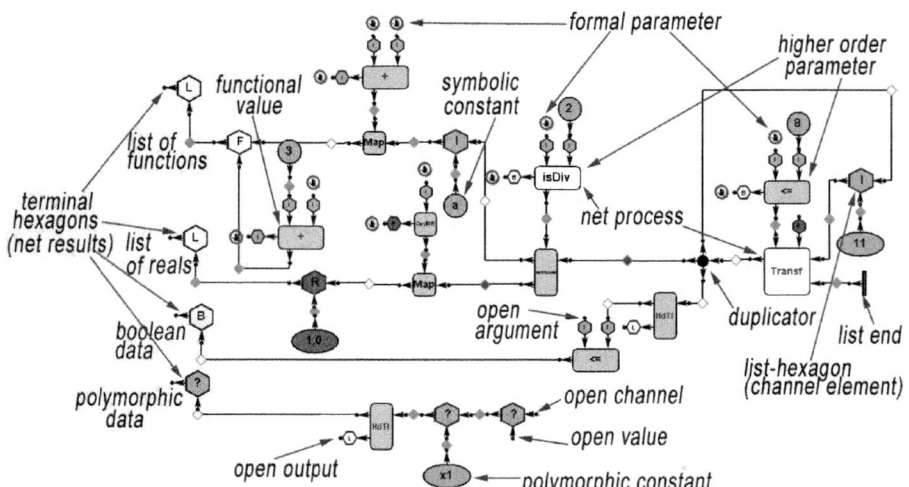

Fig. 1. NiMo program elements

2.1 Interfaces and Connections

All the mentioned nodes are *interfaces* having typed (in/out) connection ports. Interfaces are dragged from a ToolBox and dropped into the workspace where the net is being built (see top of Fig. 2). Clicking on a pair of ports connects them with an edge if both types are compatible; otherwise a failure message is generated. Process interfaces have an *F-out* port on the bottom. It is not one of their outputs but their value as a functional data.

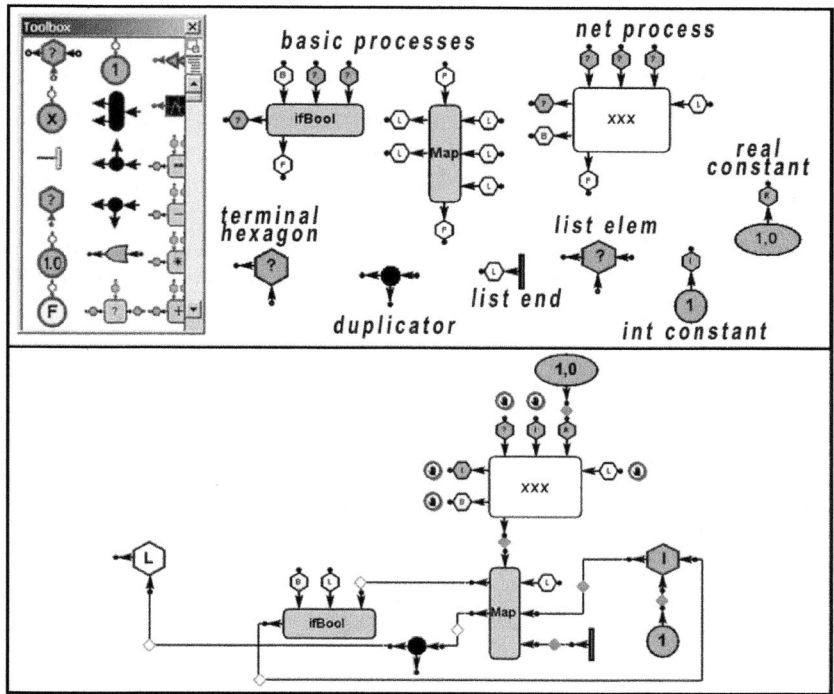

Fig. 2. Interfaces

This special out-port disappears when any output of the process is connected (becoming a potentially active process), or when all its inputs are connected (it is no longer a function). HO parameter processes are connected by their *F-out* port (as *xxx* on the bottom of Fig. 2). All the other open ports get thus blocked (⬤) to prevent new connections which would change its type. There is a set of built-in processes (grey rounded-rectangles) for basic types and stream processing. It includes multiple output versions of many Haskell prelude functions, as the process *SplitAt*, analogous to the *splitAt* function that can behave also as *take* or as *drop* just by leaving one or the other output open. We call this feature *partial production*, in analogy with the notion of partial application; i.e. there is a symmetry in parameters and results regarding partiality.

Also, some basic processes have configurable arity, as a *Map* with n input and m output channels[2] (generalizing *map*, *zipWith* and *zipWith3*), *TakeWhile* and *Filter* with n input and output channels, and an *Apply* process.

Terminal hexagon interfaces correspond to the net outputs. Subnets connected to them are considered productive, even being incomplete. In execution all the non-productive subnets are deleted by the garbage collector. For instance, the net in Fig. 2 is productive. Moreover, it is able to produce a result because Map_{3-2} already has enough inputs to act since one of its input channels has a list-end connected, thus it returns a list-end in both outputs. Then the duplicator also returns the list-end.

2.2   Net-Process Definitions

Net processes are user-defined components whose interfaces (the white rounded-rectangles) are defined by means of a parameterisation mechanism. The net in/out open ports that are to be considered as formal parameters or results, are bound to the in/out ports of a configurable interface that is given a name. Afterwards, it can be imported to the Toolbox to be used as a process in a new net and so on, allowing incremental net complexity up to any arbitrary degree.

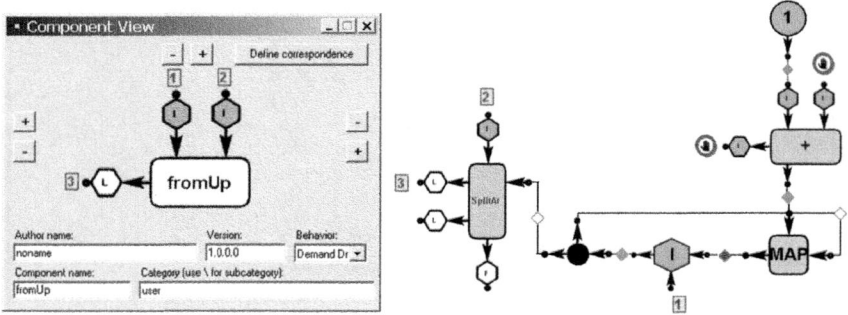

Fig. 3. Net Process definition

Fig. 3 shows an example for the process *fromUp*[3] that generates a list with k consecutive integers from the value n, where n and k correspond respectively to the parameters labelled 1 and 2. When the net process acts, the interface is replaced by the net updating the connections according to the bindings. Also, there is a *generic process interface* for building the interface of a not yet defined net process. The user sets the process name and number of channel/non-channel parameters and outputs, and optionally their types (which are all polymorphic by default). In a top down development this allows nets with not yet defined processes to execute. And it is also the means to define recursive processes, i.e. to build a net definition containing the process interface which is being defined.

---

[2] We will refer to it as Map_{n-m}.

[3] In Haskell code: *fromUp n k = x where(x, y) = splitAt k z ; z= n: map (1+) z.*

2.3   Partial Application and Production in HO

In NiMO partial application can be made in any order. In HO parameters, the effective arguments can be delayed by connecting a vertical green-arrow before connecting its F-out port. On the left of Fig. 4, process *ifBool* has the green-arrow at its first input, thus allowing its value to be completed later. It is also the way for binding this port as a second order parameter if the net is defined as a net process[4]. Moreover, in NiMo multiple output processes and even partial

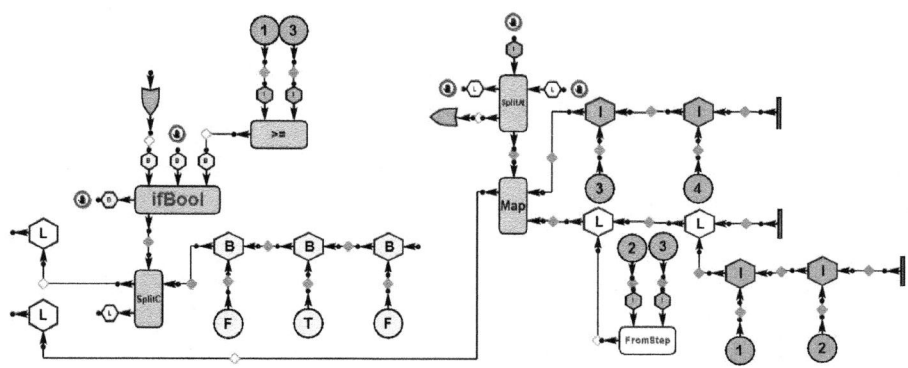

Fig. 4. Delayed argument and partial production

production are allowed in HO parameters. The horizontal green-arrow (in the middle of Fig.4) is connected to the second output of process *SplitAt*. It makes *SplitAt* to behave like *take*, becoming a suitable parameter for a single output *Map*. ◀━ is the only interface that can be connected to a process out port without elimination of the F-out port. Once the process is applied the green-arrow disappears.

3   Graphical Typing

As already said, in NiMo type checking and inference is made step by step and locally during net editing. Initially the net is empty. The user adds interfaces and connects pairs of type compatible ports. The full type information of each interface port is carried in a second kind of (optionally visible) graphs, which are updated with each new connection and help to identify what is failing when a connection is rejected. In this section we present the graph representation of types and the textual notation to describe them in a way close to the usual type expressions.

---

[4] E.g. if the increment in Fig. 3 were the third *fromUp* parameter instead of being 1.

3.1   Type Graph and Type Descriptors

The net has an associated *type graph,* which is an acyclic and maybe non-connected graph whose nodes are *type hexagons* labelled I, R, B, L, F, O and ?. All ports of every interface are tied to a node in the type graph[5], and shared sub graphs indicate identical types. In connected ports only the out is tied to the type graph (to avoid arrow duplication). The net type graph is incrementally built during the net construction starting from the type graph associated to each interface that we call its *type descriptor*(TD). TDs fully describe the type of processes and data items. Each interface port is tied to one type hexagon by means of a non-labelled arrow. This hexagon is the root of the port TD and it could be shared by, or included in, another port TD of the interface. In NiMo there are no variable names and this also applies to type variables in polymorphic types. The label ? stands for all the polymorphic types. Sharing a polymorphic hexagon is the graphical equivalent of multiple occurrences of a type variable in a polymorphic type expression. In Fig. 5 we can see the interfaces on the top

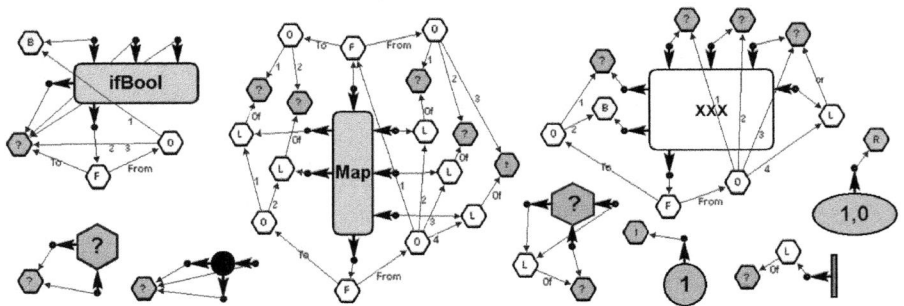

Fig. 5. Type descriptors

of Fig. 2 with their TDs. The F-out port TD of the process interfaces *ifBool,* Map_{3-2} and *xxx* describes their type as a functional value. In NiMo a *process type* is a generalization of a functional type, whose graphical representation is a graph rooted with a hexagon F with outgoing edges labelled *From* and *To.* Multiple inputs or outputs in a process type correspond to the subgraphs with an O-hexagon root and edges labelled by numbers. In case of single input or output the corresponding O-hexagon is omitted (as happens with the output of *ifBool*). Note that an O-hexagon never roots a port descriptor; it is not a NiMo type but a subgraph of a F type descriptor. It has as its children the descriptors of the inputs/outputs of the process (thus the F-out port TD contains as sub-graphs the TDs of all the other ports of the interface).

In the textual notation that we will use from now on, ∥ denotes the type constructor O for ordered parallel inputs or results, each ?-hexagon in the TD is denoted by a type variable $?_i$ (or ? if there is only one), and multiple occurrences of

---

[5] For an idea of what it looks like, Fig. 10 shows the type graph of the net in Fig. 2.

the same variable in the type expression correspond to a shared ?-hexagon. Thus the most general type for processes is denoted by $?_{i1}\|\ldots\|?_{in}\to?_{o1}\|\ldots\|?_{om}$ where $n, m \geq 0 \quad n + m > 0$. The denotation for the *ifBool* type is $B\|?\|?\to?$, for Map_{3-2} is $(?_1\|?_2\|?_3\to?_4\|?_5)\|[?_1]\|[?_2]\|[?_3]\to[?_4]\|[?_5]$, and for the user process *xxx* is $?_1\|?_2\|?_3\|[?_3]\to?_4\|B$. Some other examples of process types are $+ : I\|I\to I$; *id* : $?\to?$; *fibonacci* : $\to[I]$ and *sink* : $?\to$. The two last ones are non-functional processes; their interfaces do not have a F-out port. *fibonacci* is a process with no inputs and a single output which is an integer list, and *sink* is a process with no output that consumes its input value. It does not have a Haskell equivalent; its definition would be something like *sink x = void*.

4   Type Graph Unification

In order to connect two ports, the editor must first verify that their TDs t and t' can be *unified*; i.e. that there exists a *unifier graph* t $\approx$ t' for them. In this case the connection is made and both ports acquire this common TD; otherwise a failure message is generated. NiMoToons has an option to automatically roll-back partial unifications by recovering the original types each time a connection fails; otherwise they persist to be analyzed and can be explicitly undone afterwards[6].

The unifier graph exists when the respective TDs are *structurally equivalent*. Roughly, this means that both TDs can be overlapped and all their respective hexagons coincide (same label and number of children), except when one of them is a polymorphic hexagon, in which case the other one hides it. In Haskell-like languages the unification is always structural. A functional type has a single interpretation because all functions have a single result and also a single parameter (the first one), and to be unified both type expressions must be structurally equivalent. Curried and uncurried functions have no equivalent types. But in NiMo processes can be interpreted in one or the other way, and thus non-structural unification is allowed under certain conditions that are described in section 4.2.

4.1   Structural Unification

Fig. 6 shows an example where the F-out port TDs of interfaces f and g, are structurally equivalent. The screen-shot on the right can be obtained by moving the hexagons of both TDs to make them coincide. This allows us to visualize the unifier graph $t \approx t'$ that would result if both TDs were unified[7]. The corresponding port types are $t = I\|?_1\to[?_2]$ and $t'=?_3\|R\to?_4$. We can see that the second input of f, the first input of g, and its output, each one having a different polymorphic type on the left, have been replaced by the respective types in the other interface. The resulting type $t \approx t' = I\|R\|\to[?_2] = t\langle?_1{\Leftarrow}R; ?_6{\Leftarrow}B\rangle = t'\langle?_3{\Leftarrow}I; ?_4{\Leftarrow}?_2\rangle$

---

[6] The same happens when a connection is destroyed (individually or as a result of deleting a connected interface).

[7] Being both out-ports they cannot be connected but their TDs would be unified e.g. if they were connected as values of two list-items in a same list.

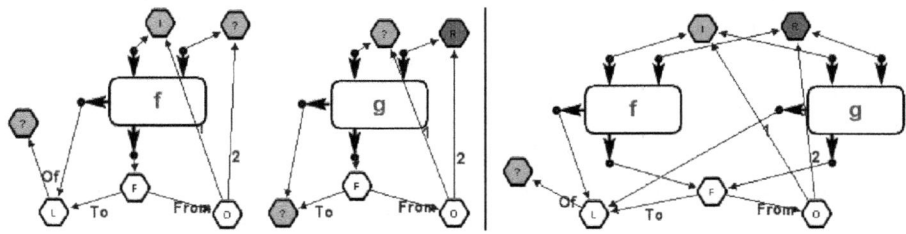

Fig. 6. Structural unification

where the notation $?_i \Leftarrow \delta$ stands for the replacement of the corresponding ?-hexagon by a subgraph δ.

If two TDs t and t' unify, the unifier graph $t \approx t'$ is obtained by the fusion of t and t' into a common type graph where, starting from the roots, each pair of corresponding hexagons *collapses* in a single node. This node has as its incoming edges the union of both sets of incoming edges.

The following rules define the (commutative and highest precedence) operator $\approx$ that obtains the unification result in case of structural equivalence:

1. $t \approx t = t$ for t rooted in $\{I, R, B\}$
2. $t \approx ? = t$ \qquad (t is not rooted O and $? \not\subset t$)
3. $[t] \approx [t'] = [\, t \approx t'\,]$
4. $(t_1 \| \ldots \| t_n) \approx (t'_1 \| \ldots \| t'_n) = t_1 \approx t'_1 \| \ldots \| t_n \approx t'_n$
5. $(ti_1 \| \ldots \| ti_n {\to} to_1 \| \ldots \| to_m) \approx (ti'_1 \| \ldots \| ti'_n {\to} to'_1 \| \ldots \| to'_m) =$
   $(ti_1 \| \ldots \| ti_n) \approx (ti'_1 \| \ldots \| ti'_n) \;\to\; (to_1 \| \ldots \| to_m) \approx (to'_1 \| \ldots \| to'_m)$

Rule 1 is for basic types, i.e two single node TDs with the same label collapsing in a single one. Rule 2 says that a ?-hexagon can be substituted by any other TD not rooted O, because O does not represent a tuple type; it is always a subgraph of a process TD. Hence, a single polymorphic input/output cannot be instantiated to multiple inputs/outputs. Besides, the ?-hexagon cannot be a proper subgraph of the other TD because a cycle would occur (infinitely recursive type). When a ?-hexagon collapses with any other node, the resulting hexagon is the other one (which acquires its incoming edges). This graph replacement of any node ? in the TD t by the graph δ[8] is denoted as $t\langle ?\Leftarrow\delta\rangle$. Rules 3 and 4 apply when both labels are L or O; the respective subgraphs are pairwise unified and the collapsed hexagon has (same number of) new outgoing edges, each one of them having as target the respective collapsed hexagons. Rule 5 applies for structurally equivalent TDs rooted F. The collapsed hexagon has as children the unifier graphs of both pairs of children.

4.2   Non Structural Unification

In NiMo two process types with different number of parameters and results can also be unified. Fig. 7 shows that, as happens in Haskell, process + is a

---

[8] It can be seen as the equivalent to the Damas-Milner instantiation rule.

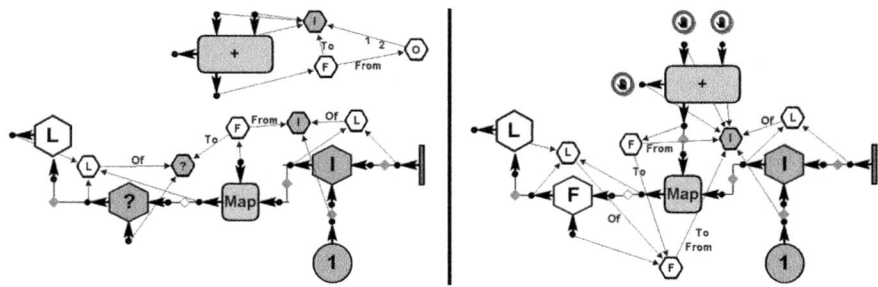

Fig. 7. Curried interpretation of multiple inputs

valid HO parameter for *Map*, in which case the elements in the input channel must be integers, and the result is a channel of functional elements of type $I{\to}I$. But the type of $+$ is $I\|I{\to}I$, and thus it should unify with $I{\to}(I{\to}I)$. I.e. in cases like this, there is an implicit conversion among non-structurally equivalent process types. Also the number of outputs could have been different, as happens in Fig. 8. In general, processes with multiple inputs and outputs can be viewed as returning intermediate functional types, i.e. the type of a process with $n > 1$ inputs and m outputs $t_1\| \ldots \|t_n \to t'_1\| \ldots \|t'_m$ can be implicitly converted to types $t_1\| \ldots \|t_k{\to}(t_{k+1}\| \ldots \|t_n{\to}t'_1\| \ldots \|t'_m)$ for any $k < n$. Thus two non-structurally equivalent process types t and t' could be unified if any of the curried interpretations of t is structurally equivalent to some of those of t'. The idea is that the process with fewer parameters must return a single output, whose type has in turn to unify with the functional type resulting of applying the other one to as many parameters as it has. In this case both F nodes collapse, and the new children are the children of the unifier graph root. i.e. the structure of the result changes. The following equation defines the unification result in these cases:

6. $(t_1\| \ldots \|t_k\|t_{k+1}\| \ldots \|t_n \to to) \approx (t'_1\| \ldots \|t'_k{\to}to')=$
$$(t_1\| \ldots \|t_k) \approx (t'_1\| \ldots \|t'_k) \to to' \approx (t_{k+1}\| \ldots \|t_n{\to}to)$$

Note that all the curried interpretations of a process can be derived from it.

In Fig. 8 the process types of $f : ?_1\|?_2\|[?_3]{\to}?_4\|?_5$ and $g : ?_6\|?_7{\to}?_8$ unify because both the first two inputs types unify ($?_1\|?_2 \approx ?_6\|?_7$) and g has a single output that unifies with a function from the third input of f to its results, i.e. $?_8{\approx}([?_3]{\to}?_4\|?_5)$. On the right side[9] $\tau f{\approx}\tau g = ?_1\|?_2{\to}([?_3]{\to}?_4\|?_5)$, where the collapsed hexagons during the unification correspond to the substitutions $\langle ?_6{\Leftarrow}?_1; ?_7{\Leftarrow}?_2; ?_8{\Leftarrow}([?_3]{\to}?_4\|?_5)\rangle$ in the type expression τg, whose result is one of the possible curried interpretations of τf.

---

[9] The right side cannot be obtained by overlapping as in Fig. 6. It was obtained by first connecting the F-out ports as the values of a pair of connected list-items (then deleted). The unification persists but can be undone by forcing type recalculation.

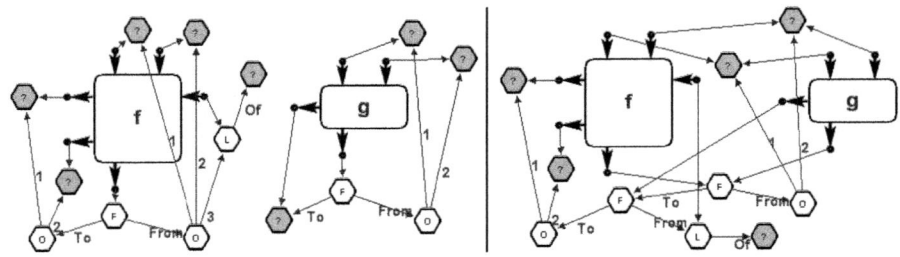

Fig. 8. Non-structural unification

5 Incremental Type Inference for Nets

In functional programming languages variables are used as formal parameters (bound variables), or locally defined elements. Free variables are considered missing definitions and rejected by the compiler. In NiMo there are no variable names. Function parameters are the process interface in-ports, data hexagons with open in-ports can be seen as anonymous free variables, and nets containing open ports are executable. Besides, the multiple outputs of a net can be produced in parallel by non-connected subnets, unlike functional interpreters that always deal with a single (and closed) expression. Hence, the incremental typing of nets has to cover all these cases.

During construction, the net is considered to have as many parameters/results as open in/out ports, which are pairwise closed with each new connection. In terms of graphs the net is a non-connected directed graph. Each new interface adds a component and each connection may reduce the number of connected components (CC). On the other hand, several port TDs in a CC could share subgraphs with ?-hexagons; then, unifying a pair of port TDs can affect any other port TD all along both CCs. But even if the port TDs are identical, the connection changes the types of both interfaces, those of their CCs and thus the net type, because all of them lose (at least) an in or an out open port. In general, connection order is irrelevant except when connecting ports of a process interface having an F-out port. This port makes a difference in the CC type as is discussed in the next section.

5.1 Functional and Non-functional Components

If N is the net under construction, $N = \cup N_i$ where N_i are its CCs. E.g. the net in Fig. 5 has nine single-interface CCs. They are connected in Fig 9 becoming the CCs N_1 and N_2 that result from connecting *xxx* with *real-const* in N_2, and all the other interfaces (in any order) in N_1. Both CCs are of a different kind.

N_2 is a functional component since it has (a process with) an open F-out port, while all processes in N_1 have lost theirs[10]. N_1 has four in and two out open ports. We denote its type as $\{B\|[I]\|(?_1\|I\|?_2{\rightarrow}I\|?_3)\|[?_1]\}{\rightarrow}\{[?_3]\|[?_3]\}$,

---

[10] Because all them have at least one output connected.

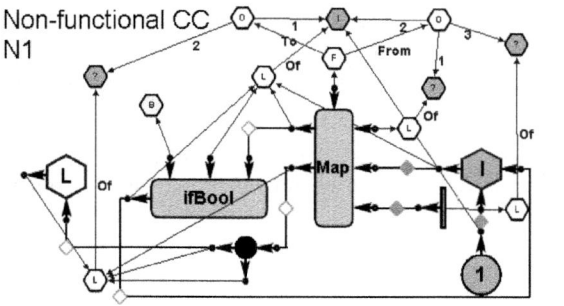 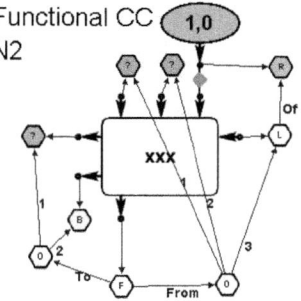

Fig. 9. Both kind of CCs

where curly brackets indicate that the given ordering is arbitrary[11]. Further connections of these ports can be made in any order; they are *free open ports*. The general form of a non functional CC type τN is $\{t_1\|\dots\|t_n\} \to \{t'_1\dots\|t'_m\}$ with $n, m \geq 0$.

The type of N_2 is different because having a F-out port the connection effect is not uniform (see 2.1 and 2.3). As a functional data xxx can be connected by its F-out port, thus disabling all its open ports. Or xxx could be applied by connecting any of its inputs and the F-out port remains, unless it had only one. But when connecting any output the F-out port disappears, except when connecting a horizontal green-arrow (but not in the only open output). This mutual dependence among the open ports of the interface (*bound open ports*) is denoted in the CC type with a down-arrow preceding the F-out TD (which has as subgraphs all the other open port TDs). In this case $\tau N_2 = \downarrow(?_4\|?_5\|[R]\to?_6\|B)$.

Also, a CC having a F-out port can have non bound in/out open ports as well, as it happens in the net in section 5.5. In this case its type is a compound type of the form $\downarrow(t_1\|\dots\|t_n \to t'_1\dots\|t'_m) \oplus \{t''_1\|\dots\|t''_{n2}\}\to\{t'''_1\|\dots\|t'''_{m2}\}$ where $\oplus$ is the composition operator described in the next section. Moreover, in the general case a CC could have more than one F-out port and also other free open ports. Therefore the most general type for a CC is:

$\downarrow(T_1 \to T'_1) \oplus \dots \downarrow(T_n \to T'_n) \oplus \{T\}\to\{T'\}$ where capital T stands for expressions of the form $t_1\|\dots\|t_m$.

5.2   Net Type Operators

The operators below perform the transformations on the CC type appropriate for connecting each kind of open port. Operators $\neg^{in}, \neg^{out}, \neg^{A-out}$ and $\neg$ are infix; the 2nd operand is the port index in the given ordering, and $\neg^{F-out}$ is postfix.

---

[11] Ordering is significant for ports of HO parameters, which are clockwise applied, but not for a non-parameterised net. If it finally becomes a net-process (see 2.2) the user selects the open ports to be the parameters and results, and sets both orderings.

1. $\{T\} \rightarrow \{T'\} \neg^{in} k = \{T \neg k\} \rightarrow \{T'\}$ — when connecting the k-th in-port
2. $\{T\} \rightarrow \{T'\} \neg^{out} k = \{T\} \rightarrow \{T' \neg k\}$ — when connecting the k-th out-port
3. $t_1 \| \ldots \| t_n \neg k = \begin{cases} t_1 \| \ldots \| t_{k-1} \| t_{k+1} \| \ldots \| t_n & \text{if } n > 1 \\ \emptyset & \end{cases}$ — to remove the k-th parallel input or output
4. $\downarrow(T \rightarrow T') \neg^{F-out} = \emptyset$ — when connecting the F-out port
5. $\downarrow(T \rightarrow T') \neg^{in} k = \downarrow(T \neg k \rightarrow T')$ — when connecting the k-th input
6. $\downarrow(T \rightarrow T') \neg^{out} k = \{T\} \rightarrow \{T \neg k\}$ — when connecting the k-th output
7. $\downarrow(T \rightarrow T') \neg^{A-out} k = \downarrow(T \rightarrow T' \neg k)$ — when connecting a green-arrow to the k-th output
8. $\downarrow(T \rightarrow \emptyset) = \{T\} \rightarrow \emptyset$ — once all the outputs have green-arrows
9. $\downarrow(\emptyset \rightarrow T) = \emptyset \rightarrow \{T\}$ — once all the inputs have been connected

If the CC has no F-out port it just loses the port (1, 2, 3). When connecting an F-out, all the open ports get closed (4). Any open input can be connected[12] and the F-out persists (5), unless it were the last one (9). When connecting any output the F-out also disappears, thus changing the kind of the CC type (6), except when it is connected with a green-arrow (7 and 8).

On the other hand, if the connected ports belong to different CCs the connection fuses both CCs in a single CC whose free in/out ports are the union of the respective free in/out ports. It is performed by the operator $\oplus$ that groups together the respective sets of types. $\oplus$ is commutative with neutral element $\emptyset$.

$\{T_1\} \rightarrow \{T_1'\} \oplus \{T_2\} \rightarrow \{T_2'\} = \{T_1 \| T_2\} \rightarrow \{T_1' \| T_2'\}$
$\downarrow(T_1 \rightarrow T_1') \oplus \{T_2\} \rightarrow \{T_2'\}$ does not reduce.

5.3 The Type Inference Algorithm

In this section we present the steps to obtain the CC type that results after connecting a pair of unifiable in/out ports. From now on we will denote the connection of an in-port p_1 with an out-port p_2 as $p_1 \prec p_2$. If component N_1 has an in-port p_1 and component N_2 has an out-port p_2, $N = N_1 p_1 \prec p_2 N_2$ is the CC resulting from the connection $p_1 \prec p_2$.

The type τN is obtained as follows:
1. both TDs are unified: $\tau p_1 \approx \tau p_2 = \tau p_1 \langle \sigma_1 \rangle = \tau p_2 \langle \sigma_2 \rangle$
2. τp_1 and τp_2 are "removed from" τN_1 and τN_2 (applying the fitting $\neg$ operator), thus resulting $\tau N_1'$ and $\tau N_2'$
3. the substitutions σ_1 σ_2 are respectively applied on $\tau N_1'$ and $\tau N_2'$
4. $\tau N = \tau N_1' \langle \sigma_1 \rangle \oplus \tau N_2' \langle \sigma_2 \rangle$

Step 1 obtains the unifier graph for both port TDs by performing the substitutions described in section 4. As a result of the unification, other TDs in both CCs might change (if they shared ?-hexagons with the connected ports). In the graph representation such substitutions are made only once on the shared subgraphs. In the equivalent CC type expressions they are performed in step 3,

---

[12] This rule applies also when connecting a vertical green-arrow; it is not a special case.

once the TDs of the ports closed by the connection have been removed from both CC types, as detailed in the previous section. The last step composes the obtained CC types, thus resulting the single connected component type.

5.4   An Example

The net in Fig. 10 is the result of connecting the components in Fig. 9 by connecting the first in-port[13] of Map_{3-2} in N_1 and the F-out port of xxx in N_2.

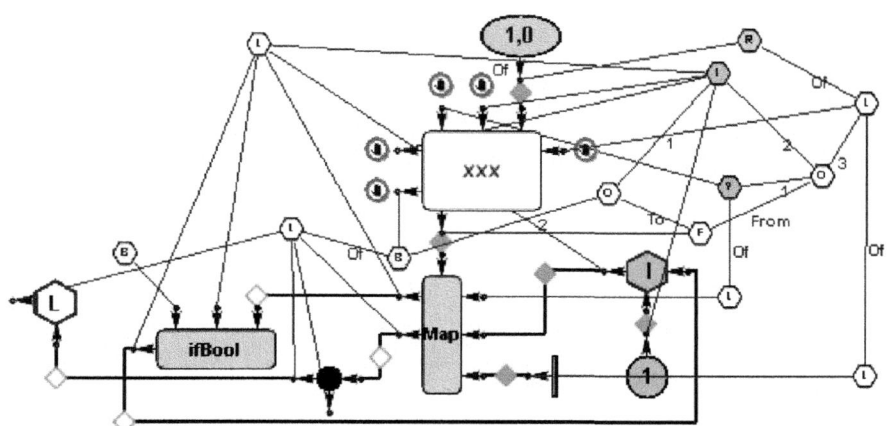

Fig. 10. Single component net

$$\tau p_1 = \tau Map_{3-2}^{in-1} = ?_1\|I\|?_2 \rightarrow I\|?_3, \text{ and } \tau p_2 = \tau xxx^{F-out} = ?_4\|?_5\|[R] \rightarrow ?_6\|B.$$

The τN calculation proceeds as follows:

1. $\tau p_1 \approx \tau p_2 = ?_1\|I\|[R] \rightarrow I\|B = \tau p_1 \langle ?_2 \Leftarrow [R]; ?_3 \Leftarrow B \rangle = \tau p_2 \langle ?_4 \Leftarrow ?_1; ?_5, ?_6 \Leftarrow I \rangle$

2. p_1 is the 3rd in-port in the given ordering for τN_1 and p_2 is the N_2 F-out:

$$\tau N_1 \neg^{in} 3 = \{B\|[I]\|\ \overbrace{(?_1\|I\|?_2 \rightarrow I\|?_3)}\ \|[?_1]\neg 3\} \rightarrow \{[?_3]\|[?_3]\}$$
$$= \{B\|[I]\|[?_1]\} \rightarrow \{[?_3]\|[?_3]\}$$
$$\tau N_2 \neg^{F-out} = \downarrow (?_4\|?_5\|[R] \rightarrow ?_6\|B)\neg^{F-out} = \emptyset$$

3. $(\{B\|[I]\|[?_1]\} \rightarrow \{[?_3]\|[?_3]\}) \langle ?_2 \Leftarrow [R]; ?_3 \Leftarrow B \rangle = \{B\|[I]\|[?_1]\} \rightarrow \{[B]\|[B]\}$
$\emptyset \langle ?_4 \Leftarrow ?_1; ?_5, ?_6 \Leftarrow I \rangle = \emptyset$

4. $\tau N = \{B\|[I]\|[?_1]\} \rightarrow \{[B]\|[B]\} \oplus \emptyset = \{B\|[I]\|[?_1]\} \rightarrow \{[B]\|[B]\}$

Note that the connected ports p_1 and p_2 now have $\tau p_1 \approx \tau p_2$ as their type, and all the port TDs that shared with them a collapsed ?-hexagon have also changed. Map_{3-2} has lost this open port, and all the in and out ports of N_2 have been closed with the connection of the F-out port.

---

[13] We use the notation X^{in-i}, X^{out-k} and X^{F-out} to refer respectively to the i-th in-port, the k-th output-port and the F-out port of an interface X.

5.5 A Second Example

Fig 11 shows the connection of functional CCs and CCs with green-arrows. On the left side, N_1 contains the horizontal green-arrow $Hgra$, N_2 the process xxx, N_3 the vertical green-arrow $Vgra$, and N_4 the interfaces $Rprod$ (*) and $HdTl$.

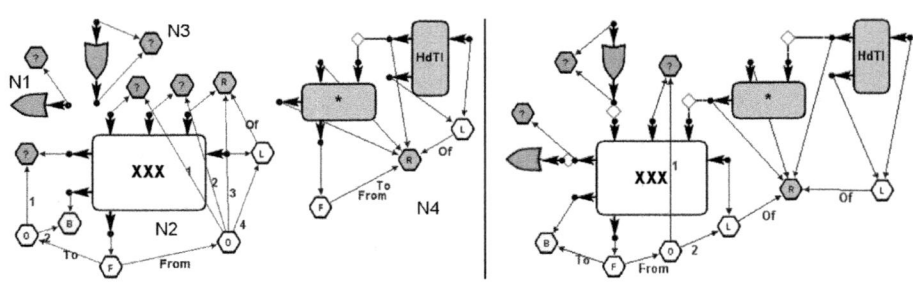

Fig. 11. Connecting green-arrows

$$\tau N_1 = \{?_4\}\rightarrow\emptyset \qquad \tau N_2 = \downarrow(?_1\|?_2\|R\|[R]\rightarrow?_3\|B)$$
$$\tau N_3 = \{?_5\}\rightarrow\{?_5\} \qquad \tau N_4 = \downarrow(R\rightarrow R) \oplus \{[R]\}\rightarrow\{[R]\}$$

The CC N on the right results from having connected in any order[14] the three pairs of ports $p_1\prec p_1'$ $p_2\prec p_2'$ and $p_3\prec p_3'$

$p_1=Hgra^{in}$ $p_1' = xxx^{out1}$; $p_2 = xxx^{in1}$ $p_2'=Vgra^{out}$; $p_3 = xxx^{in3}$ $p_3'=Rprod^{out}$

For instance, two of the six possible connection orderings are:

$((N_1\ p_1\prec p_1'\ N_2)\ p_2\prec p_2'N_3\ )p_3\prec p_3'N_4$ and $(N_1\ p_1\prec p_1'(N_2\ p_3\prec p_3'N_4)\ )p_2\prec p_2'N_3$

The final result τN is the same; e.g. in the second case it is obtained as follows:

(*connection* 1)$N_{2\cdot4} = N_2\ p_3\prec p_3'N_4$

$\tau p_3\approx\tau p_3'=R\approx R=\tau p_3\langle\rangle=\tau p_3'\langle\rangle$

$\tau(N_2\ p_3\prec p_3'N_4) = (\tau N_2\neg^{in}3)\langle\rangle \oplus (\tau N_4\neg^{out}1)\langle\rangle$

$= \downarrow(?_1\|?_2\|R\|[R]\neg3 \rightarrow ?_3\|B) \oplus (\downarrow(R\rightarrow R\neg1) \oplus \{[R]\}\rightarrow\{[R]\})$

$= \downarrow(?_1\|?_2\|[R]\rightarrow?_3\|B) \oplus \{R\}\rightarrow\emptyset \oplus \{[R]\}\rightarrow\{[R]\}$

$= \downarrow(?_1\|?_2\|[R]\rightarrow?_3\|B) \oplus \{R\|[R]\}\rightarrow\{[R]\}$

(*connection* 2)$N_{1\cdot2\cdot4} = N_1\ p_1\prec p_1'N_{2\cdot4}$

$\tau p_1\approx\tau p_1'=?_4\approx?_3=\tau p_1\langle?_4\Leftarrow?_3\rangle=\tau p_1'\langle\rangle$

$\tau(N_1\ p_1\prec p_1'\ N_{2\cdot4}) = (\tau N_1\neg^{in}1)\langle?_4\Leftarrow?_3\rangle \oplus (\tau N_{2\cdot4}\neg^{A-out}1)\langle\rangle$

$= (\{?_4\neg1\}\rightarrow\emptyset)\langle?_4\Leftarrow?_3\rangle \oplus \downarrow(?_1\|?_2\|[R]\rightarrow?_3\|B\neg1) \oplus \{R\|[R]\}\rightarrow\{[R]\}$

$= \emptyset \oplus \downarrow(?_1\|?_2\|[R]\rightarrow B) \oplus \{R\|[R]\}\rightarrow\{[R]\}$

$= \downarrow(?_1\|?_2\|[R]\rightarrow) \oplus \{R\|[R]\}\rightarrow\{[R]\}$

(*connection* 3)$N = N_{1\cdot2\cdot4}\ p_2\prec p_2'N_3$

$\tau p_2\approx\tau p_2'=?_1\approx?_5=\tau p_2\langle\rangle=\tau p_2'\langle?_5\Leftarrow?_1\rangle$

$\tau(N_{1\cdot2\cdot4}\ p_2\prec p_2'\ N_3) = (\tau N_{1\cdot2\cdot4}\neg^{in}1)\langle\rangle \oplus (\tau N_3\neg^{out}1)\langle?_5\Leftarrow?_1\rangle$

$= \downarrow(?_1\|?_2\|[R]\neg1\rightarrow B) \oplus \{R\|[R]\}\rightarrow\{[R]\} \oplus (\{?_5\}\rightarrow\{?_5\neg1\})\langle?_5\Leftarrow?_1\rangle$

$= \downarrow(?_2\|[R]\rightarrow B) \oplus \{R\|[R]\}\rightarrow\{[R]\} \oplus \{?_1\}\rightarrow\emptyset$

$= \downarrow(?_2\|[R]\rightarrow B) \oplus \{R\|[R]\|?_1\}\rightarrow\{[R]\}$

---

14 Since none of the connections closes the other ports.

6 Related Work and Final Remarks

We have presented the graphical type inference system for an incremental and highly interactive development language where editing and execution are interleaved. NiMo programs are graphs that evolve, and so is type information. Hence, the graph transformation approach is the natural framework to model type representation and inference. In this paper we have used a textual notation close to the usual type expressions to describe the type graphs and their evolution. The transformation rules for unification and typing of nets have been presented in terms of a set of operators that perform unification and connection on the equivalent type expressions. However, this textualization shadows some advantages of the graph representation, as having a single shared ?-node instead of multiple occurrences of a quantified variable (hence multiple substitutions).

Regarding the graph transformation approach for modelling types, [8] presents a general framework for typing graph rewriting systems based on the notion of annotated hypergraphs. NiMo nets might be also described in this way, since interfaces can be viewed as directed hypergraphs whose nodes are the ports, internally connected by a hyperedge. Ports are annotated by the corresponding TDs, hence the whole net can be viewed as an annotated hypergraph.

Concerning the graphical and incremental approach, an outstanding asset is that the inference system itself becomes an online visualization tool for type information and failure identification. On this aspect there are several works. GemCut [9] is a graphical viewer for functions in the Haskell-like language CAL; the editor uses CAL compiler's inference system to prevent type errors. TypeTool [10] and System I [11] are web-based tools for visualizing type inference of lambda terms; they are intended to teaching the basis of type inference algorithms for functional languages. Other research focus on tracing the origin of unification failure. [12] proposes a guideline for evaluating the quality of type error diagnosis of type inference systems. It compares several systems and presents the algorithm *Unification Assumption Environments*. The inference process records the local inferences so as to identify all possible sources of inconsistencies. In NiMo, whenever a pair of type hexagons cannot be collapsed, all type ports related to them can be visually identified. Other work on this regard, (not a graphical tool either) is [13] that uses a graph representation with nodes labelled by lambda terms and types from which information is extracted to help in error debugging.

In general, inference systems work on complete terms that can be erroneous, thus producing an error message. In NiMo erroneous nets cannot be edited; messages just indicate incompatibility. Moreover, port compatibility can be tried before connecting simply by moving both TDs hexagons to make them coincide (except in cases of non-structural equivalence).

Another significant point about inference in NiMo is the total absence of type variables; transformations take place directly on the graph structure of the type expressions. The assumption environment is distributed and tied to each term (CC) since every token carries its own type and partially built expressions are always well typed and also carry their type. Besides, NiMo code is bi-dimensional and can be built in any order; most of the port connections are applications and in NiMo partial application can be made in any order (not only from left to right), hence incremental inference can be made in the user-stated port connection order. On polymorphism handling, interface TDs are originally as polymorphic as they can ever be; hence there is no equivalent for generalization. Instantiation corresponds to the ?-hexagons collapse that occurs when unifying the port TDs.

The other differences come from the data-flow ingredient plus incompleteness. Multiple inputs and outputs required a non-trivial generalization to handle the process type. Non-structural unification is the means to have multiple inputs (then partial application in any order), while keeping the advantages of currying in HO constructs without explicit conversions. On the other hand, typing NiMo nets required treatment of incompleteness and multiple outputs produced by non-connected subnets, in contrast to inference systems that deal with a single and closed term. Application corresponds to connecting a process input in a functional CC. Having multiple inputs and outputs, partial application in any order and partial production also in HO parameters, we needed different operators to define the connection effect vs. the single rule used in functional languages.

Considering the overall development of NiMo, the paradigms fusion was a big challenge that required figuring out many creative solutions to make both models compatible and the graphical realization feasible. But we think it was worth it; the graphic-functional-dataflow nature of NiMo and its incompleteness tolerance result in a very powerful computation model where everything is visible and dynamically modifiable, even the evaluation policy. This allows us to exploit implicit parallelism in a very intuitive way, and to perform symbolic execution in the same framework. We are now exploring its possibilities in simulation and modelling, as well as in generative and multistage programming.

As regards future development, the mixed model opens a range of possible extensions, some of which are hard to imagine in other languages; think for instance that here functions are showable and polymorphic expressions executable. Conversely, some relevant functional language features are not yet included; in particular overloading, type classes, and user defined types (now algebraic types are emulated with functional types), with the consequent implications for inference. But again, the first challenge is making their graphical equivalents stylistic-consistent and manageable, which requires facilities for the compact viewing of complex values. We are now extending the visualization features for net-processes and data channels to cope with any subnet. Besides, in the current version net-process definitions have a single rule with a single interface on the left, whereas Haskell-like languages allow definitions by cases using patterns, making them more modular and readable. The inclusion of this mechanism in NiMo would be a major upgrade far beyond expressiveness, because symbolic execution together with graph patterns open the door to program transformation in the same framework; hence even dynamically.

Acknowledgments. We thank the reviewers for their detailed and helpful comments.

References

1. Turner, D.A.: Miranda: a non-strict functional language with polymorphic types. In: Jouannaud, J.-P. (ed.) FPCA 1985. LNCS, vol. 201, pp. 1–16. Springer, Heidelberg (1985)
2. Clerici, S., Zoltan, C.: A graphic functional-dataflow language. In: Loidl, H.W. (ed.) Trends in Functional Programming. Intellect, vol. 5, pp. 129–144 (2004)
3. AGG: Agg home page (2009), http://user.cs.tu-berlin.de/~gragra/agg/
4. Clerici, S., Zoltan, C.: A dynamically customizable process-centered evaluation model. In: PPDP 2009: Proceedings of the 11th ACM SIGPLAN Conference on Principles and Practice of Declarative Programming, pp. 37–48. ACM, New York (2009)
5. Clerici, S., Zoltan, C.: Graphical type inference. a graph grammar definition. Technical Report LSI-07-24-R, Dept. Llenguatges i Sistemes Informàtics, Universitat Politècnica de Catalunya (July 2007)
6. Clerici, S., Zoltan, C., Prestigiacomo, G.: Nimotoons: a totally graphic workbench for program tuning and experimentation. Electr. Notes Theor. Comput. Sci. 258(1), 93–107 (2009)
7. NiMo: Nimo home page (2010), http://www.lsi.upc.edu/~nimo/Project
8. König, B.: A general framework for types in graph rewriting. Acta Inf. 42(4), 349–388 (2005)
9. Resources (2009), http://resources.businessobjects.com/labs/cal/gemcutter-techpaper.pdf
10. Simões, H., Florido, M.: TypeTool - a type inference visualization tool. In: Proceedings of the 13th International Workshop on Functional and (Constraint) Logic Programming (2004), http://www.dcc.fc.up.pt/typetool/cgi-bin/tt.pl
11. Church Project: System I (2010), http://types.bu.edu/modular/compositional/system-i/
12. Yang, J., Michaelson, G., Trinder, P., Wells, J.B.: Improved Type Error Reporting. In: Proceedings of 12th International Workshop on Implementation of Functional Languages, pp. 71–86 (2000)
13. McAdam, B.J.: Generalising techniques for type debugging. In: Trinder, P.W., Michaelson, G., Loidl, H.W. (eds.) Scottish Functional Programming Workshop. Trends in Functional Programming, Intellect, vol. 1, pp. 50–58 (1999)

Hygienic Macros for ACL2

Carl Eastlund and Matthias Felleisen

Northeastern University
Boston, MA, USA
{cce,matthias}@ccs.neu.edu

Abstract. ACL2 is a theorem prover for a purely functional subset of
Common Lisp. It inherits Common Lisp's unhygienic macros, which are
used pervasively to eliminate repeated syntactic patterns. The lack of
hygiene means that macros do not automatically protect their producers
or consumers from accidental variable capture. This paper demonstrates
how this lack of hygiene interferes with theorem proving. It then explains
how to design and implement a hygienic macro system for ACL2. An
evaluation of the ACL2 code base shows the potential impact of this
hygienic macro system on existing libraries and practices.

1 Unhygienic Macros Are Not Abstractions

ACL2 [1] is a verification system that combines a first-order functional subset of
Common Lisp with a first-order theorem prover over a logic of total functions.
It has been used to model and verify large commercial hardware and software
artifacts. ACL2 supports functions and logical statements over numbers, strings,
symbols, and s-expressions. Here is a sample program:

(**defun** double (x) (+ x x))

(**defthm** double⇒evenp (**implies** (**integerp** x) (**evenp** (double x))))

The **defun** form defines double, a function that adds its input to itself. The
defthm form defines double⇒evenp, a conjecture stating that an integer input to
double yields an even output. The conjecture is implicitly universally quantified
over its free variable x. ACL2 validates double⇒evenp as a theorem, using the
definition of double and axioms about **implies**, **integerp**, and **evenp**.

From Common Lisp, ACL2 inherits *macros*, which provide a mechanism for
extending the language via functions that operate on syntax trees. According to
Kaufmann and Moore [2], *"one can make specifications more succinct and easy
to grasp ... by introducing well-designed application-specific notation."* Indeed,
macros are used ubiquitously in ACL2 libraries: there are macros for pattern
matching; for establishing new homogenous list types and heterogenous structure
types, including a comprehensive theory of each; for defining quantified claims
using skolemization in an otherwise (explicit) quantifier-free logic; and so on.

In the first-order language of ACL2, macros are also used to eliminate repeated
syntactic patterns due to the lack of higher-order functions:

R. Page, Z. Horváth, and V. Zsók (Eds.): TFP 2010, LNCS 6546, pp. 84–101, 2011.
© Springer-Verlag Berlin Heidelberg 2011

```
(defmacro defun-map (map-fun fun)
  '(defun ,map-fun (xs)
     (if (endp xs)
         nil
         (cons (,fun (car xs)) (,map-fun (cdr xs))))))
```

This macro definition captures the essence of defining one function that applies another pointwise to a list. It consumes two inputs, map-fun and fun, representing function names; the body constructs a suitable **defun** form. ACL2 *expands* uses of defun-map, supplying the syntax of its arguments as map-fun and fun, and continues with the resulting function definition. Consider the following term:

```
(defun-map map-double double)
```

Its expansion fills the names map-double and double into defun-map's template:

```
(defun map-double (xs)
  (if (endp xs)
      nil
      (cons (double (car xs)) (map-double (cdr xs)))))
```

Unfortunately, ACL2 macros are *unhygienic* [3], meaning they do not preserve the meaning of variable bindings and references during code expansion. The end result is accidental capture that not only violates a programmer's intuition of lexical scope but also interferes with logical reasoning about the program source. In short, macros do not properly abstract over syntax.

To make this concrete, consider the **or** macro, which encodes both boolean disjunction and recovery from exceptional conditions, returning the second value if the first is **nil**:

```
(defthm excluded-middle (or (not x) x))
```

```
(defun find (n xs) (or (nth n xs) 0))
```

The first definition states the law of the excluded middle. Since ACL2 is based on classical logic, either (**not** x) or x must be true for any x. The second defines selection from a list of numbers: produce the element of xs at index n, or return 0 if **nth** returns **nil**, indicating that the index is out of range.

A natural definition for **or** duplicates its first operand:

$$(\textbf{defmacro}\ \text{or}\ (a\ b)\ {}^\backprime(\textit{if}\ ,a\ ,a\ ,b)) \qquad (1)$$

This works well for excluded-middle, but the expanded version of find now traverses its input twice, doubling its running time:

```
(defun find (n xs) (if (nth n xs) (nth n xs) 0))
```

Macro users should not have to give up reasoning about their function's running time. Consequently, macros should avoid this kind of code duplication.

The next logical step in the development of **or** saves the result of its first operand in a temporary variable:

$$(\textbf{defmacro}\ \text{or}\ (a\ b)\ {}^\backprime(\textit{let}\ ((x\ ,a))\ (\textit{if}\ x\ x\ ,b))) \qquad (2)$$

This macro now produces efficient and correct code for find. Sadly though, the expanded form of excluded-middle is no longer the expected logical statement:

(**defthm** excluded-middle (**let** ((x (**not** x))) (**if** x x x)))

The **or** macro's variable x has captured excluded-middle's second reference to x. As a result, the conjecture is now equivalent to the statement (**not** x).

ACL2 resolves this issue by dealing with the **or** macro as a special case. For symbolic verification, **or** expands using code duplication. For execution, it expands by introducing a fresh variable. The regular macro language of ACL2 does not come with the same expressive power, however. Allowing the creation of fresh variables would introduce uninterned symbols that violate ACL2's axioms and thus corrupt its carefully crafted logical foundation; allowing a separation of executable behavior from the logical semantics would also invite unsoundness.

The **case-match** macro, also provided with ACL2, does not have any such special cases. This macro is used for pattern matching and case dispatch. Its implementation is designed to work around ACL2's lack of hygiene: the macro's expansion never binds any temporary variables. Here is an example use of **case-match** to destructure a 3-element list:

(**let** ((x (**quote** (1 2 3))))
  (**case-match** x ((a b c) (list a b c))))

The macro expands into the following code:

(**let** ((x (**quote** (1 2 3))))
  (**if** (**if** (**consp** x)
          (**if** (**consp** (**cdr** x))
              (**if** (**consp** (**cdr** (**cdr** x)))
                  (eq (**cdr** (**cdr** (**cdr** x))) **nil**)
                nil)
            nil)
        nil)
      (**let** ((a (**car** x)) (b (**car** (**cdr** x))) (c (**car** (**cdr** (**cdr** x)))))
        (**list** a b c))
    nil))

Note that the input to **case-match** is a variable. The macro requires that the user bind the input to a variable, because the input is duplicated many times in the macro's output and the macro cannot safely bind a variable itself. Applications of **car** and **cdr** to walk down the input list are duplicated for the same reason; as a result, the size of the output increases quadratically.

In a hygienic system, **case-match** would be able to safely bind temporary variables in its expanded form. Thus, the user would not need to explicitly bind the input to **case-match** to a variable:

(**case-match** (**quote** (1 2 3)) ((a b c) (**list** a b c)))

This also makes **case-match** available for use by other macros. In ACL2's unhygienic macro system, other macros cannot safely bind a variable to store **case-match**'s input without risking unintended capture.

Furthermore, the intermediate results of **car** and **cdr** could be bound to temporary variables, yielding fewer function calls in the expanded code. Here is the expansion of the above use of **case-match** produced by one possible implementation in a hygienic macro system:

```
(let ((x₀ (quote (1 2 3))))
  (flet ((fail₀ () nil))
    (if (consp x₀)
        (let ((x₁ (car x₀)) (y₁ (cdr x₀)))
          (if (consp y₁)
              (let ((x₂ (car y₁)) (y₂ (cdr y₂)))
                (if (consp y₂)
                    (let ((x₃ (car y₂)) (y₃ (cdr y₂)))
                      (if (eq y₃ nil)
                          (let ((a x₁) (b x₂) (c x₃)) (list a b c))
                          (fail₀))))
                    (fail₀)))
              (fail₀))
        (fail₀))))
```

This version of **case-match** uses temporary variables to perform each **car** and **cdr** only once, producing output with a linear measure.

In general, macro writers tread a fine line. Many macros duplicate code to avoid introducing a variable that might capture bindings in the source code. Others introduce esoteric temporary names to avoid accidental capture. None of these solutions is universal, though. Finding itself in the same place, the Scheme community introduced the notion of *hygienic* macros [3,4,5]. This paper presents an adaptation of hygienic macros to ACL2. It motivates the design and the ACL2-specific challenges, sketches an implementation, and finally presents a comprehensive evaluation of the system vis-a-vis the ACL2 code base.

2 The Meaning of Hygiene for ACL2

Hygienic macro systems ensure that variables in macro-generated code respect the intended lexical scope of the program. Hence, our first step is to analyze the notion of lexical scope in ACL2 and to formulate appropriate goals and policies for the adaptation of hygienic expansion. This section presents the design goals and interprets them in the context of ACL2.

2.1 Design Goals

Our hygienic macro expander is designed to observe four key principles.

Referential transparency means that variables derive their meaning from where they occur and retain that meaning throughout the macro expansion process. Specifically, variable references inserted by a macro refer to bindings inserted by the macro or to bindings apparent at its definition site. Symmetrically, variable references in macro arguments refer to bindings apparent at the macro call site. Following tradition, a hygienic macro system comes with a disciplined method for violating the hygiene condition on individual variables as needed.

Next, *separate compilation* demands that libraries can be expanded, verified, and compiled once and loaded many times. There is no need to re-expand, re-verify, or re-compile a library each time it is used in a new context.

Thirdly, we preserve *logical soundness*. We do not change the logical axioms of ACL2, nor its verification system or compiler. Our few changes to its runtime system are made carefully to observe ACL2's existing axioms. Existing reasoning in the logic of ACL2 remains valid in our system, and execution remains in sync with symbolic reasoning.

Finally, *source compatibility* means that most well-behaved macros continue to function as before. When the revised expansion process affects the behavior of an existing program, the changes are due to a potentially flawed macro.

Unfortunately, we are not able to provide a formal statement of correctness of our macro system with respect to these principles. The correctness of hygienic macros is an open research problem; early proof attempts have since been shown to be flawed. The only known proof of correctness of a hygienic macro system [6] does not support such features as recursive macros, case dispatch during macro expansion, or decomposing lists of arbitrary length during expansion.

2.2   Reinterpreting ACL2

Our hygienic macro system redefines the existing **defmacro** form in ACL2. We do not introduce hygienic macros as a separate mechanism alongside unhygienic macros because hygiene is a property of an entire macro system, rather than a property of individual macro definitions. The implementation of hygiene requires the collaboration of all macros to track the scope of variables; expanding a single macro unhygienically can ruin the benefits of hygiene for all other macros.

Figure 1 specifies the essential core of ACL2. A program is a sequence of definitions. In source code, any definition or expression may be replaced by a macro application; individual functions may be defined outside of **mutual-recursion**; and string or number literals do not require an explicit **quote**. The grammar is written in terms of symbols (sym), strings (str), and numbers (num). A sequence of elements of the form a is denoted $\overrightarrow{a}$, or $\overrightarrow{a}^{\,n}$ when its length is significant. We use this core language to explain ACL2-specific challenges to hygienic macro expansion.

Lexical Bindings: ACL2 inherits Common Lisp's namespaces: function and variable bindings are separate and cannot shadow each other. The position of a variable reference determines its role. In an expression position, a variable refers to a value, in application position to a function or macro. For example, the following code uses both kinds of bindings for **car**:

(**let** ((car (**car** x))) (**car** car))

$$def = (\textbf{mutual-recursion } \overrightarrow{(\textbf{defun } sym \ (\overrightarrow{sym}) \ exp)}) \quad \text{mutually recursive functions}$$

	$\mid \ (\textbf{defmacro } sym \ (\overrightarrow{sym}) \ exp)$	macro definition
	$\mid \ (\textbf{defthm } sym \ exp \ (sym \ \overrightarrow{(sym \ exp)}))$	conjecture with proof hints
	$\mid \ (\textbf{include-book } str)$	library import
	$\mid \ (\textbf{encapsulate } (\overrightarrow{(sym \ num)}) \ \overrightarrow{def})$	definition block
	$\mid \ (\textbf{local } def)$	local definition
$exp =$	sym	variable reference
	$\mid \ (sym \ \overrightarrow{exp})$	function call
	$\mid \ (\textbf{let } (\overrightarrow{(sym \ exp)}) \ exp)$	lexical value bindings
	$\mid \ (\textbf{flet } (\overrightarrow{(sym \ (\overrightarrow{sym}) \ exp)}) \ exp)$	lexical function bindings
	$\mid \ (\textbf{quote } sexp)$	literal value
$sexp =$	$num \mid str \mid sym \mid (\overrightarrow{sexp})$	s-expression

Fig. 1. Abridged syntax of fully-expanded ACL2 programs

Hygienic expansion must track both function and variable bindings for each possible reference. After all, during expansion, the role of a symbol is unknown until its final position in the expanded code is determined.

Hygienic expansion must also be able to distinguish macro-inserted lexical bindings from those in source code or in other macros. With hygienic expansion, version (2) of the **or** macro in section 1 should work. For example, the excluded-middle conjecture should expand as follows:

(**defthm** excluded-middle (**let** ((x_2 (**not** x_1))) (**if** x_2 x_2 x_1)))

The macro expander differentiates between the source program's x_1 and the macro's x_2, as noted by the subscripts; the conjecture's meaning is preserved.

Function Bindings: Functions bound by **flet** are substituted into their applications prior to verification. To prevent unintended capture of free variables during unhygienic expansion, **flet**-bound functions may not refer to enclosing bindings. Consider the following expression that violates this rule:

```
(let ((five 5))
  (flet ((add5 (x) (+ five x))) ;; illegal reference to five, bound to 5
    (let ((five "five"))
      (add5 0))))
```

Under unhygienic expansion, the reference to five in add5 would be captured:

```
(let ((five 5))
  (let ((five "five"))
    (let ((x 0)) (+ five x)))) ;; five is now bound to "five"
```

Hygienic macro expansion allows us to relax this restriction, as lexical bindings can be resolved before substitution of **flet**-bound functions. The same expression expands as follows:

```
(let ((five₁ 5))
  (let ((five₂ "five"))
    (let ((x 0)) (+ five₁ x))))
```

Quantification: ACL2 conjectures are implicitly universally quantified:

```
;; claim: ∀x(x > 0 ⇒ x ≥ 0)
(defthm non-negative (implies (> x 0) (≥ x 0)))
```

Here the variable x is never explicitly bound, but its scope is the body of the **defthm** form. ACL2 discovers free variables during the expansion of conjectures and treats them as if they were bound.

This raises a question of how to treat free variables inserted by macros into conjectures. Consider the following definitions:

```
(defmacro imply (var) '(implies x ,var))
```

```
(defthm x⇒x (imply x))
```

The body of x⇒x expands into (**implies** x_2 x_1), with x_1 from x⇒x and x_2 from imply. In x⇒x, x is clearly quantified by **defthm**. In the template of imply, however, there is no apparent binding for x. Therefore, the corresponding variable x_2 in the expanded code must be considered unbound. Enforcing this behavior yields a new design rule: macros must not insert new free variables into conjectures.

We must not overuse this rule, however, as illustrated by the macro below:

```
(defmacro disprove (name body) '(defthm name (not ,body)))
```

```
(disprove x=x+1 (= x (+ x 1)))
```

Here we must decide what the apparent binding of x is in the body of x=x+1. In the source syntax, there is nothing explicit to suggest that x is a bound or quantified variable, but during expansion, the macro **disprove** inserts a **defthm** form that captures x and quantifies over it. On one hand, allowing this kind of capture violates referential transparency. On the other hand, disallowing it prevents abstraction over **defthm**, because of the lack of explicit quantification.

To resolve this dilemma, we allow **defthm** to quantify over variables from just a single source—surface syntax or a macro. This permits the common macros that expand into **defthm**, but rejects many cases of accidental quantification, a source of bugs in the ACL2 code base. A more disruptive yet sounder alternative would be to introduce explicit quantification into ACL2.

Definition Scope: ACL2 performs macro expansion, verification, and compilation on one definition at a time. Forward references are disallowed, and no definition may overwrite an existing binding.

Nevertheless, just as hygiene prevents lexical bindings from different sources from shadowing each other, it also prevents definitions from different sources from overwriting each other.

Consider the following macro for defining a semigroup based on a predicate recognizing a set and a closed, associative operation over the set:

```
(defmacro semigroup (pred op)
  '(encapsulate ()
     (defthm closed
       (implies (and (,pred a) (,pred b)) (,pred (,op a b))))
     (defthm associative
       (implies (and (,pred a) (,pred b) (,pred c))
         (equal (,op a (,op b c)) (,op (,op a b) c)))))))
```

The **semigroup** macro takes two function names as arguments and proves that they form a semigroup. The name, number, and form of definition used in the proof is not part of the macro's interface. In order to leave these names free for reuse, such as in subsequent reuses of the **semigroup** macro, they must not be visible outside the individual macro application.

```
(semigroup integerp +)
(semigroup stringp string-append)
```

Macros must be able to use defined names that originate outside them, however. For instance, the monoid macro uses the previously defined **semigroup** macro to establish a closed, associative operation with an identity element.

```
(defmacro monoid (pred fun zero)
  '(encapsulate ()
     (semigroup ,pred ,fun)
     (defthm identity
       (implies (,pred a)
         (and (equal (,fun ,zero a) a) (equal (,fun a ,zero) a))))))
```

```
(monoid rationalp * 1)
```

Macros frequently rely on prior definitions; therefore these definitions must remain visible to the expanded form of macros.

Because prior definitions are visible inside macros, macros must not redefine any name that is visible at their definition. Such a redefinition would allow a logical inconsistency, as the macro would be able to refer to both the old and new meanings for the defined name. The following example shows how redefinition could be used to prove (f) equal to both **t** and **nil**.

```
(defun f () t)
```

```
(defmacro bad ()
  '(encapsulate ()
     (defthm f=t (equal (f) t))
     (defun f () nil)
     (defthm f=nil (equal (f) nil))))
```

Our policy for the scope of definitions during hygienic expansion is therefore three-fold. First, defined names from inside macros are not externally visible. Second, macros may refer to any name that is visible at their definition. Third, macros may not redefine any name that is visible at their definition.

Encapsulated Abstractions: The **encapsulate** form in ACL2 delimits a block of definitions. Definitions are exported by default; these definitions represent the block's *constraint*, describing its logical guarantees to the outside. Definitions marked **local** represent a *witness* that can be used to verify the constraint, but they are not exported.

For example, the following block exports a constraint stating that $1 \leq 1$:

```
(encapsulate ()
  (local (defthm x≤x (≤ x x)))
  (defthm 1≤1
    (≤ 1 1) ;; use the following hint:
    (x≤x (x 1)))))
```

The local conjecture states that $(\leq x\ x)$ holds for all values of x. The conjecture 1≤1 states that $(\leq 1\ 1)$ holds; the subsequent hint tells ACL2 that the previously verified theorem x≤x is helpful, with *1* substituted for x.

Once the definitions in the body of an **encapsulate** block have been verified, ACL2 discards hints and local definitions (the witness) and re-verifies the remaining definitions (the constraint) in a second pass. The end result is a set of exported logical rules with no reference to the witness. Local theorems may not be used in subsequent hints, local functions and local macros may no longer be applied, and local names are available for redefinition.

An **encapsulate** block may have a third component, which is a set of *constrained functions*. The header of the **encapsulate** form lists names and arities of functions defined locally within the block. The function names are exported as part of the block's constraint; their definitions are not exported and remain part of the witness.

The following block exports a function of two arguments whose witness performs addition, but whose constraint guarantees only commutativity:

```
(encapsulate ((f 2))
  (local (defun f (x y) (+ x y)))
  (defthm commutativity (equal (f x y) (f y x))))
```

Definitions following this block can refer to f and reason about it as a commutative function. Attempts to prove it equivalent to addition fail, however, and attempts to call it result in a run-time error.

Our hygienic macro system preserves the scoping rules of **encapsulate** blocks. Furthermore, it enforces that names defined in the witness are not visible in the constraint, ensuring that a syntactically valid **encapsulate** block has a syntactically valid constraint prior to verification. Our guarantee of referential transparency also means that local names in exported macros cannot be captured. For instance, the following macro m constructs a reference to w:

```
(encapsulate ()
  (local (defun w (x) x))
  (defmacro m (y) `(w ,y)))

(defun w (z) (m z)) ;; body expands to: (w z)
```

When a new **w** is defined outside the block and **m** is applied, the new binding does not capture the **w** from **m**. Instead, the macro expander signals a syntax error, because the inserted reference is no longer in scope.

Books: A *book* is the unit of ACL2 libraries: a set of definitions that is verified and compiled once and then reused. Each book acts as an **encapsulate** block without constrained functions; it is verified twice—once with witness, and once for the constraint—and the constraint is saved to disk in compiled form. When a program includes a book, ACL2 incorporates its definitions, after ensuring that they do not clash with any existing bindings.

ACL2 allows an exception to the rule against redefinition that facilitates compatibility between books. Specifically, a definition is considered *redundant* and skipped, rather than rejected, if it is precisely the same as an existing one. If two books contain the same definition for a function f, for instance, the books are still compatible. Similarly, if one book is included twice in the same program, the second inclusion is considered redundant.

This notion of redundancy is complicated by hygienic macro expansion. Because hygienic expanders generally rename variables in their output, there is no guarantee that identical source syntax expands to an identical compiled form. As a result, redundancy becomes a question of α-equivalence instead of simple syntactic equality. Coalescing redundant definitions in compiled books would thus require renaming all references to the second definition. This code rewriting defeats the principle of separate compilation.

Rather than address redundancy in its full generality, we restrict it to the case of loading the same book twice. If a book is loaded twice, the new definitions will be syntactically equal to the old ones because books are only compiled once. That is, this important case of redundancy does not rely on α-equivalence, and thus allows us to load compiled books unchanged.

Macros: Macros use a representation of syntax as their input and output. In the existing ACL2 system, syntax is represented using primitive data types: strings and numbers for literals, symbols for variables, and lists for sequences of terms.

Hygienic macro systems must annotate syntax with details of scope and macro expansion. Kohlbecker et al. [3] incorporate these annotations into the existing symbol datatype; in contrast, Dybvig et al. [5] introduce a separate class of *syntax objects*. To preserve existing ACL2 macros, we cannot introduce an entirely new data type; instead, we adopt the former method.

In adapting the symbol datatype, we must be sure to preserve the axioms of ACL2. On one hand, it is an axiom that any symbol is uniquely distinguished by the combination of its name and its *package*—an additional string used for manual namespace management. On the other hand, the hygienic macro expander must distinguish between symbols sharing a name and a package when one originates in the source program and another is inserted by a macro. We resolve this issue by leaving hygienic expansion metadata transparent to the logic: only macros and unverified, *program mode* functions can distinguish between two symbols with the same name and package. Conjectures and verified, *logic mode* functions cannot make this distinction, i.e., ACL2's axioms remain valid.

The symbols inserted by macros must derive their lexical bindings from the context in which they appear. To understand the complexity of this statement, consider the following example:

```
(defun parse-compose (funs arg)
  (if (endp funs) arg '(,(car funs) (compose ,(cdr funs) ,arg))))

(defmacro compose (funs arg) (parse-compose funs arg))

(compose (string-downcase symbol-name) (quote SYM))
;; ⇒ (string-downcase (compose (symbol-name) (quote SYM)))
```

The auxiliary function parse-compose creates recursive references to compose, but compose is not in scope in parse-compose. To support this common macro idiom, we give the code inserted by macros the context of the macro's definition site. In the above example, the symbol *compose* in parse-compose's template does not carry any context until it is returned from the compose macro, at which point it inherits a binding for the name. This behavior allows recursive macros with helper functions, at some cost to referential transparency: the reference inserted by parse-compose might be given a different meaning if used by another macro.

This quirk of our design could be alleviated if these macros were rewritten in a different style. If the helper function parse-compose accepted the recursive reference to compose as an argument, then the quoted symbol *compose* could be passed in from the definition of compose itself, where it has meaning:

```
(defun parse-compose (compose funs arg)
  (if (endp funs) arg '(,(car funs) (,compose ,(cdr funs) ,arg))))

(defmacro compose (funs arg) (parse-compose (quote compose) funs arg))
```

Symbols in macro templates could then take their context from their original position, observing referential transparency. However, to satisfy our fourth design goal of source compatibility and accommodate common ACL2 macro practice, our design does not mandate it.

Breaking Hygiene: There are some cases where a macro must insert variables that do not inherit the context of the macro definition, but instead intentionally capture—or are captured by—variables in the source program. For instance, the defun-map example can be rewritten to automatically construct the name of the map function from the name of the pointwise function:

```
(defmacro defun-map (fun)
  (let ((map-fun-string (string-append "map-" (symbol-name fun))))
    (let ((map-fun (in-package-of map-fun-string fun)))
      '(defun ,map-fun (xs)
         (if (endp xs)
             nil
             (cons (,fun (car xs)) (,map-fun (cdr xs))))))))

(defun-map double) ;; expands to: (defun map-double (xs) ... )
```

$$
\begin{aligned}
state &= \langle str, bool, bool, ren, table, \{\overrightarrow{sym}\}, \{\overrightarrow{key}\}\rangle & \text{expansion state} \\
table &= [\overrightarrow{sym \mapsto rec}] & \text{def. table} \\
rec &= \langle sig, fun, thm\rangle & \text{def. record} \\
sig &= \mathsf{fun}(bool, num) \mid \mathsf{macro}(id, num) \mid \mathsf{thm}(\{\overrightarrow{sym}\}) \mid \mathsf{special} & \text{def. signature} \\
fun^n &= \cdot \mid \overrightarrow{sexp}^n \to sexp & n\text{-ary function} \\
thm &= \cdot \mid \cdots & \text{theorem formula} \\
sexp &= num \mid str \mid id \mid \mathsf{cons}(sexp, sexp) & \text{s-expression} \\
id &= sym \mid \mathsf{id}(sym, \{\overrightarrow{mark}\}, ren, ren) & \text{identifier} \\
sym &= \mathsf{sym}(str, str, \{\overrightarrow{mark}\}) & \text{symbol} \\
bool &= \mathsf{t} \mid \mathsf{nil} & \text{boolean} \\
ren &= [\overrightarrow{key \mapsto sym}] & \text{renaming} \\
key &= \langle sym, \{\overrightarrow{mark}\}\rangle & \text{identifier key} \\
mark &= \langle str, num\rangle & \text{mark}
\end{aligned}
$$

Fig. 2. Representation of expansion state and s-expressions

In this macro, the name double comes from the macro caller's context, but map-double is inserted by the macro itself. The macro's intention is to bind map-double in the caller's context, and the caller expects this name to be bound.

This implementation pattern derives from the Common Lisp package system. Specifically, the **in-package-of** function builds a new symbol with the given string as its name, and the package of the given symbol. In our example, map-double is defined in the same package as double.

We co-opt the same pattern to transfer lexical context. Thus the name map-double shares double's context and is visible to the macro's caller. Macro writers can use **in-package-of** to break the default policy of hygiene.

3   Hygienic Macro Expansion

The ACL2 theorem prover certifies saved books and verifies interactive programs using a process of iteratively expanding, verifying, and compiling each term in turn. The expansion process takes each term and produces a corresponding, fully-expanded definition; it also maintains and updates an *expansion state* recording the scope and meaning of existing definitions so far. Our hygienic macro system requires these changes: an augmented representation of unexpanded terms and expansion state; an adaptation of Dybvig et al.'s expansion algorithm [5]; and new versions of ACL2's primitives that manipulate the new forms of data while satisfying existing axioms.

Figure 2 shows the definition of expansion states. An expansion state contains seven fields. The first names the source file being expanded. The second and third determine expansion modes: global versus local definition scope and logic mode versus program mode. Fields four and five provide mappings on the set of compiled definitions; the fourth is added for hygienic expansion to map bindings in source code to unique compiled names, and the fifth is ACL2's mapping from compiled names to the meaning of definitions. The sixth field is the subset of compiled definition names that are exported from the enclosing scope, and the seventh is the set of constrained function names that have been declared but not yet defined; we update this final field with hygienic metadata to properly track macro-inserted bindings.

A *definition table* maps each definition to a record describing its signature, executable behavior, and logical meaning. We use ACL2's existing definition signatures; we augment macro signatures to carry an identifier representing the lexical context of the macro's definition. An executable function implements a function or macro, and a logical formula describes a function or theorem equationally; we do not change either representation.

Figure 2 also shows the low-level representation of s-expressions. Symbols and sequences as shown in figure 1 are represented using the sym and cons constructors, respectively. An s-expression is either a number, a string, an identifier, or a pair of s-expressions. Numbers and strings are unchanged. The most important difference to a conventional representation concerns *identifiers*, which extend symbols to include information about expansion. An identifier is either a symbol or an annotated symbol. A symbol has three components: its name, its package, and a set of *inherent marks* used to support unique symbol generation. Annotated symbols contain a symbol, a set of *latent marks* used to record macro expansion steps, and two renamings; unlike standard identifier representations, we must differentiate function and value bindings. We represent booleans with symbols, abbreviated **t** and **nil**.

Identifiers represent variable names in unexpanded programs; unique symbol names are chosen for variables in fully expanded programs. The mapping between the two is mediated by *keys*. Each function or value binding's key combines the unique symbol corresponding to the shadowed binding—or the unmodified symbol if the name has no prior binding—and the (latent) marks of the identifier used to name the binding. A *renaming* maps keys to their corresponding symbols.

A *mark* uniquely identifies an event during macro expansion: a variable binding or single macro application. Each one comprises its source file as a string—to distinguish marks generated during the compilation of separate books, in an adaptation of Flatt's mechanism for differentiating bindings from separate modules [7]—as well as a number chosen uniquely during a single session.

This representation of s-expressions is used both for syntax during macro expansion and for values during ordinary runtime computation. Hence, ACL2 functions that deal with symbols must be updated to work with identifiers in a way that observes the axioms of regular symbols. The basic symbol observations name, package, eq, and symbolp are defined to ignore all identifier metadata. The symbol constructor intern produces a symbol with empty lexical context, while in-package-of copies the context of its second argument.

We also introduce four new identifier comparisons: $=^b_f$, $=^r_f$, $=^b_v$, and $=^r_v$. They are separated according to the ACL2 function and value namespaces, as signified by the subscripts, and to compare either binding occurrences or references, as signified by the superscripts. *These procedures do not respect ACL2's axioms.*

They can distinguish between symbols with the same name and package, so we provide them in program mode only. As such, they may be used in macros as variable comparisons that respect apparent bindings.

4   Evaluating Hygiene

Our design goals for hygienic ACL2 macros mention four guiding principles: referential transparency, separate compilation, logical soundness, and source compatibility. As explained, the macro expansion process preserves referential transparency by tracking the provenance of identifiers, with two key exceptions: symbols inserted by macros take their context from the macro definition site rather than their own occurrence, and conjecture quantification can "capture" free variables in macro inputs. Furthermore, our representation for compiled books guarantees separate compilation. We preserve logical soundness by obeying ACL2's axioms for symbols in operations on identifiers, and by reusing the existing ACL2 compiler and theorem proving engine. Only the principle of source compatibility remains to be evaluated.

Our prototype does not support many of the non-macro-related features of ACL2 and we are thus unable to run hygienic expansion on most existing books. To determine the degree of compatibility between our system and existing macros, we manually inspected all 2,954 **defmacro** forms in the books provided with ACL2 version 3.6, including the separate package of books accumulated from the ACL2 workshop series. Of these, some 488 nontrivial macros might be affected by hygiene. The rest of the section explains the details.

Code Duplication: The behavior of macro-duplicated code does not change with hygienic expansion; however, hygiene encourages the introduction of local variables in macros and thus avoids duplication. With our system, all 130 code-duplicating macros can be rewritten to benefit from hygiene.

Variable Comparison: Comparing variable names with eq does not take into account their provenance in the macro expansion process and can mistakenly identify two symbols with the same name but different lexical contexts. We found 26 macros in ACL2 that compare variable names for assorted purposes, none of which are served if the comparison does not respect the variable's binding. The new functions $=_f^b$, $=_f^r$, $=_v^b$, and $=_v^r$ provide comparisons for variables that respect lexical context. Once again, the result of eq does not change in our system, so these macros will function as they have; however, macro writers now have the option of using improved tools. Each of the 26 macros can be rewritten with these functions to compare variable names in a way that respects lexical bindings during macro expansion.

Free Variables: Free variables in macros usually represent some protocol by which macros take their meaning from their context; i.e., they must be used in a context where the names in question have been bound. Much like mutable state in imperative languages, free variables in macros represent an invisible channel of communication. When used judiciously, they create succinct programs, but they can also be a barrier to understanding. Of the 90 macros that insert free variables, 83 employ such a protocol. Our hygienic macro expander rejects such macros; they must be rewritten to communicate in an explicit manner.

Five further cases of free variables are forward references, in which a macro's body constructs a reference to a subsequent definition. To a macro writer, this may not seem like a free reference, but it is, due to the scope of ACL2 definitions. Therefore this use of forward references does not satisfy the principle of referential transparency. These macros must also be rewritten or reordered to mesh with hygienic macro expansion.

The final two cases of free variables in a macro are, in fact, symptoms of a single bug. The macro is used to generate the body of a conjecture. It splices several expressions into a large implication. One of the inputs is named top, and its first reference in the macro is accidentally quoted—instead of filling in the contents of the input named top, the macro inserts a literal reference to a variable named top. By serendipity, this macro is passed a variable named top, and nothing goes wrong. Were this macro ever to be used with another name, it would construct the wrong conjecture and either fail due to a mysterious extra variable or succeed spuriously by proving the wrong proposition. Our hygienic macro system would have flagged this bug immediately.

Variable Capture: We found 242 instances of variable (85) or definition (157) names inserted by macros that introduce bindings to the macro's input or surrounding program. Of the macros that insert definition names, there were 95 that used in-package-of to explicitly bind names in the package of their input, 44 that used intern to bind names in their own package, 16 that used hard-coded names not based on their input at all, and two that used the make-event facility [8] to construct unique names.

The package-aware macros will continue to function as before due to our interpretation of in-package-of. As written, the intern-based macros guarantee neither that the constructed names bind in the context of the input, nor that they don't, due to potential package mismatches. Hygienic expansion provides a consistent guarantee that they don't, making their meaning predictable. Hard-coded names in macros will no longer bind outside of the macro itself. These are the other side of free variable protocols; they must be made explicit to interoperate with hygiene. The make-event utility allows inspection of the current bindings to construct a unique name, but nothing prevents that name from clashing with any subsequent binding. Hygiene eliminates the need to manually scan the current bindings and guarantees global uniqueness.

Lexical variables account for the other 85 introduced bindings. We discovered nine whose call sites exploited these bindings as part of an intentional protocol. These macros can be made hygienic by taking the variable name in question as an argument, thus making the macro compatible with hygienic expansion, freeing up a name the user might want for something else, and avoiding surprises if a user does not know the macro's protocol.

Of the other 76 macros that bind local variables in the scope of their arguments, 59 attempt to avoid capture. There are 12 that choose long, obscure names; for instance, gensym::metlist (meaning "metlist" in the "gensym" package), indicating

	Improves for free	Improves with work	Unchanged	Broken; improves	Broken; restores
Code Duplication	–	130	–	–	–
Free variable	2	–	–	83	5
Lexical capture	29	47	–	9	–
Definition capture	–	2	95	44	16
Variable comparison	–	26	–	–	–
Total	31	205	95	136	21

Fig. 3. Impact of hygienic expansion on nontrivial ACL2 macros

a wish for the Lisp symbol-generating function gensym, which is not available in ACL2. There is also a convention of adding -do-not-use-elsewhere or some similar suffix to macro-bound variables; in one case, due to code copying, a variable named hyp--dont-use-this-name-elsewhere is in fact bound by *two* macros in different files. Obscure names are a poor form of protection when they are chosen following a simple formula, and a macro that binds a hard-coded long name will never compose properly with itself, as it always binds the same name.

A further 40 macros generate non-capturing names based on a known set of free variables, and seven more fail with a compile error if they capture a name as detected by check-vars-not-free. These macros are guaranteed not to capture, but the latter still force the user to learn the name bound by the macro and avoid choosing it for another purpose. Some of these macros claim common names, such as val and x, for themselves.

Finally, we have found 17 macros in the ACL2 books that bind variables and take no steps to avoid capture. All of the accidentally variable-capturing macros will automatically benefit from hygienic expansion.

Exceptions: The notable exceptions to hygiene we have not addressed are make-event, a tool for selective code transformation, and **state**, a special variable used to represent mutation and i/o. We have not yet inspected most uses of make-event in the ACL2 code base, but do not anticipate any theoretical problems in adapting the feature. For **state** and similar "single-threaded" objects, our design must change so as to recognize the appropriate variables and not rename them.

Summary: Figure 3 summarizes our analysis. We categorize each macro by row according to the type of transformation it applies: code duplication, free variable insertion, capture of lexical or definition bindings, and variable comparison. We omit the trivial case of simple alias macros from this table.

We split the macros by column according to the anticipated result of hygienic expansion. In the leftmost column, we sum up the macros whose expansion is automatically improved by hygienic expansion. Next to that, we include macros that work as-is with hygiene, but permit a better definition. In the center, we tally the macros whose expansion is unaffected. To the right, we list macros that must be fixed to work with hygienic macro expansion, but whose expansion becomes more predictable when fixed. In the rightmost column, we list those macros that must be fixed, yet do not benefit from hygienic expansion.

Many libraries and built-in features of ACL2 rely on the unhygienic nature of expansion and use implicit bindings; as a result, our system cannot cope with every macro idiom in the code base. These macros must be rewritten in our system. We anticipate that all of the macros distributed with ACL2 can be fixed straightforwardly by either reordering definitions or adding extra arguments to macros. However, this process cannot be automated and is a potential source of new errors. Fortunately, the bulk of macros will continue to work, and we expect most of them to benefit from hygiene. The frequent use of code duplication, obscure variable names, and other capture prevention mechanisms shows that ACL2 users recognize the need for a disciplined approach to avoiding unintentional capture in ACL2 macros.

5 Related Work and Conclusions

ACL2 is not the only theorem prover equipped with a method of syntactic extensions. PVS has macros [9]; however, they are restricted to definitions of constants that are inlined during the type-checking phase. As a result, preserving the binding structure of the source program is simple.

The Agda, Coq, Isabelle, and Nuprl theorem provers all support extensible notation. These include issues of parsing, precedence, and associativity that do not arise in ACL2's macros, which are embedded in the grammar of s-expressions. The notation mechanisms of Agda and Isabelle are limited to "mixfix" operator definitions [10,11]. These definitions do not introduce new variable names in their expansion, so the problem of variable capture does not arise.

Nuprl and Coq have notation systems that permit the introduction of new binding forms. Nuprl requires each notational definition to carry explicit binding annotations. These annotations allow Nuprl to resolve variable references without the inference inherent in hygienic macro systems [12]. The notation system of Coq ensures that introduced variables do not capture source program variables and vice versa [13], although the precise details of this process are undocumented. Neither Nuprl nor Coq allow case dispatch or self-reference in notational definitions. Our work combines the predictability of variable scope present in Nuprl and Coq notation with the expressive power of ACL2 macros.

Hygienic macros have been a standardized part of the Scheme programming language for over a decade [14]. They have been used to define entire new programming languages [15,16], including an implementation of the runtime components of ACL2 in Scheme [17]. These results are feasible because of hygiene and are facilitated by further advances in macro tools [7,18].

With hygienic macros, ACL2 developers gain the power to write more trustworthy and maintainable proofs using macros. Furthermore, adding a scope-respecting macro mechanism is a necessary step for any future attempt to make ACL2 reason about its source programs directly instead of expanded terms. Our techniques may also be useful in adapting hygienic macros to languages other than Scheme and ACL2 that have different binding constructs, different scope mechanisms, multiple namespaces, implicit bindings, and other such features.

At the 2009 ACL2 Workshop's panel on the future of theorem proving, panelist David Hardin of Rockwell Collins stated a desire for domain-specific languages in automated theorem proving. This paper is the first of many steps toward user-written, domain-specific languages in ACL2.

References

1. Kaufmann, M., Manolios, P., Moore, J.S.: Computer-Aided Reasoning: an Approach. Kluwer Academic Publishers, Dordrecht (2000)
2. Kaufmann, M., Moore, J.S.: Design goals of ACL2. Technical report, Computational Logic, Inc. (1994)
3. Kohlbecker, E., Friedman, D.P., Felleisen, M., Duba, B.: Hygienic macro expansion. In: Proc. 1986 ACM Conference on LISP and Functional Programming, pp. 151–161. ACM Press, New York (1986)
4. Clinger, W., Rees, J.: Macros that work. In: Proc. 18th Annual ACM SIGPLAN-SIGACT Symposium on Principles of Programming Languages, pp. 155–162. ACM Press, New York (1991)
5. Dybvig, R.K., Hieb, R., Bruggeman, C.: Syntactic abstraction in Scheme. Lisp and Symbolic Computation 5(4), 295–326 (1992)
6. Herman, D., Wand, M.: A theory of hygienic macros. In: Gairing, M. (ed.) ESOP 2008. LNCS, vol. 4960, pp. 48–62. Springer, Heidelberg (2008)
7. Flatt, M.: Composable and compilable macros: you want it when? In: Proc. 7th ACM SIGPLAN International Conference on Functional Programming, pp. 72–83. ACM Press, New York (2002)
8. Kaufmann, M., Moore, J.S.: ACL2 Documentation (2009), http://userweb.cs.utexas.edu/users/moore/acl2/current/acl2-doc.html
9. Owre, S., Shankar, N., Rushby, J.M., Stringer-Calvert, D.W.J.: PVS Language Reference (2001), http://pvs.csl.sri.com/doc/pvs-language-reference.pdf
10. Danielsson, N.A., Norell, U.: Parsing mixfix operators. In: Proc. 20th International Symposium on the Implementation and Application of Functional Languages, School of Computer Science of the University of Hertfordshire (2008)
11. Wenzel, M.: The Isabelle/Isar Reference Manual (2010), http://isabelle.in.tum.de/dist/Isabelle/doc/isar-ref.pdf
12. Griffin, T.G.: Notational definition—a formal account. In: Proc. 3rd Annual Symposium on Logic in Computer Science, pp. 372–383. IEEE Press, Los Alamitos (1988)
13. The Coq Development Team: The Coq Proof Assistant Reference Manual (2009), http://coq.inria.fr/coq/distrib/current/refman/
14. Kelsey, R., Clinger, W., Rees, J. (eds.): Revised[5] report on the algorithmic language Scheme. ACM SIGPLAN Notices 33(9), 26–76 (1998)
15. Gray, K., Flatt, M.: Compiling Java to PLT Scheme. In: Proc. 5th Workshop on Scheme and Functional Programming, pp. 53–61 (2004)
16. Tobin-Hochstadt, S., Felleisen, M.: The design and implementation of Typed Scheme. In: Proc. 35th Annual ACM SIGPLAN-SIGACT Symposium on Principles of Programming Languages, pp. 395–406. ACM Press, New York (2008)
17. Vaillancourt, D., Page, R., Felleisen, M.: ACL2 in DrScheme. In: Proc. 6th International Workshop on the ACL2 Theorem Prover and its Applications, pp. 107–116 (2006)
18. Culpepper, R.: Refining Syntactic Sugar: Tools for Supporting Macro Development. PhD dissertation, Northeastern University (2010)

What's the Matter with Kansas Lava?

Andrew Farmer, Garrin Kimmell, and Andy Gill

Information Technology and Telecommunication Center,
Department of Electrical Engineering and Computer Science,
The University of Kansas,
2335 Irving Hill Road,
Lawrence, KS 66045, USA
{anfarmer,kimmell,andygill}@ku.edu

Abstract. Kansas Lava is a functional hardware description language implemented in Haskell. In the course of attempting to generate ever larger circuits, we have found the need to effectively test and debug the internals of Kansas Lava. This includes confirming both the simulated behavior of the circuit and its hardware realization via generated VHDL. In this paper we share our approach to this problem, and discuss the results of these efforts.

1 Introduction

Lava is a Domain Specific Language (DSL) embedded in Haskell that allows for the description of hardware circuits using Haskell functions [1]. It turns out that such a DSL, known as a functional hardware description language, represents a natural way to express circuits. For instance, the definition of a half adder, which takes two bits as inputs, adds them, and returns the result bit and a carry bit, is:

```
halfAdder :: Bit -> Bit -> (Bit, Bit)
halfAdder a b = (carry,sum)
  where carry = and2 a b
        sum   = xor2 a b
```

The half adder can be run like a normal Haskell function. We call this mode of running the circuit *simulation*.

```
ghci> halfAdder true true
(T,F)
```

We can also, under the correct conditions, capture our half adder function as an abstract syntax tree, which we can render into a traditional hardware description language, such as VHDL. We call this process *synthesis*.

R. Page, Z. Horváth, and V. Zsók (Eds.): TFP 2010, LNCS 6546, pp. 102–117, 2011.
© Springer-Verlag Berlin Heidelberg 2011

1.1   What is Kansas Lava?

Kansas Lava is an effort to create a modern Lava implementation that allows direct specification of circuits like traditional Lava. Kansas Lava makes extensive use of recent design patterns, like Applicative Functors, to permit concise and natural expression of hardware concerns as Haskell functions. Kansas Lava also heavily leverages advanced extensions to GHC's type system, like scoped type variables and type functions, to offer a high degree of control over signal representations, accurate simulation, and assurances of correctness.

Notice that the `halfAdder` circuit above, when defined in Kansas Lava, can be used in two contexts: as a combinatorial circuit and as a circuit operating on a sequence of clocked values:

```
ghci> :t halfAdder
halfAdder :: (Signal sig) =>
    sig Bool -> sig Bool -> (sig Bool, sig Bool)
ghci> :t true
true :: Comb Bool
ghci> halfAdder true true
(T,F)
ghci> let x = toSeq $ cycle [False,False,True,True]
ghci> let y = toSeq $ cycle [False,True]
ghci> halfAdder x y
(F :~  F :~  F :~  T :~ ..., F :~  T :~  T :~  F :~ ...)
```

1.2   In This Paper

Programmatically generating hardware presents new challenges when it comes to testing and debugging. Often, traditional lightweight testing strategies are adept at discovering errors, via simulation, but offer little help in determining the cause of the error.

When used in this debugging context, they often scale poorly to large circuits since they don't permit inspection of intermediate values, and require a functional decomposition to expose these internal streams that may be unnatural or time consuming. What is needed in such a situation is a debugging tool that permits the inspection of intermediate values and the testing of parts of a circuit in isolation.

Additionally, none of these tools allows a means of testing the synthesized circuit. This is a prime concern both for the implementors of Kansas Lava and users in the late stages of circuit design – who need to refine circuits to meet the constraints imposed by their chosen hardware substrate.

In this paper we present a solution to this problem for Kansas Lava. Specifically, we:

- show why existing solutions like QuickCheck are often ineffective in this domain (Section 2).

- introduce the notion of probes, a means of observing intermediate values without loss of modularity (Section 3), and explain their implemention (Section 4).
- show that probes offer a natural way to compare the simulated circuit to the sythesized version (Section 5).
- demonstrate the powerful ability of probes to demarcate subcircuits, permitting a form of automated algorithmic debugging which compares the behavior of the simulation to that of the synthesized VHDL (Section 6).

Using these tools has allowed us to debug large, real-world Lava circuits in a more straightforward manner than in the past.

2   Testing Functional Circuits

We specifically want to test two aspects of circuits in Kansas Lava. First, that they behave correctly in simulation, like any Haskell function. Secondly, that the generated VHDL behaves exactly the same as the simulated circuit, clock for clock.

A popular method of testing Haskell functions is to use the QuickCheck tool [2]. QuickCheck allows the Haskell programmer to define logical assertions about the bahavior of functions, known as properties, and then attempts to find counter-examples by generating random inputs to each property and checking the result. The programmer is given a means to control how the random inputs are generated via a typeclass called `Arbitrary`.

Since Lava circuits are Haskell functions, using QuickCheck is straightforward. For instance, given Kansas Lava's implementation of boolean conjunction and a suitable instance of QuickCheck's `Arbitrary` type class, one can verify properties like the following, which shows that the and2 implementation is commutative:

```
prop_andComm x y = (x ‘and2‘ y) == (y ‘and2‘ x)
   where types = (x :: Comb Bool, y :: Comb Bool)
```

While this approach is quick and easy to implement, it is of limited use.

Foremost, equality over sequential inputs is problematic. Two sequences can certainly be unequal, and they can have equivalent prefixes, but they are unbounded data structures, so it is impossible to assert equivalence. We can use a hack to say, effectively, that equivalent prefixes are good enough:

```
prop_andCommSeq x y = prefix (x ‘and2‘ y) == prefix (y ‘and2‘ x)
   where types = (x :: Seq Bool, y :: Seq Bool)
         prefix = (take 100) . toList
```

but this is less than ideal. Nevertheless, an instance of QuickCheck's `Arbitrary` type class is defined for `Seq`, in case it proves useful for other kinds of tests.

Secondly, QuickCheck tests properties by generating random inputs based on type information. While this may be effective for small circuits, larger circuits often require complex non-random input. For instance, we may want to isolate a case where a specific control sequence elicits bad behavior and repeatedly test that case. In essence, we need a unit test instead of a randomized test.

Most problematic for us, as the developers of the Kansas Lava DSL, is the fact that QuickCheck doesn't test the generated VHDL at all. Equality between signal types, over which all Kansas Lava circuits are defined, only compares the simulation values (and in the case of sequences, as mentioned above, doesn't even do that).

It is not obvious how to define equality over the generated code, short of comparing the resulting circuit graphs for isomorphism. The worst case complexity of such a solution is often exponential.

2.1 Observing Intermediate Values

Kansas Lava circuits are opaque Haskell functions which only permit observation of the relationship between inputs and outputs. Intermediate values, defined as local Haskell bindings, cannot be observed without modifying the underlying circuit.

As a simple example, consider this archetypal (and buggy) Lava definition of a full adder, constructed by combining two half adder circuits:

```
fullAdder a b cin = (sum,cout)
  where (s1,c1) = halfAdder a a
        (sum,c2) = halfAdder cin s1
        cout = xor2 c1 c2
```

In this example, the intermediate values s1, c1, and c2 are not exposed as outputs to the function, and are consequently not observable. In fact, the above definition has a bug in the calculation of (s1,c1) where the input parameter a is used as the second argument to the half adder instead of the parameter b. Observing the input/output behavior of the fullAdder function (with QuickCheck for example) will reveal incorrect behavior, but does not provide any insight into the location of the error. Rather, we need to be able to observe the input/output behavior of the first halfAdder *in the context of its use in the full adder.*

One approach to locating the bug is to simply return the intermediate values as additional outputs to the circuit:

```
fullAdder a b cin = ((sum,cout),debug)
  where (s1,c1) = halfAdder a a
        (sum,c2) = halfAdder cin s1
        cout = xor2 c1 c2
        debug = (s1,c1,c2)
```

While this succeeds in exposing the intermediate values, we have changed the interface to the circuit. This necessitates a modification to all the circuits depending on fullAdder, and in general leads to a loss of modularity. Moreover, the clarity of the type signature is lost completely:

Before:

```
fullAdder :: (Signal sig) => sig Bool -> sig Bool -> sig Bool
                            -> (sig Bool, sig Bool)
```

After:

```
fullAdder :: (Signal sig) => sig Bool -> sig Bool -> sig Bool
    -> ((sig Bool, sig Bool), (sig Bool, sig Bool, sig Bool))
```

If the incorrect behavior were to be observed when defining a circuit which *uses* the full adder, then that circuit must in turn be modified to propagate the debugging output.

This leaves the user with two options, both with significant drawbacks. They can either export *all* of the intermediate circuit values and sort through the global collection, or they can iteratively export a subset of the intermediate values, checking for correct behavior, until the troublesome circuit is located. The first solution requires changing large amounts of code and muddying function interfaces, the second is incredibly time consuming.

3   Circuit Instrumentation Using Probes

Kansas Lava provides a solution that sidesteps this problem using the notion of a *probe*, based on the design in the Hawk Architectural Design Language [3]. When using this construct, intermediate values can be observed without changing the circuit interface. Only those intermediate values that are probed will be observable, allowing probes to be inserted and removed as the circuit is searched to locate the source of an error.

Using this function, we can instrument the fullAdder circuit to expose intermediate values without changing the circuit interface:

```
fullAdder a b cin = (sum,cout)
    where (s1,c1)  = halfAdder a a
          (sum,c2) = halfAdder cin (probe "s1" s1)
          cout     = xor2 (probe "c1" c1) (probe "c2" c2)
```

Two functions are provided for extracting probe values. First, probeCircuit takes a circuit with probes and generates an association list of probe names and values. Then getProbe looks up a probe name in this list and returns the associated value. The test function, shown below, demonstrates the use of these two functions.

```
test = do
    probes <- probeCircuit $ fullAdder false true false
    case (getProbe probes "s1") of
        Just (ProbeValue probeName xstrm) ->
            return $ showXStream xstrm
```

Calling `test` at the ghci prompt yields the following trace of outputs for the s1 probe:

```
ghci> test
"F" :~   "F" :~   "F" :~   "F" :~ ...
```

The probe mechanism automatically lifts combinational Kansas Lava values into a stream of values.

While the above example demonstrated a way to observe intermediate Kansas Lava values, it doesn't shed a great deal of light on the particular bug in the full adder circuit. We have only observed the output of the `halfAdder`, whereas the bug is due to the incorrect input value. To make it possible to observe both the input and output of a function, we can apply `probe` to the *function itself*:

```
fullAdder a b cin = (sum,cout)
  where (s1,c1)  = (probe "ha1" halfAdder) a a
        (sum,c2) = halfAdder cin s1
        cout     = xor2 c1 c2
```

To print out traces from all of the probes, we modify our `test` function:

```
test = do
    probes <- probeCircuit $ fullAdder false true false
    mapM_ printProbe probes
    where printProbe (i, (ProbeValue name xstrm)) = do
        putStr $ name ++ ": "
        putStrLn $ show xstrm
```

The `probe` function generates names by simply enumerating each argument (along with the result) and adding the enumerated index to the given probe name, ha1:

```
ghci> test
ha1_0: "F" :~ "F" :~ "F" :~ "F" :~ ...
ha1_1: "F" :~ "F" :~ "F" :~ "F" :~ ...
ha1_2: "(F,F)" :~ "(F,F)" :~ "(F,F)" :~ "(F,F)" :~...
```

In this example, `ha1_0` is the first argument to `halfAdder`, `ha1_1` is the second, and `ha1_2` is the result. The fact that the two inputs to `halfAdder` are the same is now obvious.

4   Implementation

4.1   Implementing Probes on Values

There are two concrete types in Kansas Lava: `Seq` and `Comb`, which represent sequential and combinatorial values, respectively. Combinatorial values exclude the notion of a clock, whereas sequential values encode a series of values over time:

```
data Comb a = Comb <shallow value> <deep structure>
data Seq a = Seq (Stream <shallow values>) <deep structure>
```

Both are instances of the Signal type class, over which most primitives are defined.

The shallow embedding is a regular Haskell value which can be manipulated by Haskell functions. The deep embedding is a structure of primitive entities that can be reified to a netlist, from which we generate VHDL for compilation. Kansas Lava primitives manipulate both embeddings, freeing the user to focus on circuit composition.

The ability to observe intermediate values is a pleasing consequence of maintaining both embeddings. In essense, when the probe function is invoked on a circuit, the deep embedding is annotated with the result of the shallow embedding.

The probe function itself takes a string representing a user-significant name for the intermediate value and a Kansas Lava circuit. To allow probe to be utilized for a variety of types, the function is overloaded via a type class and instances are provided for the range of types representable as Kansas Lava circuits.

```
class Probe a where
    probe :: String -> a -> a
```

To allow any Kansas Lava value to be stored in the deep representation, we construct an existential type, ProbeValue:

```
data ProbeValue = forall a. (Show a, RepWire a, Typeable a) =>
                        ProbeValue String (XStream a)
            deriving Typeable
```

The Typeable constraint on a allows us to use Haskell's Data.Dynamic library to store and recover the printed representation of the value. One downside of this implementation decision is that we can no longer manipulate observed values directly, only their string representations. The XStream data type can be thought of as a Seq that has no deep embedding:

```
data XStream a = XStream (Stream a)
data Seq a = Seq (Stream a) (D a)
```

For Seq values, the result of the shallow embedding is simply repackaged into an XStream and added to a special attribute list in the deep data structure:

```
instance (Show a, RepWire a, Typeable a) => Probe (Seq a) where
    probe name (Seq shallow (D deep)) =
        Seq shallow (D (addAttr name stream deep))
            where stream = XStream shallow :: XStream a
```

The addAttr function handles the various possible entities that may make up the deep embedding at this point. Using the common case of a Port as an example, we see addAttr create a ProbeValue and add it to the attribute list:

```
addAttr :: forall a . (...) =>
    String -> XStream a -> Driver E -> Driver E
addAttr name value (Port v (E (Entity n outs ins attrs))) =
    let p = [("simValue", toDyn (ProbeValue name value))]
    in  Port v (E (Entity n outs ins $ attrs ++ p))
```

To retrieve the probe values, we use the probeCircuit function, which reifies the circuit and returns an association list of probe names and values:

```
probeCircuit :: (...) => a -> IO [(String,ProbeValue)]
probeCircuit circuit = do
    rc <- reifyCircuit circuit
    return [(n,p) | (_,Entity _ _ _ attrs) <- theCircuit rc
                  , ("simValue", val) <- attrs
                  , Just p@(ProbeValue n v) <- [fromDynamic val]]
```

The reifyCircuit function uses IO-based reification [4] to return a netlist representation of the circuit. Each item is a tuple of a unique id and the Entity from the deep embedding. We search through this list for any attributes that are probes, and recover the ProbeValue.

4.2   Implementing Probes on Functions

To probe a function, we apply probes to each argument as it arrives, and then probe the result value. In order to identify which probe matches which argument, we add a function to our Probe class, which is like probe, but additionally accepts a name supply:

```
class Probe a where
    probe :: String -> a -> a
    probe' :: String -> [Var] -> a -> a

instance (Show a, Probe a, Probe b) => Probe (a -> b) where
    probe name f = probe' name vars f
        where vars = [Var $ show i | i <- [0..]]

    probe' name ((Var v):vs) f x =
        probe' name vs $ f (probe (name ++ "_" ++ v) x)
```

The initial call to probe on a function f will generate a list of names and call probe'. As f is applied to each argument x, that argument has an appropriately named probe wrapped around it. Once the function is fully applied, probe' will be called on a Seq or Comb value. The probe' function for these values calls probe with the annotated name, discarding the name supply:

```
instance (Show a, RepWire a, Typeable a) => Probe (Seq a) where
    probe name (Seq shallow (D deep)) = ...

    probe' name ((Var v):_) seq = probe (name ++ "_" ++ v) seq
```

Using the `probesFor` function, we can filter the output of `probeCircuit` to
find the specific set of probes related to a probed function:

```
probesFor :: String -> [(String,ProbeValue)]
                    -> [(String,ProbeValue)]
probesFor name plist =
    sortBy (\(n1, _) (n2, _) -> compare n1 n2) $
    filter (\(n, _) -> name `isPrefixOf` n) plist
```

5   Testing the Deep Embedding

As we attempt to use Kansas Lava to generate ever larger circuits, confirming
that the shallow and deep embedding are equivalent is increasingly important.
Subtle issues like differences in timing behavior between the simulated shallow
functions and the VHDL entities often only manifest themselves in larger circuits.

To address this, we use recovered probe values to drive the VHDL simulation
and then compare the results. The function that does this is called `testCircuit`:

```
testCircuit "mux2"
    (mux2 :: Seq Bool -> (Seq U4, Seq U4) -> Seq U4)
    (\ f -> let sel  = toSeq $ cycle [True,False,True,True,False]
                inp  = toSeq $ cycle [0..15]
                inp2 = toSeq $ cycle $ reverse [0..15]
            in f sel (inp, inp2))
```

The implementation of `testCircuit` takes a user-significant name, the circuit,
and a function that applies that circuit to inputs:

```
testCircuit :: (...) => String -> a -> (a -> b) -> IO ()
testCircuit name circuit apply = do
    let probed = probe name circuit
    plist <- probeCircuit $ apply probed

    mkInputs name 50 $ probesFor name plist
    mkTestbench name probed
```

First, `testCircuit` wraps a probe around the circuit. Since the circuit is a
function, that means both inputs and outputs will be observed. Next, the `apply`
function applies the sample input provided by the user to this probed circuit.
Using `probeCircuit` and `probesFor`, the probe data is recovered.

The `mkInputs` function transforms the `XStream` values in each probe into two
ASCII files. One is a human readable info file which gives a clock value followed
by each input and the output, in both Haskell and wire representations. The
other file is meant to be read by the VHDL testbench:

```
mux2.info                                    mux2.shallow
(0) T/1 -> (0,15)/11110000 -> 0/0000         1111100000000
(1) F/0 -> (1,14)/11100001 -> 14/1110        0111000011110
(2) T/1 -> (2,13)/11010010 -> 2/0010         1110100100010
(3) T/1 -> (3,12)/11000011 -> 3/0011         1110000110011
(4) F/0 -> (4,11)/10110100 -> 11/1011        0101101001011
(5) T/1 -> (5,10)/10100101 -> 5/0101         1101001010101
...                                          ...
```

Running the VHDL testbench created by `mkTestbench` will generate a `mux2.deep` file that corresponds to the `mux2.shallow` file. If these two files are the same, then the simulated and compiled versions of the circuit behaved in the same way.

6 Handling Large Circuits

The framework we just described suffers because it only uses the probe data for the overall circuit. This is fine when the circuit is small, but becomes problematic for larger circuits because, while it effectively reports that something is wrong, it offers no help in pinpointing the bug.

The user can place many probes within a single circuit, so our framework should be able to generate tests for each of them. This allows the user to narrow down the problem by finding probe tests that fail within the larger circuit.

6.1 Extracting Subcircuits

Whereas probing intermediate values is a useful analogue to actual hardware probes, effectively allowing the user to watch a stream of values move along a wire in the circuit, probing functions is much more powerful. Since each input to the function is itself probed, along with the output, we have effectively tagged the boundaries of the function within the circuit graph.

To illustrate, reifying our probed `fullAdder` gives the graph in Fig. 1. Notice that nodes are annotated with the names of probes applied to them. To find the nodes that make up the `halfAdder` function named `ha2`, we start at its output node (`ha2_2`, the highest numbered `ha2` probe) and do a breadth first search (BFS) backward along the input edges. If we encounter a node that also has an `ha2` probe on it, then we have reached one of the arguments to the function. This marks the boundary of the function within the graph. Nodes encountered during this search make up the subgraph that implements the `halfAdder` function.

Using this subgraph, we can create a new sink based on the output type of the `ha2_2` node. The leaves, which all have probes on them, are sorted in argument order based on the probe name. Each leaf is replaced with a `Pad` (an externally driven input), using the output type of the leaf as the new input and output type of the `Pad`. This allows us to pass the captured probe data as input. The newly extracted self-contained circuit can be seen in Fig. 2.

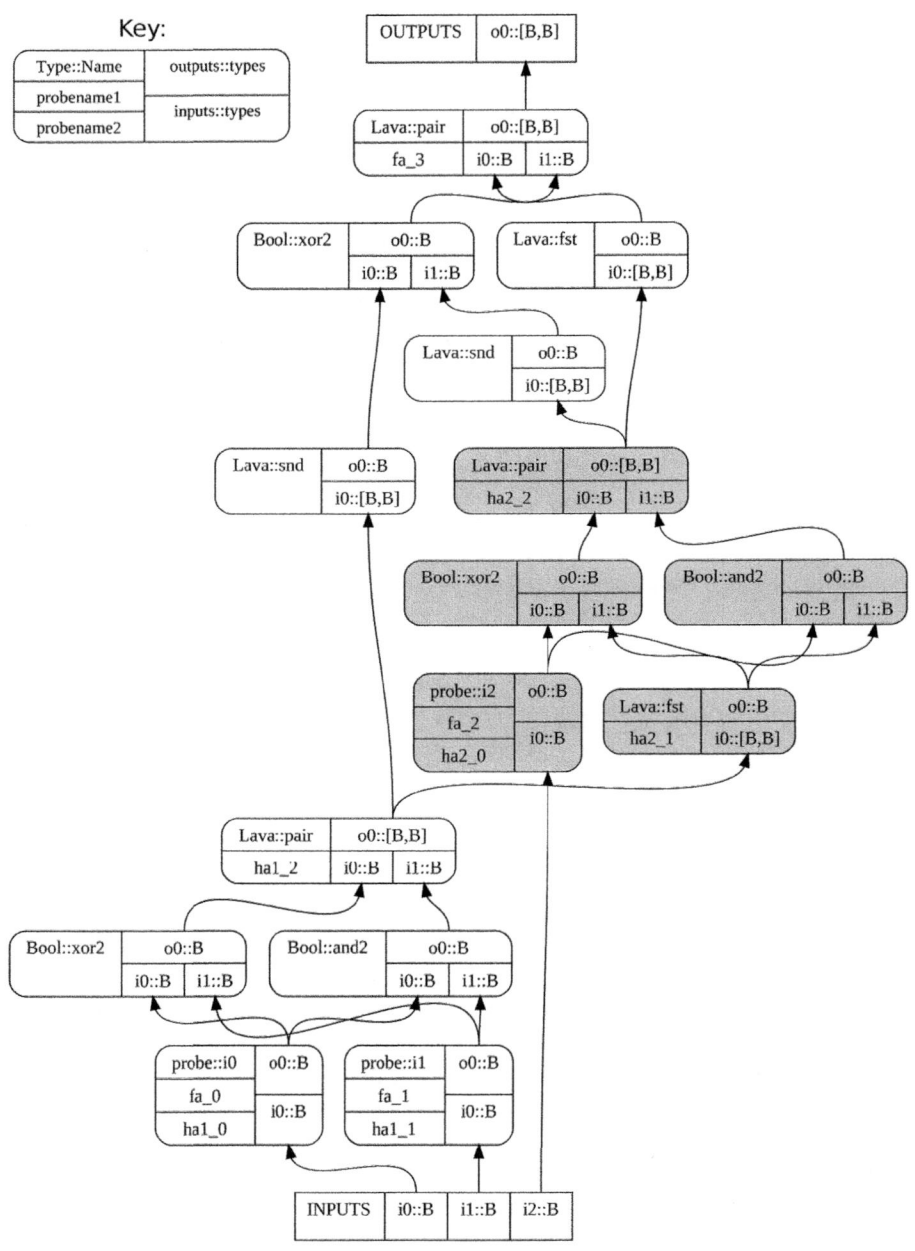

Fig. 1. A circuit graph for the `fullAdder`. Note that we have attached probes to each `halfAdder` as well as the entire circuit. Using a BFS backwards along the inputs of the ha2_2 node, we find the subcircuit making up the second probed `halfAdder`. These nodes are shaded in gray.

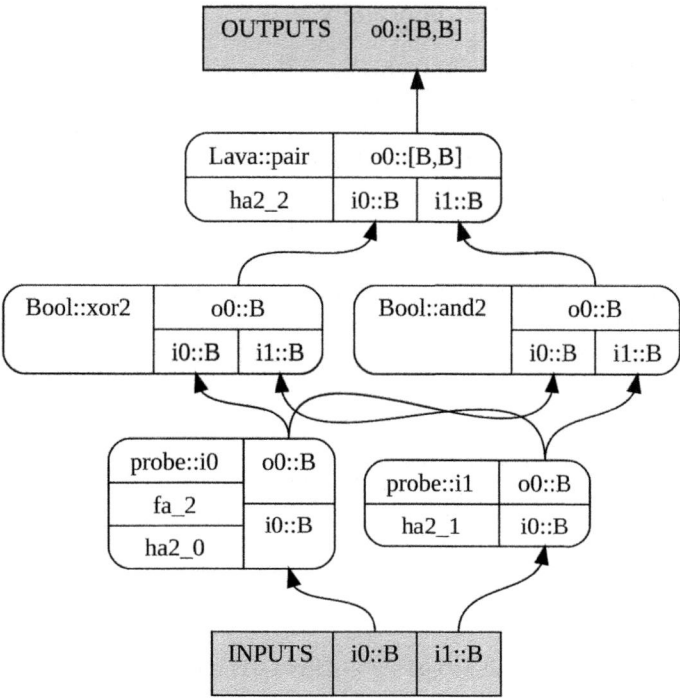

Fig. 2. The circuit for the `ha2` probe, extracted from the `fullAdder` circuit in Fig. 1. Leaf nodes have been converted to `Pads`, and new sources and sinks are derived based on type information.

We provide a function named `extract` to implement this algorithm. It takes a probe name and a reified circuit and returns a reified subcircuit which implements the probed function:

```
extract :: String -> ReifiedCircuit -> ReifiedCircuit
```

Using `extract`, we can write a more versatile version of `testCircuit` which allows us to specify *which* probed function we would like to test in the context of the overall circuit:

```
testSubcircuit :: (...) => String -> a -> (a -> b) -> IO ()
testSubcircuit name circuit apply = do
    let probed = probe "whole" circuit

    reified <- reifyCircuit probed
    plist <- probeCircuit $ apply probed

    mkInputs name 50 $ probesFor name plist
    mkTestbenchFromRC name $ extract name reified
```

6.2 Locating Errors Automatically

The ability to extract and individually test subcircuits allows us to liberally probe a circuit and use our intuition to locate the cause of a problem.

However, since we are testing the correspondence of the shallow and deep embeddings, which comes down to diffing the generated outputs, there is no reason not to automate this process.

To do so, we implement a form of algorithmic debugging [5]. The general idea is to build an execution tree, and for each node ask an oracle if the result at that node is correct, eventually finding the node that is causing the error. Normally the oracle is the programmer, but in this case we can use the recorded probe data, effectively making the shallow embedding an oracle for the deep embedding.

We do this by walking the circuit graph in breadth first order from the sinks, recording the relationship among the various probes in the circuit into a simple Rose Tree structure that records the name of the probe, the node's unique identifier, and a list of children:

```
data ProbeTree = Node String Unique [ProbeTree]
   deriving (Eq, Show)

probeForest :: ReifiedCircuit -> [ProbeTree]
```

In the context of a hardware circuit, our execution tree must capture the *contained-in* relationship between probed functions (as opposed to the *depends-on* relationship). This encodes the failure relationships between probed subcircuits. If subcircuit A is wholly contained by subcircuit B, then A's failure will most likely also cause B to fail. As such, A is a child of B. Otherwise, A and B are siblings. For the fullAdder example, probeForest returns:

```
[Node "fullAdder" 3 [Node "ha2" 5 [],Node "ha1" 9 []]]
```

Note that while ha2 depends on the output of ha1 in the circuit, ha1 is not contained *within* ha2. A failure within ha1 will not necessarily lead to a failure of ha2, merely bad input. Both are within the fullAdder subcircuit, whose failure could be caused by either, meaning ha1 and ha2 are siblings.

Now that we have this tree structure, we use it to implement our debugger. There are various strategies for traversing the execution tree. Most of these focus on improving the experience for human oracles by reducing the number nodes tested and avoiding dramatic context switches that can slow the oracle down. Since we are using the shallow embedding as our oracle, we chose a strategy known as Top-Down Search [6]. While not the most advanced strategy available, it is both simple to implement and effective at pruning the execution tree.

Beginning at the root, we call a modified testSubcircuit on each node to extract and compare the deep and shallow embeddings of the probed subcircuit. If the test fails, we start testing each child, on the premise that the failure was caused by a failing child. If the test succeeds, we assume all child subcircuits functioned properly (since they are part of the circuit we just tested), and move on to a sibling in the tree:

```
algDebug :: ReifiedCircuit            -- circuit
         -> [(String, ProbeValue)] -- probe data
         -> IO ()
algDebug circuit pdata = go "" $ probeForest circuit
    where go []        [] = putStrLn "Embeddings act the same."
          go parent [] = putStrLn $ parent ++ " failed."
          go parent ((Node name _ children):siblings) = do
                code <- testSubcircuit circuit pdata name
                case code of
                    ExitSuccess -> go parent siblings
                    ExitFailure _ -> go name children

testSubcircuit :: ReifiedCircuit
               -> [(String, ProbeValue)]
               -> String
               -> IO ExitCode
testSubcircuit circuit pdata name = do
    mkInputs name 50 $ probesFor name pdata
    mkTestbenchFromRC name $ extract name circuit
```

The search terminates in two ways:

- All siblings at the top level test successfully, meaning all probed portions of the circuit are behaving equally in both embeddings.
- All siblings at another level test successfully, meaning their parent node (which failed) is the likely culprit.

As you can see, each run of this algorithmic strategy only locates a single failing subcircuit, so we may be required to run the search multiple times if there are multiple errors.

We change our testCircuit definition once again to take advantage of this automated search:

```
testCircuit :: (...) => String -> a -> (a -> b) -> IO ()
testCircuit name circuit apply = do
        let probed = probe name circuit

        rc <- reifyCircuit probed
        pdata <- probeCircuit $ apply probed

        algDebug rc pdata
```

7 Related Work

There are many ongoing efforts to create effective testing and debugging tools for lazy functional languages. As we have seen, QuickCheck is one of those tools. Others include HPC, a code coverage tool [7], and ThreadScope, a means of visualizing parallel computations [8].

Probes are a means of tracing, a well explored area when it comes to debugging functional languages. Chitil *et al.* compare three popular solutions for tracing Haskell program execution [9], including Freja [10], Hat [11], and Hood [12]. Our probe implementation is most like that of Hood in spirit. Both are lightweight tools that allow observation of intermediate values without greatly impacting performance. Freja and Hat are extensions to Haskell compilers, and each offers a guided traversal of the trace information to locate bugs, much like our efforts in Section 6.2. Hat in particular is known to have a large runtime overhead.

Algorithmic debugging is a promising approach to automating debugging tasks [5]. Functional languages appear to be a good match for this technique due to their lack of side effects. Laziness, however, presents a problem in that values presented to the user might not be evaluated yet. Nilsson and Fritzson make an in-depth examination of algorithmic debugging in the context of lazy functional languages [13].

8 Conclusion and Future Work

Traditional Haskell testing tools like QuickCheck are of limited use when testing Lava circuits. Many properties that are easy to express over finite data structures like Comb are more cumbersome over unbounded ones such as Seq. They also offer no easy way to test the generated VHDL code.

Probes present a method of observing intermediate values in the shallow embedding without modifying the circuit interface. Their use is intuitive in the to a hardware designer accustomed to thinking of wires and observing waveforms. The dual shallow/deep embedding used by Kansas Lava signals is crucial for their implementation. In order to test VHDL generation, they permit an automated comparison of the deep and shallow embeddings.

While the current system is primarily useful to the developers of Kansas Lava, one possible future direction is to adapt the framework to be a true algorithmic debugger, with the Lava user as the oracle. Alternatively, this framework could be used to test circuit optimizations, using the unoptimized circuit as an oracle for the optimized one.

The full implications of the ability of probes to bound and extract subcircuits also remains to be explored. We can envision a hybrid execution model, running some parts of the circuit in hardware while simulating others using the shallow embedding. Efforts to visualize circuits can also be greatly improved. Large circuits may contain millions of nodes, but probes would allow us to group related parts of the circuit and view it at a more abstract level.

References

1. Bjesse, P., Claessen, K., Sheeran, M., Singh, S.: Lava: Hardware design in haskell. In: International Conference on Functional Programming, pp. 174–184 (1998)
2. Claessen, K., Hughes, J.: Quickcheck: A lightweight tool for random testing of haskell programs. ACM SIGPLAN Notices, 268–279 (2000)
3. Matthews, J.R.: Algebraic Specification and Verification of Processor Microarchitectures. PhD thesis, University of Washington (1990)
4. Gill, A., Bull, T., Kimmell, G., Perrins, E., Komp, E., Werling, B.: Introducing Kansas Lava. In: Morazán, M.T., Scholz, S.-B. (eds.) IFL 2009. LNCS, vol. 6041, pp. 18–35. Springer, Heidelberg (2010)
5. Silva, J.: A comparative study of algorithmic debugging strategies. In: Puebla, G. (ed.) LOPSTR 2006. LNCS, vol. 4407, pp. 143–159. Springer, Heidelberg (2007)
6. Av-Ron, E.: Top-Down Diagnosis of Prolog Programs. PhD thesis, Weizmanm Institute (1984)
7. Gill, A., Runciman, C.: Haskell Program Coverage. In: Proceedings of the 2007 ACM SIGPLAN Workshop on Haskell. ACM Press, New York (2007)
8. Jones Jr., D., Marlow, S., Singh, S.: Parallel performance tuning for haskell. In: Haskell 2009: Proceedings of the 2nd ACM SIGPLAN Symposium on Haskell, pp. 81–92. ACM, New York (2009)
9. Chitil, O., Runciman, C., Wallace, M.: Freja, hat and hood - a comparative evaluation of three systems for tracing and debugging lazy functional programs. In: Mohnen, M., Koopman, P. (eds.) IFL 2000. LNCS, vol. 2011, pp. 176–193. Springer, Heidelberg (2001)
10. Nilsson, H.: Declarative Debugging for Lazy Functional Languages. PhD thesis, Linköping, Sweden (May 1998)
11. Claessen, K., Runciman, C., Chitil, O., Hughes, J., Wallace, M.: Testing and tracing lazy functional programs using quickcheck and hat. In: Jeuring, J., Jones, S.L.P. (eds.) AFP 2002. LNCS, vol. 2638. Springer, Heidelberg (2003)
12. Gill, A.: Debugging haskell by observing intermediate data structures. In: Proceedings of the 2000 ACM SIGPLAN Workshop on Haskell, Technical report of the University of Nottingham (2000)
13. Nilsson, H., Fritzson, P.: Algorithmic debugging for lazy functional languages. Journal of Functional Programming 4, 337–369 (1994)

Types and Type Families for
Hardware Simulation and Synthesis
The Internals and Externals of Kansas Lava

Andy Gill, Tristan Bull, Andrew Farmer, Garrin Kimmell, and Ed Komp

Information Technology and Telecommunication Center,
Department of Electrical Engineering and Computer Science,
The University of Kansas,
2335 Irving Hill Road,
Lawrence, KS 66045
{andygill,tbull,anfarmer,kimmell,komp}@ittc.ku.edu

Abstract. In this paper, we overview the design and implementation
of our latest version of Kansas Lava. Driven by needs and experiences
of implementing telemetry circuits, we have made a number of recent
improvements to both the external API and the internal representations
used. We have retained our dual shallow/deep representation of signals
in general, but now have a number of externally visible abstractions
for combinatorial, sequential, and enabled signals. We introduce these
abstractions, as well as our new abstractions for memory and memory
updates. Internally, we found the need to represent unknown values inside
our circuits, so we made aggressive use of type families to lift our values
in a principled and regular way. We discuss this design decision, how
it unfortunately complicates the internals of Kansas Lava, and how we
mitigate this complexity.

1 Introduction

Kansas Lava is a modern implementation of a Haskell hosted hardware description language that uses Haskell functions to express hardware components, and
leverages the abstractions in Haskell to build complex circuits. Lava, the given
name for a family of Haskell based hardware description libraries, is an idiomatic
way of expressing hardware in Haskell which allows for simulation and synthesis
to hardware. In this paper, we explore the internal and external representation
of a `Signal` in Kansas Lava, and how different representations of signal-like
concepts work together in concert.

By way of introducing Kansas Lava, consider the problem of counting the
number of instances of `True` in each prefix of an infinite list. Here is an executable
specification of such a function in Haskell:

```
counter :: [Bool] -> [Int]
counter xs = [ length [ () | True <- take n xs ] | n <- [0..]]
```

R. Page, Z. Horváth, and V. Zsók (Eds.): TFP 2010, LNCS 6546, pp. 118–133, 2011.

Of course, this function is not a reasonable implementation. In practice, we could use a function defined in terms of its previous result.

```
counter :: [Bool] -> [Int]
counter xs = res
   where res = [ if b then v + 1 else v | (b,v) <- zip xs old ]
         old = 0 : res
```

Haskell programmers get accustomed to using lazy lists as one of the replacements for traditional assignment. The counter function here can be considered a mutable cell, with streaming input and output, even though referential transparency has not been compromised.

Functional programmers share common thinking with hardware designers when designing cooperating processes communicating using lazy streams. Lava descriptions of hardware are simply Haskell programs, similar in flavor to the second counter function, that tie together primitive components using value recursion for back edge creation. Our counter example could be written as follows in Lava.

```
counter :: Signal Bool -> Signal Word32
counter inc = res
   where res = mux2 inc (old + 1,old)
         old = delay 0 res
```

Lava programs are constructed out of functions like counter, and blocks of functionality with stored state communicate using signals of sequential values, just like logic gates and sequential circuits in hardware. These descriptions of connected components get translated into hardware gates, other entities, and signals between them.

2   Kansas Lava

At KU, we developed a new version of Lava, which we call Kansas Lava[6], to help generate of a specific set of rather complex circuits that implement high-performance high-rate forward error correction codes. This paper discusses our experiences of attempting to use our new Lava. By way of background, the three main features in this original version of Kansas Lava were:

- Dual-use Signal. That is, we can use the same Signal for interpretation and for generation of VHDL circuits. The above circuit example could be directly executed inside GHCi, or reified into VHDL without *any* changes to our circuit specification.
- Use of lightweight *sized-types* to represent sized vectors. Our vector type, called Matrix takes two types, a representation of size, and the type of the elements in the matrix itself.
- Use of IO-based reification [5] for graph capture. The loop in the counter example above becomes a list of primitives and connections internally, making VHDL generation straightforward.

So what went wrong and what worked well with Kansas Lava? In summary, we found the need to make the following changes:

- We fracture our `Signal` type (as used above) into two types `Seq` and `Comb`, for representing values generated by sequential and combinatorial circuits, and connect the two types with a type class (section 3).
- We then introduce functions for commuting types that contain our `Seq` and `Comb`, giving a representation agility we found necessary (section 4).
- We add a phantom type for clock domains, which allows us to represent circuits with multiple clocks in a way that ensures we have not misappropriated our clocks (section 5).
- We introduce the possibility of unknown values into our simulation embedding (section 6).
- With these building blocks, we provide various simple *protocols* for hardware communications (section 7).

Furthermore, this paper makes the following contributions:

- We document the shortcomings of our original straightforward implementation of the Lava ideas and our new solutions and design decisions.
- Some options we have chosen were not available to the original Lava developers. In particular, type families [3] are a recent innovation. This paper gives evidence of the usefulness of type families, and documents the challenges presented by using type families in practice.
- Representation agility, that is the ability to be flexible with the representations used for communication channels, turned out to be more important than we anticipated. We document why we need this flexibility and our solution, a variant of commutable functors.

3   Sequential and Combinatorial Circuits

Haskell is a great host for Domain Specific Languages (DSL), like Kansas Lava. Flexible overloading, a powerful type system, and lazy semantics facilitate this. An embedded DSL in Haskell is simply a library with an API that makes it feel like a little language, customized to a specific problem domain. There are two flavors of embedded DSLs:

- First, DSLs that use a **shallow embedding**, where values are computed with directly. Most definitions of Monads in Haskell are actually shallow DSLs, for example. The result of a computation in a shallow DSL is a value.
- Second, DSLs that use a **deep embedding** build an abstract syntax tree. The result of a computation inside a deep DSL is a structure, not a value, and this structure can be used to compute a value.

In our first iteration of the embedded DSL Kansas Lava [6], we decided to provide a principal type, `Signal`, and all Kansas Lava functions used this type to represent values over wires that change over time. Kansas Lava is unusual, in that it contains a shallow and deep embedding at the same time. This is so the same Signal can be both executed and reified into VHDL, as directed by the Kansas Lava user. The shallow embedding (direct values) was encoded as an infinite stream of direct values and the deep embedding (abstract syntax tree) was a phantom typed [9] abstract syntax tree. Slightly simplified for clarity, we used:

```
data Signal a = Signal (Stream a) (D a)

data Stream a = a :~ Stream a          -- No null constructor

type D a = AST

data AST = Var String                  -- Simplified AST
         | Entity String [AST]
         | Lit Integer
```

We can see that Signal is an abstract tuple of the shallow Stream a, and the deep abstract syntax tree, D a. Using Signal in this form, we can write operations that support both the shallow and deep components of Signal. We could write functions like and2, which acted over Signal Bool in this manner.

```
and2 :: Signal Bool -> Signal Bool -> Signal Bool
and2 (Signal a ae) (Signal b be) = Signal (zipWith (&&) a b)
                                          (Entity "and2" [ae,be])
```

Here, we can see that the definition of and2 splits both arguments into the deep and shallow components, then recombines them. The shallow result is implemented using an appropriately typed zipWith over the boolean stream, and the deep result a single node with the name "and2".

The first issue we faced was one of semantic conciseness. For representing a sequential use of and2, values that change over time stream in and the result, also a value that changes over time, streams out. However, often we were writing combinatorial circuits, to be later instantiated as components inside a larger sequential circuit. Combinatorial circuits have no state; like a function call they take and return values without history. So the *types* of our functions were saying streams of values (which can have an arbitrary historical memory), but we wanted to think of our circuits as being run many times, independently.

The analog in functional programming is base values compared to infinite lists or streams of these base values. We wanted a way of taking an operation over a base value, like Bool, and lifting it into an operation over streams, where the original operation is applied point-wise. Haskell has many such lift functions: map, zipWith, liftM, liftA2, to name a few. With this in mind, we defined the retrospectively obvious relationship.

```
data Comb a = Comb a AST        -- working definition; to be refined
data Seq a = Seq (Stream a) AST -- working definition; to be refined
```

```
liftSeq0 :: Comb a -> Seq a
liftSeq1 :: (Comb a -> Comb b) -> Seq a -> Seq b
liftSeq2 :: (Comb a -> Comb b -> Comb c) -> Seq a -> Seq b -> Seq c
```

In this way, we can be completely explicit about what a value means, and how it would be generated. But what type do we give for and2? Both a Seq and a Comb variant are reasonable, for we certainly do not want to use a lift every time we define or use an operation over Seq.

It is worth noting at this point the connection with our "Observable" value O in ChalkBoard [10], which serves the same purpose as Comb here. In ChalkBoard, there is a clear and expressive distinction between using O (operating over individually sampled pixels) and Board (operating of regions of sampled pixels). The idea of separating circuit definitions into Comb and Seq came directly from our work on ChalkBoard. However, in circuits, we want some way of writing the same circuit for sequential and combinatorial use. So at this point, we use a classical Haskell type class, Signal, to join together Comb and Seq.

```
class Signal sig where
  liftSig0 :: Comb a -> sig a
  liftSig1 :: (Comb a -> Comb b) -> sig a -> sig b
  liftSig2 :: (Comb a -> Comb b -> Comb c) -> sig a -> sig b -> sig c

instance Signal Comb where { ... }
instance Signal Seq where { ... }
```

We use the name $\mathtt{liftSig}_n$ to reflect we are now lifting into Signal, and both Comb and Seq support this overloading. With this new class, we can give a more general type for and2:

```
and2 :: (Signal sig) => sig Bool -> sig Bool -> sig Bool
and2 = liftSig2 $ \ (Comb a ae) (Comb b be)
                      -> Comb (a && b) (Entity "and2" [ae,be])
```

By making all primitives that can be both combinatorial and sequential use the type class Signal, we can write circuits and give them either a combinatorial (Comb) type, a sequential (Seq) type, or allow the general overloading. The types are driving the specification of what we can do with the code we have written.

If a specific primitive is used that is sequential, then the entire circuit will correctly inherent this. One combinator that makes this happen is register.

```
register :: Comb a -> Seq a -> Seq a -- working definition; to be refined
```

This takes a default combinatorial value, and a sequential signal to be delayed by one (implicit) clock cycle. The types make the shapes of values – how they might be built – explicit.

To summarize, changing Signal into a class rather than a data-type and providing overloaded combinatorial and sequential logic gives us three possible ways of typing many circuits. We can use the Signal *class*, and say this is a circuit that can be executed as either combinatorially or sequentially; we can use Comb to specify the one shot at a time nature of combinatorial logic; or we can use `Seq` to specify that the circuit is to be only used in a sequential context. Furthermore, we can mix and match these three possible representation specifications, in the way `register` takes both a `Comb` and a `Seq`. For this extra flexibility to work in a pragmatic way, we need some way of normalizing the `Comb`-based function into a suitable type for lifting, which can be done using the type commuting functionality discussed in the next section.

4   Commutable Functors and Signals

Which of these two types for `halfAdder` makes more sense?

```
halfAdder :: (Comb Bool,Comb Bool) -> (Comb Bool,Comb Bool)
halfAdder :: Comb (Bool,Bool) -> Comb (Bool,Bool)
```

The first is easier to write, because we can directly address and return the tuple. The second may be used by using our lift functions above. We found ourselves going around in circles between the two approaches. Both could have the same interpretation or meaning, but can we somehow support both inside Kansas Lava without favoring one or the other? To enable this, we invoke type families [3].

We have a class `Pack`, which signifies that a `Signal` can be used inside or outside a specific structure. The type translation from the packed (structure inside, `Signal` on the outside) to unpacked (structure outside, `Signal` on the inside) is notated using an type family inside the class `Pack`:

```
class (Signal sig) => Pack sig a where
 type Unpacked sig a
 pack :: Unpacked sig a -> sig a
 unpack :: sig a -> Unpacked sig a
```

This class says we can `pack` an `Unpacked` representation, and `unpack` it back again. In the same way that overloaded functions operate at different types, overloaded type families provide type synonyms at different types. For example, `type Unpacked sig a` means any overloading of the class `Pack` at the specifics types `sig` and `a` can be provided with a synonym `Unpacked` specialized for these types.

The reason for two operations is that a packed structure does not need to be isomorphic to its unpacked partner. Though every packed structure with an instance will have one specific unpacked representation to use, two types can share unpacked representations.

Reconsidering the example above, which was over the *structure* two-tuple, we have the instance:

```
instance (Wire a, Wire b, Signal sig) => Pack sig (a,b) where
    type Unpacked sig (a,b) = (sig a, sig b)
        -- types given, not the code
        pack :: (sig a, sig b) => sig (a,b)
        unpack :: sig (a,b) -> (sig a, sig b)
```

(The types are given rather than the tedious details of the implementation here.)
As can be seen from the types, pack packs the two-tuple structure inside a signal,
and unpack lifts this structure out again.

Consider the alternative implementations of the two halfAdder flavors given
at the start of this section.

```
-- unpacked version
halfAdder :: (Comb Bool,Comb Bool) -> (Comb Bool,Comb Bool)
halfAdder (a,b) = (a `xor2` b,a `and2` b)

-- packed version
halfAdder :: Comb (Bool,Bool) -> Comb (Bool,Bool)
halfAdder inp = pack (a `xor2` b,a `and2` b)
  where (a,b) = unpack inp
```

As can be seen, there is not a huge difference in clarity, because of the generic
nature of the pack/unpack pair. In general both styles are useful, and can be
used depending on context and needs.

Sometimes, the Pack class allows access to underlying representation. For
example, consider Comb (Maybe Word8). This is a Comb of optional Word8's. A
hardware representation might be 8 bits of Word8 data, and 1 bit of validity. Our
Unpack instance for Maybe reflects this representation.

```
instance (Wire a, Signal sig) => Pack sig (Maybe a) where
    type Unpacked sig (Maybe a) = (sig Bool,sig a)
        -- types given, not the code
        pack :: (sig Bool,sig a) => sig (Maybe a)
        unpack :: sig (Maybe a)  -> (sig Bool,sig a)
```

Consider an alternative type for unpacking a Signal of Maybe.

```
unpack :: (...) => sig (Maybe a) -> Maybe (sig a) -- WRONG
```

Here, the result is a single result, and can not encode a stream of Nothings
and Just values. So in general, the unpacked structure *must* be able to notate
the complete space of the signal to be packed. Table 1 lists the types pack and
unpack supports.

This Pack class has turned out to be Really Useful in practice. This ability
cuts to the heart of what we want to do with Kansas Lava, using types in an
agile way to represent the intent of the computation. These transposition like

Table 1. Packed and Unpacked Pairs in Kansas Lava

Packed	Unpacked
sig (a,b)	(sig a, sig b)
sig (a,b,c)	(sig a, sig b,sig c)
sig (Maybe a)	(sig Bool,sig a)
sig (Matrix x a)	Matrix x (sig a)
sig (StdLogicVector x)	Matrix x (sig Bool)

operations might look familiar to some readers. The `pack` and `unpack` operations over pairs of *functors* are sometimes called `dist` [11]. In our case the `pack` and `unpack` are tied to our `Signal` overloading; we are commuting (or moving) the `Signal`.

5 Phantom Types for Clock Domains

What does `Seq a` mean? `Seq` is a sequence of values, either separated by `:~` in our shallow embedding, or by sampling values at the rising edge of an implicit clock. Our telemetry circuits have, by design, multiple clock domains. That is, different parts of a circuit beat to different drums. The question is: can we use the Haskell type system to express separation of these clock domains?

We use a phantom type [9] to express the clock domain. Our new `Comb` and `Seq` have the following definitions.

```
data Comb a = Comb a AST            -- working definition; to be refined
data Seq clk a = Seq (Stream a) AST -- working definition; to be refined
```

`Comb` remains unaffected by clocks, and the lack of `clk` in the type reflects this. `Seq` now has a phantom clock value, which is notationally a typed connection to the clock that will be used to interpret the result. How do we use this clocked `Seq`? For basic gates, the same interpretation (and therefore phantom type) is placed on the inputs as the output. Consider `and2`, at the `Seq clk` type:

```
and2 :: Seq clk Bool -> Seq clk Bool -> Seq clk Bool
```

As would be expected, both inputs to `and2`, as well as the output, have the same clock for interpretation of timing.

For latches and registers, we maintain this type annotation of shared interpretation. We can now give our final type for `register`:

```
register :: (...) => Env clk -> Comb a -> Seq clk a -> Seq clk a
```

We can see that `register` combinator takes a combinatorially generated default value and an input which is interpreted using the same clock domain as the output.

The `Env` is a way of passing an environment to the `register` combinator. Specifically, one of the design questions is: do you have an implicit or explicit clock? From experience, we found adding an enable signal to our registers useful, because we could test our FPGA circuits at a much slower speed than real clock speed. Also, we needed to pass in a reset signal. Both clock enable and reset are something that you could imagine wanting to generate from other Kansas Lava circuits under some circumstances. We chose to explicitly have a typed environment, and pass in the clock enable, the reset, and at the same time, an explicit clock.

```
data Env clk = Env { clockEnv  :: Clock clk
                   , resetEnv  :: Seq clk Bool
                   , enableEnv :: Seq clk Bool
                   }
```

Env is *not* exported abstractly, and is an explicitly passed value. So the programmer is free to pattern match on Env if needed, adding extra logic to the reset and/or enable.

Figure 1 illustrates the timing properties of register, and clarifies what register actually does in the context of an environment. The clk, rst, and en are the environment. As reflected in the type, there are two inputs, and one output.

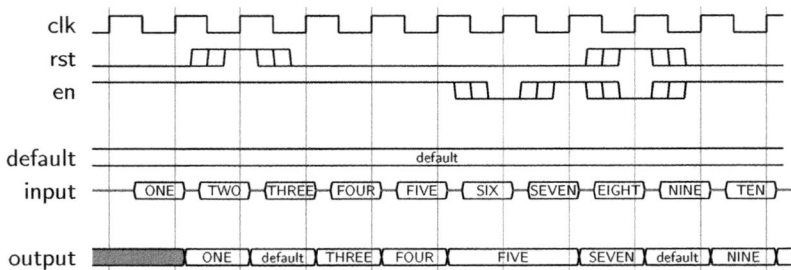

Fig. 1. register timing diagram

One remaining question is the representation of the data type Clock itself. Clock is not a sequence of values interpreted using a clock; it *is* the clock. We considered something like Seq clk (), but this would make it possible to invent nonsense clocks, and leads to convoluted semantics. So we have a new type for Clock which, like Seq, has a shallow (simulation) and deep (generation) aspect.

```
data Clock clk = Clock Rational (D clk)
```

The Rational is the clock frequency, in Hz, and the D clk is the circuit used to generate this clock (typically provided as an input to the whole circuit). Accurate simulation of possible race conditions based on two differently clocked circuits is a hard problem, but we use the Rational argument to approximate different clock rates at the interaction boundaries between clock domains.

6   Venturing into the Unknown

Often in hardware, the value of a wire is unknown. Not defaulting to some value like zero or high, but genuinely unknown. The IEEE definition of bit in VHDL captures this with an X notation. Such unknowns are introduced externally, or from reset time, and represent a value outside the standard values in Haskell. For example, when modeling hardware and transmitting a boolean, we essentially want a lifted domain.

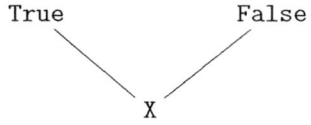

In this form, we have a `Maybe` type. But the situation is more complex for structured types. Consider a `Signal` (`Seq` or `Comb`) that represents `(Bool,Bool)`. Through experience, we want the two elements of the tuple to have *independently* lifted status. If we give the `Signal` a single unknown that represents both elements, then circuits in practice will over-approximate to unknown, hampering our shallow embedding simulation. This makes sense if we consider our hardware targets, in which a two-tuple of values will be represented by two independent wires.

We again solve this problem using type families. We introduce a new class, `Wire`, which captures the possibility of unknowns and other issues concerning the representation of the values in wires.

```
class Wire w where
    -- A way of adding unknown inputs to this wire.
    type X w
    -- check for bad things
    unX :: X w -> Maybe w
    -- and, put the good or bad things back.
    optX :: Maybe w -> X w
```

```
pureX :: (Wire w) => w -> X w    -- the pure of the X type
pureX = optX . Just
```

The type family X means lifted value, and there is a way of extracting the value from the X, using `unX`, and a way of injecting a value into an X, using `optX`. In this way, X of a specific type represents a type that can admit unknown value(s). For example, our instance for X `Bool` uses `Maybe`.

```
instance Wire Bool where
    type X Bool   = Maybe Bool
    optX (Just b) = return b
    optX Nothing  = Nothing
    unX (Just v)  = return v
    unX (Nothing) = Nothing
```

Our instance for tuples uses tuples of X.

```
instance (Wire a, Wire b) => Wire (a,b) where
        type X (a,b)      = (X a, X b)
        optX (Just (a,b)) = (pureX a, pureX b)
        optX Nothing      = ( optX (Nothing :: Maybe a)
                            , optX (Nothing :: Maybe b)
                            )
        unX (a,b) = do x <- unX a
                       y <- unX b
                       return (x,y)
```

Diagrammatically, we represent `(Bool,Bool)` that can admit failure using.

$$\text{X (Bool,Bool)} \quad\Rightarrow\quad \text{(X Bool,X Bool)} \quad\Rightarrow\quad \left(\ \underset{\displaystyle\diagdown\diagup \atop \displaystyle X}{\text{True False}}\ ,\ \underset{\displaystyle\diagdown\diagup \atop \displaystyle X}{\text{True False}}\ \right)$$

So there are 9 possible values for the pairing of the two boolean signals.

We can now give our complete types for Comb and Seq:

```
data Comb a   = Comb (X a) (D a)
data Seq clk a = Seq (Stream (X a)) (D a)
```

One complication is that all function primitives now need to be written over our X type. However, only the primitives will know how they want to handle unknowns anyway, and we use the built-in support for the Maybe monad where possible. So what happens in practice? Some functions are straightforward, because the X type maps to (say) the Maybe data type. Maybe is a monad, so liftM2 can be used:

```
and2 = liftS2 $ \ (Comb a ae) (Comb b be) ->
               Comb (liftM2 (&&) a b)
                    (Entity "and2" [ae,be])
```

The tricky part comes when we work with any type of polymorphism, including containers or selectors. Consider the type for mux2:

```
mux2 :: (Signal sig, Wire a) => sig Bool -> (sig a,sig a) -> sig a
```

We can see from the type that we have two arguments, a signal of Bool, which is our conditional control, and a pair of signals. Semantically, mux2 dynamically chooses one of the tupled signals depending on the Bool signal. We want to capture this behavior in our shallow embedding.

  Our implementation (remember this is *internal* code, not what the Kansas Lava user would see or need to write) for mux2 is:

```
mux2 :: forall sig a . (Signal sig, Wire a)
     => sig Bool -> (sig a,sig a) -> sig a
mux2 i ~(t,e)
     = liftSig3 (\ ~(Comb i ei)
                   ~(Comb t et)
                   ~(Comb e ee)
                     -> Comb (mux2shallow (witness :: a) i t e)
                             (Entity "mux2" [ei,et,ee])
                ) i t e

mux2shallow :: forall a . (Wire a) => a -> X Bool -> X a -> X a -> X a

witness = error "witness"
```

At first glance, this is similar in flavor to and2. The main new trick here is the creation of a type witness to pass to mux2shallow, using a scoped type variable [8], and the explicit use of forall to force the scoping. Without the type witness, mux2 will never type-check the call to mux2shallow. The problem is that without the witness, there is no way to unify the other arguments of mux2shallow to their expected types. Type families, like X, are not injective, so X a ~ X b (X a unifies with X b) does not imply a ~ b, unlike (most) traditional type constructors. We use this trick for passing type witnesses all over our implementation.

The implementation of `mux2shallow` can now focus on the problem at hand, choosing a signal.

```
mux2shallow :: forall a . (Wire a) => a -> X Bool -> X a -> X a -> X a
mux2shallow _ i t e =
    case unX i :: Maybe Bool of
        Nothing -> optX (Nothing :: Maybe a)
        Just True -> t
        Just False -> e
```

We extract the value from the X Bool, which we consider abstract here, and if it is True or False, we choose a specific signal, or generate an unknown value if X Bool is the unknown. Again, we need to use scoped type variables, though the behavior of `mux2shallow` should be clear from its definition. This way of thinking about supporting unknowns, where we extract values from X, handle unknowns algorithmically, and repackage things using X again is a common pattern. We have the flexibility to include a basic hardware style thinking about unknown values, and make extensive and pervasive use of use of it to provide hardware style semantics to Kansas Lava users.

7   Protocols for Signals

On top of the generality of the above types, we have constructed a number of type idioms that make building circuits easier. We have three idioms, validity (`Enabled`), memory (`Memory`), and updates to memory (`Pipe`).

Validity of a value on a wire is a general concept. Often, this is done using an *enable* boolean signal that accompanies another value signal. When the enable signal is True, the value signal is present, and should be consumed. When the enable signal is False, then the value signal is arbitrary, and should be ignored. In Kansas Lava, we define this enable concept using:

```
type Enabled a = Maybe a
```

We could have used a literal pairing of (Bool,a), but we found this to be cumbersome in practice. Instead, we let the *representation* be the pair, and the *value* be lifted using a Maybe.

```
instance (Wire a) => Wire (Maybe a) where
    type X (Maybe a) = (X Bool, X a)
        . . .
```

Using `Enabled`, we signify a value that may not always be valid. Kansas Lava provides combinators that allow combinatorial circuits to be lifted into `Enabled` circuits, and our implementations have a data-flow feel where the enable is the token flowing through the circuit. The concept of `Enabled`, however, is distinct from our concept of unknown. `Enabled` is a user *observable* phenomenon, and user-level decisions can be make based on the validity bit; while unknown values are a lower-level shallow embedding implementation trick to allow our combinatorial circuits to behave more like hardware.

Reading memory is a sequential function, from addresses to contents:

```
type Memory clk a d = Seq clk a -> Seq clk d
```

Given a `Memory` we can send in addresses using function application, and expect back values, perhaps after a short discrete number of clock cycles. We defer the actual *creation* of the `Memory` for a moment, but observe that the read requests and the values being read share the same clock.

Writing memory is done using a sequence of address-datam write request pairs. Specifically:

```
type Pipe a d = Enabled (a,d)
```

The pipe idiom gives an optional write command, saying write this datam (d) to this address (a), if enabled. The name `Pipe` is used as a mnemonic for pushing something small though a pipe, one piece at a time. Of course, `Pipe` is a general concept, and could be used as a simple protocol in its own right.

Returning to the question of how we actually construct a `Memory`, we make two observations. Our first observation is that there is an interesting symmetry between `Memory`, which has a datum answer for every address, and `Pipe`, for which, if we look backwards in time, we can also observe the relevant address write. Given access to history, both represent the same thing: access to values larger than those which a single signal can encode, though the expected implementation for both is completely different. This symmetry gives our design of memory generation. Specifically, we have a function that takes a `Seq` of `Pipe` and returns a `Memory`:

```
-- working definition; to be refined
pipeToMemory :: (...) => Env clk -> Seq clk (Pipe a d) -> Memory clk a d
```

Our second observation is that the clocking choices from the `Pipe` input can be completely independent to the clocking choices for the reading of the memory. There is no reason in hardware, other than the complexity of implementation, that a memory *must* read and write based on the same clock. We can reflect this possibility in our type. So, given a stream of such `Pipe`-based write requests, we can construct a `Memory`:

```
pipeToMemory :: (...)
          => Env clk1
          -> Env clk2
          -> Seq clk1 (Pipe a d)
          -> Memory clk2 a d
```

Here, `pipeToMemory` has two clock domains, `clk1` and `clk2`. If the clocks are actually the same clock, then Kansas Lava can generate simpler hardware that can rely on this, but the full generality is to available to the user.

Given a sequence of enabled addresses, we can also turn a `Memory` back into a `Pipe`:

```
memoryToPipe :: (...)
             => Env clk
             -> Memory clk a d
             -> Seq clk (Enabled a)
             -> Seq clk (Pipe a d)
```

This time, because we are *reading* memory, we are in the same clock domain for all arguments to `memoryToPipe`. The types force this, and make this design choice clear. A dual clock domain version of `memoryToPipe` is possible, but the semantics do not generalize into the same single clock domain version, because an extra latch would be required to handle the clock domain impedance.

Together `Enabled`, `Memory` and `Pipe` form a small and powerful algebraic framework over `Seq`, able to express many forms of sequential communications. We intend to exploit this in the future, using it for guiding Kansas Lava program derivations.

8 Related Work

The ideas behind Lava, or in general, programs that describes and generate hardware circuits, are well explored. The original ideas for Lava itself can be traced back to the hardware description language μFP [13]. A pattern in the research that followed was the common thinking between functional programming and hardware descriptions. A summary of the principles behind Lava specifically can be found in [2] and [4].

The ForSyDe system [12], which is also embedded in Haskell, addresses many of the same concerns as Kansas Lava. Like Kansas Lava, ForSyDe provides both a shallow and deep embedding, though in ForSyDe this is done via two distinct types and using the Haskell `import` mechanism. Additionally ForSyDe provides a rich design methodology on top of the basic language, and supports many "models of computation" [7]. The principal differentiator of Kansas Lava is its use of type families, which allow a *single* executable model to be utilized effectively. Kansas Lava has also pushed further with the family of connected signal types, and has taken a type-based approach to supporting multiple clock domains. A more complete formal comparison of the two systems remains to be done.

Kansas Lava is a modeling language. It models communicating processes, currently via synchronous signals. There are several other modeling languages that share this basic computational basis, for example Esterel [1]. There are many other models for communicating processes, and each model family has many language-based implementations. The overview paper written by Jantsch, et. al. [7] gives a good summary of this vast area of research.

9 Conclusions

In this paper, we have seen a number of improvements to Kansas Lava, unified by a simple principle: how can we use types to express the nature and limitation of the computation being generated by this Kansas Lava expression? We have made many more changes than we anticipated to Kansas Lava to turn it into a useful VHDL generation tool. For now, however, Kansas Lava as a language has somewhat stabilized.

Each change was initiated because of a specific shortcoming. We separated the types of combinatorial and sequential circuits because we were writing combinatorial circuits and imprecisely using the universal signal type, which was sequential. We provided generic mechanisms for commuting signals, so that we could have our cake (write functions in the style we find clearest) and eat it too (lift these functions if necessary). We used phantom types for clock domains, because we do not trust ourselves to properly render circuits with multiple clocks without type assistance. Finally, we allow the representation of the unknown in our simulations despite the pervasive consequence of the choice, because our simulations were not matching our experience with generated VHDL.

We hope that we can build up a stronger transformationally based design methodology round Kansas Lava. Currently we have a number of large circuits where we have translated high level models systematically into Lava circuits, where large is defined as generating millions of non-regular discrete logic units. Our largest circuit to date is about 1500 lines of Kansas Lava Haskell. The commuting of signals has turned out to be extremely useful when deriving our circuits from higher-level specifications. Writing correct, efficient circuits is hard, and we hope to address at least some of these circuits as candidates for our methodologies.

Acknowledgments

We would like to thank the TFP referees for their useful feedback.

References

1. Berry, G.: The constructive semantics of pure Esterel (1999),
   http://www-sop.inria.fr/esterel.org/files/
2. Bjesse, P., Claessen, K., Sheeran, M., Singh, S.: Lava: Hardware design in haskell. In: International Conference on Functional Programming, pp. 174–184 (1998)
3. Chakravarty, M.M.T., Keller, G., Jones, S.P.: Associated type synonyms. In: ICFP 2005: Proceedings of the Tenth ACM SIGPLAN International Conference on Functional Programming, pp. 241–253. ACM, New York (2005)
4. Claessen, K.: Embedded Languages for Describing and Verifying Hardware. PhD thesis, Dept. of Computer Science and Engineering, Chalmers University of Technology (April 2001)
5. Gill, A.: Type-safe observable sharing in Haskell. In: Proceedings of the 2009 ACM SIGPLAN Haskell Symposium (September 2009)
6. Gill, A., Bull, T., Kimmell, G., Perrins, E., Komp, E., Werling, B.: Introducing Kansas Lava. In: Morazán, M.T., Scholz, S.-B. (eds.) IFL 2009. LNCS, vol. 6041, pp. 18–35. Springer, Heidelberg (2010)

7. Jantsch, A., Sander, I.: Models of computation and languages for embedded system design. IEE Proceedings on Computers and Digital Techniques 152(2), 114–129 (2005); Special issue on Embedded Microelectronic Systems
8. Jones, S.P., Shields, M.: Lexically scoped type variables, http://research.microsoft.com/en-us/um/people/simonpj/papers/scoped-tyvars/
9. Leijen, D., Meijer, E.: Domain specific embedded compilers. In: 2nd USENIX Conference on Domain Specific Languages (DSL 1999), Austin, Texas, pp. 109–122 (October 1999)
10. Matlage, K., Gill, A.: ChalkBoard: Mapping functions to polygons. In: Morazán, M.T., Scholz, S.-B. (eds.) IFL 2009. LNCS, vol. 6041, pp. 55–71. Springer, Heidelberg (2010)
11. McBride, C., Patterson, R.: Applicative programing with effects. Journal of Functional Programming 16(6) (2006)
12. Sander, I.: System Modeling and Design Refinement in ForSyDe. PhD thesis, Royal Institute of Technology, Stockholm, Sweden (April 2003)
13. Sheeran, M.: mufp, a language for vlsi design. In: LFP 1984: Proceedings of the 1984 ACM Symposium on LISP and Functional Programming, pp. 104–112. ACM, New York (1984)

Testing with
Functional Reference Implementations

Pieter Koopman and Rinus Plasmeijer

Institute for Computing and Information Sciences (ICIS),
Radboud University Nijmegen, The Netherlands
{pieter,rinus}@cs.ru.nl

Abstract. This paper discusses our approach to test programs that determine which candidates are elected in the Scottish Single Transferable Vote (STV) elections. Due to the lack of properties suited for model-based testing, we have implemented a reference implementation in a pure functional programming language. Our tests revealed issues in the law regulating these elections as well as the programs implementing the rules that are offered for certification. Hence, certification by testing with a reference implementation is able to reveal problems in the software to be certified. Functional programming languages appeared to be an excellent tool to implement reference implementations. The reference implementation was developed quickly and none of the differences found was due to an error in the reference implementation.

1   Introduction

In traditional testing techniques the test cases are designed by a test engineer. The test engineer specifies some inputs and the expected output of the implementation under test (iut). These test cases are executed by hand, or by a special purpose automatic test tool. The automatic execution of tests has the advantage that it is faster and more reliable. This is especially convenient for repeated testing (called regression testing) after changes in the iut.

Model-based testing is a powerful technique to increase the confidence in the quality of software. In model-based testing the test engineer specifies a general property rather than concrete input-output pairs. Usually the inputs for the test can be derived automatically. Even if this is not possible, the model-based approach has the advantage that the specified property makes it clearer what is tested, it is easy to execute more tests, and it is much easier to adapt the tests if changed system properties require this.

In order to use model-based testing it is crucial to have a property relating input and output in a sufficiently powerful way, or a set of these properties. Usually such properties can be deduced from the specification of the program, even if the specification is informal. In this paper we show how model-based testing can be used if it is not possible to formulate sufficiently powerful properties relating input and output. We construct a reference implementation, ri, for the iut and require that this ri produces the same results as the iut for all

R. Page, Z. Horváth, and V. Zsók (Eds.): TFP 2010, LNCS 6546, pp. 134–149, 2011.

inputs. This is expressed by the property: $\forall\, i \in$ Input . iut $i =$ ri i. This property is tested by evaluating it for a large number of inputs i. Preferably these inputs are generated automatically. Even if the inputs are generated manually instead of automatically, this approach is beneficial when we want to execute a large number of tests since we have to create and maintain only one ri instead of a large number of handcrafted input-output pairs. Obviously this approach only works if we can create a reference implementation for reasonable costs.

The main requirements for ri are clearness and a low cost and fast development. Execution speed is less important, a slow ri will only slowdown the test execution, but not the iut. Also a nice user interface is not required, in the automatic tests we compute iut $i =$ ri i by a program rather than manually. Maintainability is not required for single certification of the iut, but becomes important if we want to perform regression tests on the iut. Given these requirements for the ri, functional programming languages are the ideal tool to construct the ri. Given that the iut is usually not developed in a functional programming language and that the ri is developed completely independently of the iut, it is very unlikely that both implementations contain the same mistakes and hence pass these tests unnoticed. Hence, correctness of the ri is desirable, but not absolutely required.

In this paper we illustrate this approach of software testing by a real world example. We were asked to certify two different election programs to be used in Scottish local elections by testing. This software has to implement a specific version of a Single Transferable Vote (STV) system [9,10].

The trend we indicate in this paper is the use of functional programs as reference implementation during the testing phase of programs written in mainstream languages like Java. This paper presents an example that shows that this can work very well.

In our tests we focus on input-output of the systems under test, this is called functional testing in standard test terminology. Since we are not able to monitor what happens inside the implementation under test our test are usually called black-box tests: the iut is treated as a black-box. Since our tests cover the entire system this level of testing is called system testing (in contrast to for example unit testing that concentrates on testing individual functions or methods). Our tests are based on a general property or model of the system, hence this way of testing is called model-based testing. Model-based testing is significantly more advanced than automated testing. In automated testing a user defined test suite, set of tests, is executed automatically by some program. In model-based testing the test tool generates a test suite, usually on-the-fly, executes these tests and gives a verdict based on the test results.

In Section 2 we explain the STV election rules in some more detail. We explain how the iut was tested in Section 3. Some details about the implementations tested are given in Section 4 and details about the reference implementation in Section 5. The issues found during testing are categorized in Section 6 and discussed in Section 7. Finally we draw conclusions in Section 8.

2   STV Election Rules

STV is a preferential voting system designed to minimize wasted votes and to provide proportional representation while votes are explicitly for candidates and not for party lists. When STV is used in multi-seat constituencies as in this case, it is also called proportional representation through the single transferable vote (PR-STV). STV usually refers to PR-STV as it does here. In Australia STV is known as the Hare-Clark Proportional method, while in the United States it is sometimes called choice voting or preference voting.

The key idea is that each voter gives a preference list of candidates as a vote. This list contains at least one candidate and at most all candidates in order of preference. When a candidate has more votes than needed to be elected or is eliminated in the voting process, the additional votes are transferred (partly) to the next candidate on the ballots. The orders of vote transfer and elimination are important. The exact rules to be followed are very operationally specified in the law for these elections. The law states how a human being should determine the result of the election by sorting ballots and transferring ballots from one pile to another pile with a specific weight.

For a real election there are a large number of ballots and the STV system often needs a large number of stages to decide which candidates are elected. We have seen up to 100 stages during the tests. To compute the election results fast and accurately it is necessary to use a computer program that implements the law and determines which candidates are elected based on the ballots. Obviously such a program should be correct. Since there is no way to check the election results for voters and candidates, one has to trust such a program. In order to improve the confidence in this software we were asked to certify it by performing black box tests for this system. For the certification of one iut we had to verify the results of a test suite of over 800 elections, for the other iut no test suite was specified.

As authors of the model-based test tool G∀st [5,6] we initially planned to state a sufficiently strong set of logical properties and test the election software with G∀st. G∀st is a model-based test system that automatically tries to find behavior of the iut that is not allowed by the specification. A specification is either a logical property, or an extended state machine. It appeared however impossible to derive sufficiently strong logical properties relating the election results to the input of the program (the ballots). For instance, one odd aspect of STV is that it is non-monotonic. This means that getting more votes may prevent a candidate from being elected in some rare situations [1,4]. Also a candidate that occurs on the second position of each and every ballot is not necessarily elected [2]. Since the voting software only receives one input, the set of ballots, a state-based approach does not work either.

Instead of trying to derive logical properties from the law specifying this version of the STV elections we decided to construct a ri that implements the law and check for all test cases if it yields the same result as the iut. We used the functional programming language Clean [8] to implement this ri. In this example Input is the set of all possible elections E. This set is infinite. Even if we pose upper bounds on the number of candidates and ballots, the set of elections with realistic upper bounds is way too large to enable exhaustive testing. In order to ensure that differences between the iut and ri are found during testing our first customer supplied a set S of about 800 elections to be used as test suite. S contains hand crafted normal elections, borderline cases for the STV-rules, as well as real elections from STV-elections[1] used world wide, see e.g. [11]. We also generated test suites and investigated their capability to find errors. Our experiments show that generated test suites are able to spot the same issues as the test suite S.

2.1   Specification of the Scottisch STV

In the first step of the election process the votes are given to the first candidate in the ballots. The quota Q is computed as:

$$Q = \lfloor \frac{\text{number\_of\_votes}}{\text{number\_of\_seats} + 1} \rfloor + 1$$

The floor brackets $\lfloor x \rfloor$ indicate rounding down of the number x. The fraction of x, if any, is simply removed. This definition is called the *Droop quota* [3], it ensures that the number of candidates that reach the quota is at most equal to the number of seats. Each candidate that reaches the quota is elected. When a candidate is elected and has more votes than required, the surplus of votes is transferred proportionally to the next candidates on the ballots assigned to that candidate. Similarly, if a candidate is eliminated, their votes transfer to the next candidates on the ballots of that candidate.

The election rules [10], give an operational description that guides a human to determine the result of the election by putting ballots on piles and transferring ballots to other piles. In more abstract terms this algorithm is:

```
assign_ballots_to_the_first_candidate;
while (not all_seats_are_filled)
{
    declare_any_candidate_having_Q_votes_or_more_elected;
    if (number_of_candidates == number_of_seats)
        elect_all_remaining_candidates;
    else if (there_are_candidates_with_untransfered_surplus_of_votes)
        transfer_votes_of_candidate_with_the_most_votes;
    else
        eliminate_candidate_with_fewest_votes_and_transfer_votes;
}
```

In the situation that there is more than one candidate with the highest number of votes, we look back in the history. If one of the candidates had more votes on one of the previous iterations of the algorithm, the surplus of that candidate is transferred first. Otherwise there is a *tie*. The law prescribes that a candidate is

---

[1] There are many variants of the STV rules used world wide. Although different rules might yield different results, these elections still provide realistic test cases.

chosen by lot in these situations. In a real election a human has to decide which candidate is treated first. During testing various fixed orders of elimination are used in order to speed up testing and to obtain reproducible results. If there are several candidates with the least number of votes for elimination the same algorithm is used: look for a difference in the history, if that is not available it is a tie.

Initially all votes have value one. In the transfer of votes they get a new value. The transfer value, tv is computed as

$$tv = \frac{(votes\_of\_candidate - Q) \times current\_value}{votes\_of\_candidate}$$

The tv is truncated to five decimal places.

The votes are transferred per ballot pile to the next candidate on that ballot that is neither elected nor eliminated. If there is not such a candidate available, the votes are marked as nontransferable votes. Also fractions of votes that are lost by truncation to five decimal places are added to the nontransferable votes. The nontransferable votes are only recorded to monitor that no votes are lost.

2.2   Format of the Test Cases

Each test case is stored in a separate text file. Some typical examples are listed in the tables 1 and 3. The first line of the file contains the number of candidates and the number of seats. Then there is optionally a line indicating which candidates are withdrawn, indicated by a sequence of negative numbers. Withdrawals are not possible in the Scottish elections, the data format contains them since they occur in some other STV elections used as test case. Then there is a series of lines indicating the values on the ballot papers. This sequence is terminated by a line beginning with 0. Each line starts with the number of ballot papers with this vote distribution, followed by the numbers of the candidates and terminated with 0.

After the votes, there are some lines containing the names of the candidates between quotes and the name of the election. Optionally this data is followed by some comments.

2.3   Example Election

A very small example election is the selection of 3 out of 5 candidates with 402 votes is shown in Table 1. On the left we show the actual data, on the right an explanation. This example is designed such that fractions do no occur, all candidates will have a natural number of votes during the entire election process.

Table 2 contains the transfer table of votes produced by election 1. The row labeled void contains the nontransferable votes.

Since there are 402 votes (all valid) and 3 seats, the quota Q equals $\frac{402}{3+1} + 1 = 101$. This implies that Alice and Bob are elected immediately. Since Alice has

Table 1. The input data for example election 1 and an explanation of this input

5 3	5 candidates, 3 positions
200 1 2 4 0	200 ballots with preference 1 2 4
125 2 5 0	125 ballots with preference 2 5
1 4 0	1 ballot with only candidate 4
76 5 0	76 ballots with only candidate 5
0	end of ballots
"Alice"	name of candidate 1
"Bob"	name of candidate 2
"Carol"	...
"Dave"	
"Ed"	
"Example election 1"	Name of this election

Table 2. The transfer table of example election 1

name	initial	trans 1	votes	trans 2	votes	elim 3	votes	elim 5	votes	final
Alice	200.0	-99.0	101.0	-	101.0	-	101.0	-	101.0	Elected
Bob	125.0	-	125.0	-24.0	101.0	-	101.0	-	101.0	Elected
Carol	-	-	-	-	-	-	-	-	-	
Dave	1.0	99.0	100.0	-	100.0	-	100.0	-	100.0	Elected
Ed	76.0	-	76.0	24.0	100.0	-	100.0	-100.0	-	
void	0.0	0.0	0.0	0.0	0.0	0.0	0.0	100.0	100.0	
total	402.0		402.0		402.0		402.0		402.0	

more votes than Bob her votes are transferred first (column trans 1). After each transfer there is a column indicating the new number of votes for all candidates. Since Bob is already elected, he does not receive votes from Alice. In the next iteration the votes of Bob are transferred (trans 2).

Now there are no votes to transfer and we have to eliminate a candidate. Since Carol has less votes than Dave and Ed, she is eliminated first (elim 3). This empty column indicating the transfer of zero votes. The absence of votes for a candidate is indicated with a −.

Next Dave or Ed has to be eliminated since none of the remaining candidates reaches the quota. In the current round they have an equal amount of votes, but in a previous round Dave had more votes than Ed. So, Ed is eliminated. There is no next candidate on the ballots of Ed, this implies that the votes are non-transferable. Note that we start at the last vote distribution and look back in history. If we would start at the first round, Dave is eliminated instead of Ed, since he had less votes there.

The remaining candidate, Dave, is now deemed to be elected since the number of remaining candidates and the number of seats to be filled are equal. Note that Dave never reached the quota. This ends the election algorithm.

2.4 Paradoxes

A number of strange effects are known in STV elections. These effects are often called paradoxes. Paradoxes are relevant for model-based testing since they make it harder to state properties that can be used in model-based testing.

Table 3 illustrates that being elected is nonlinear in the number of votes. The only difference between example election 2 and 3 is that two voters swapped their ballots from 4 3 (Dave, Carol) to 3 4 (Carol, Dave). As a consequence Carol has more votes in the initial stage of election 3 than in election 2. Nevertheless Carol is elected in election 2, but not in election 3. In these examples there are 26 votes and 2 candidates need to be elected, hence $Q = 9$. This paradox is not due to the small number of votes. The same effect occurs if we multiply the number of votes by any positive constant.

These kind of paradoxes limit the general properties one can use for testing election software. Among the best properties encountered are: 1) the total amount of votes (including nontransferable votes) is equal in all stage of the election, and 2) if a candidate reaches the quota in the first round she is always elected. These properties are way too weak for serious tests of election software. For this reason we have to test with a reference implementation.

An obvious condition to be satisfied is that no votes are lost in this algorithm. The sum of the votes of the candidates and the nontransferable votes should be equal to the initial number of valid votes after each iteration of the algorithm.

Table 3. Examples showing nonlinearity of STV

```
4 2
9 1 0
5 2 3 0
6 3 0
4 4 2 0
2 4 3 0
0
Alice
Bob
Carol
Dave
example 2
```

```
4 2
9 1 0
5 2 3 0
6 3 0
4 4 2 0
2 3 4 0
0
Alice
Bob
Carol
Dave
example 3
```

name	initial	elim 2	votes	final
Alice	9.0	-	9.0	Elected
Bob	5.0	-5.0	-	
Carol	6.0	5.0	11.0	Elected
Dave	6.0	-	6.0	
void	0.0	0.0	0.0	
total	26.0	26.0	26.0	

name	initial	elim 3	votes	final
Alice	9.0	-	9.0	Elected
Bob	5.0	4.0	9.0	Elected
Carol	8.0	-	8.0	
Dave	4.0	-4.0	-	
void	0.0	0.0	0.0	
total	26.0	26.0	26.0	

3   Testing Election Software

Testing the election software is approximating the property $\forall e \in E.$iut $e =$ ri e by executing $\forall e \in S\,.$iut $e =$ ri e for some finite set of elections $S \subset E$. The test suite S must be large enough to spot differences between the iut and the ri with high probability, but as small as possible to obtain results quickly. Since we had to do certification of tested software, we expected a correct iut. Hence we did not optimize the order of elements in S and preferred coverage above a small size.

3.1   The Notion of Equivalence of Election Results

In order to determine if iut $e =$ ri e holds for some election e we need to compare election results. In first approximation one is tempted to compare if the same candidates are elected. We use a much more precise notion of equivalence. Both programs yield a vote transfers table as shown above. Our notion of equivalence checks for textual equivalence of these vote transfer tables.

This notion of equivalence appears to be much more sensitive for slight differences in the iut and the ri. By looking only at the elected candidates we need a test case where such a difference influences the results of the election in order to note the difference. Although there will always exists such test cases that reveal the differences between the iut and the ri based on the elected candidates for all relevant problems, it will take much more effort to find those test cases. This would require special attention in the creation of test cases and most likely requires much larger test suites. Our more precise notion of equivalence is always right and spots differences quicker.

3.2   Test Suites

For our first certification we had to check a test suite of 808 test cases. This test suite contained handcrafted elections to test the correct implementation of specific aspects of the law as well as test cases taken from STV-elections world wide. Since this test suite was largely undocumented we added our own test cases to test borderline cases of the rules. It was easier and faster to design these test cases than to check if these things were covered in the provided test suite.

For the next certification we developed a similar test suite. During certification we added test cases to check our assumptions on incorrect behaviour of the iut. By coincidence the final test suite also contains 808 test cases.

The size of the test cases ranges from 2 candidates to over 100 candidates, and from a few votes to 99999. In the resulting vote transfer tables this takes up to 98 stages to determine the election result.

3.3   Test Suite Generation

To investigate the power of automatic test case generation we developed a straightforward data type representing elections (number of candidates, number of candidates to be elected, and a list of ballots). We created a generator that generates valid instances of this data type (number of candidates to be elected smaller or equal to the number of candidates, and only valid ballots), see [7]. We can tune the size of the test cases by setting upper bounds for the number of candidates and the number of ballots. The generated instances were turned to election files and handled like the other test suites.

It appeared that even with small test cases the issues found by the standard test suites are also found by the generated test suite. We typically need more test cases to find an issue, but that is compensated by the ease of test suite generation. Even the total test time to find the issues was not larger for the generated test suite since the test cases are smaller and hence testing is faster.

4   Implementations Under Test

We tested two programs to compute election results in this setup. Both programs were only available as an executable, no source code or additional information was available. Hence the only option was black box testing. When an issue was found we had to deduce from the transfer tables what happened. We could not look into the code of the iut to verify our expectations of possible errors.

iut A   This program was written in Delphi. Actually there were two versions of this program. One interactive version (2.6 MB) suited for experiments and single election results, and one bulk test driver (525 KB) that executes all elections in a given directory.

iut B   This program was given as two Java archives (3.1 MB and 7.4 MB). We used an external script to apply it to all test cases in a given directory.

The programs obtained for testing were tested by their manufacturers and were given to us for certification. Our tests were no beta tests, but final testing to obtain certification.

5   The Functional Reference Implementation

The reference implementation was written in the functional programming language Clean. Since the reference implementation, ri, was written in first approach to test one iut, maintainability of the program was not considered to be an issue. We did not expect to test a second implementation ever in the future. Since the program ri was used as reference implementation correctness was considered to be very important. Since the program ri would be used for certification and the speed of certification was not an issue, we always chose simple and obviously correct solutions instead of smart and more efficient solutions. For instance we always used lists of values and candidates instead of search trees or some other advanced data structure.

Whenever possible we used G∀st in the standard way to test components of this program.

5.1   Numbers with Five Digit Precision

Numbers with five digit precision and truncation after operations play an important role in the election software. All calculations of votes and vote transfers have to be done in five digit precision. For our reference implementation we need a stable implementation of those numbers.

In order to avoid rounding errors and possible overflows we represent numbers with five digit precision used for administration of the number of votes by multiplying them by 10^5 and storing this number as an integer with infinite precision (BigInt).

```
:: Fixed = Fixed BigInt

class toFixed a :: a → Fixed
instance toFixed Int where toFixed i = Fixed (FACTOR * toBigInt i)

FACTOR =: toBigInt (10^PRECISION)
PRECISION =: 5
```

The most important numerical operations on this type are implemented as:

```
instance + Fixed where (+) (Fixed x) (Fixed y) = Fixed (x + y)
instance − Fixed where (−) (Fixed x) (Fixed y) = Fixed (x − y)
instance * Fixed where (*) (Fixed x) (Fixed y) = Fixed ((x*y)/FACTOR)
instance / Fixed where (/) (Fixed x) (Fixed y) = Fixed ((FACTOR*x)/y)
```

The implementation of these operations is tested by stating some standard properties of numbers as property in G∀st.

```
pAssocAddFixed :: Fixed Fixed Fixed → Bool
pAssocAddFixed a b c = (a+b)+c = a+(b+c)

pAddSubFixed :: Fixed Fixed Fixed → Bool
pAddSubFixed a b c = a−b−c = a−(b+c)
```

Due to truncation many arithmetic properties do not hold for Fixed numbers. Some examples are:

```
pDistMulFixed :: Fixed Fixed Fixed → Bool
pDistMulFixed a b c = (a+b)*c = a*c+b*c

pAssocMulFixed :: Fixed Fixed Fixed → Bool
pAssocMulFixed a b c = (a*b)*c = a*(b*c)
```

As expected properties pAssocAddFixed and pAddSubFixed test successfully in G∀st. When testing the properties pDistMulFixed and pAssocMulFixed it quickly finds relevant counterexamples. The first counterexample found for pDistMulFixed after 75 tests was −0.33333 1.0 0.5. The first counterexample for pAssocMulFixed was 0.33333 0.5 2.0 after 259 tests.

Our test results shoes clearly that using some form of floating point numbers, e.g. doubles, and a special print function that truncates to five digits does not work correctly. One of the systems under test used such an implementation in early versions. This was a source of a large number of problems.

It is obvious that rounding problems can be avoided by performing all computations with rational numbers of infinite precision. However, this is not what the law on the elections prescribes. Computing with such rational numbers and truncating them to five digit precision whenever they are needed would introduce a source of new computational differences.

5.2   Administration of Candidates

A pile of identical ballots is represented by the type Ballot.

```
:: Ballot
= { count   :: Fixed    // number of ballots in this pile
  , value   :: Fixed    // the value of these ballots, initially the value is one
  , order   :: [Int]    // the order of candidates on this ballot
  }
```

In a similar way we use a record to store the information about candidates.

```
:: Candidate
= { ballots  :: [Ballot]  // the ballots currently assigned to this candidate
  , votes    :: Fixed     // the current number of votes
  , status   :: Status    // the status of this candidate, see below
  , cName    :: String    // the candidate name
  , cNumber  :: Int       // the candidate number
  , trace    :: [String]  // trace info to build transfer table
  , history  :: [Fixed]   // the number of votes in previous stages
  }
```

```
:: Status = Eliminated | Elected | Running
```

The implementation of the election algorithm is basically just a parser for a data file and careful bookkeeping according to the rules in the law.

5.3   Size of Executable

The size of the executable that generates the vote transfer table for ri and compares it with the table generated by iut is only 141 KB. This is more than an order of magnitude smaller than the iut's. This is partly caused by the absence of a GUI in the ri. Our ri consists of 591 lines of Clean code.

There is no information available about the development time of the iut's. Hence we cannot compare it with the time needed to develop our ri. Our ri was developed and tested within a week.

6   Issues Found

The test system signals an issue each time the vote transfer tables generated by the iut and ri are not identical. All issues are examined manually to find the reasons causing these differences. These reasons can be categorized in the following groups.

1. Syntactical differences in the generated output. Since the vote transfer tables are compared textually the system is very sensitive to further irrelevant layout details. Some examples of differences in this class are:

   Trailing zeros. A single vote can be formatted as 1, 1.0 and 1.00000. Although these representations are clearly equivalent, they are textually different.

   Votes of eliminated candidates. All votes that were assigned to an eliminated candidate are transferred to other candidates, or added to the nontransferable votes. Hence these candidates will always have no votes left at all. This can be indicated by a blank field, a -, or 0.0.

   Different number layout. One of the iut's used the database Microsoft SQL Server 2005. The way the numbers are printed and parsed by this database system depends on the language settings. If Microsoft Vista is set to Dutch the number 1.0 is displayed as 1,0.

   Removing spaces from names. This obviously has no meaning for the election result, but does cause textual differences in the vote transfer table.

   String quotes. There were different rules used to enclose strings (like the names of candidates) in string quotes (i.e. "Koopman" or Koopman).

   Most issues are solved by adapting the generated vote transfer table of the reference implementation to the iut since this was the fastest way to progress.

2. Syntactically incorrect number of votes (e.g. 9 digits precision instead of 5).

3. Losing the last vote in a completely full ballot. This was an error in the iut that was corrected.

4. One of the iuts looses candidates if the number of candidates in a test case was larger than some fixed number. This results in unpredictable behavior since results of previous elections might be used instead of the current election. This was caused by the loader component of the iut that used a upper bound of the number of candidates that was too small (25 in the first approach, 100 in a later version). The problem is handled by setting this upper bound of the iut sufficiently large for all test cases.

5. Unexpected characters (like digits and characters like '-') in the name of candidates caused similar effects.

6. The law [10] states in rule 48 about vote transfer that *"the calculation being made to five decimal places (any remainder being ignored)"*. In the calculation

$$\text{tranfer} = \frac{\text{surplus} \times \text{value\_of\_ballot}}{\text{total\_number\_of\_votes}}$$

   this can be interpreted in two ways: **1)** truncate to 5 places after each operation, or **2)** truncate to 5 places after the entire computation. In some cases this produces different results. Hence it might influence which candidates are elected.

7. The law [10] states in rule 50:

   (3) *"The returning officer shall, in accordance with this article, transfer each parcel of ballot papers referred to in paragraph (2)(a) to the continuing candidate for whom the next available preference is given on those papers* *and shall credit such continuing candidates with an additional number of votes calculated in accordance with paragraph (4)."*

(5) *"This rule is subject to rule 52."*

Where rule 52 states: (2) *"Where the last vacancies can be filled under this rule, no further transfer shall be made"*.

For the election of candidates it does not matter if we give (3) preference over (5) or the other way around, for the resulting vote transfer tables it does matter. All programs give rule 50 (3) preference over rule 50 (5), and hence rule 52.

8. If the rules specify that some candidate has to be eliminated, the candidate with the lowest number of votes has to be eliminated. If two or more candidates have this amount of votes we have to look into the history to see if there was a difference in amount of votes. One of the implementations did this wrong.

9. The rules do not specify how to treat blank ballots. In some election systems a blank vote is valid. In this system they are invalid. This is done since blank votes have an influence on the quota Q if they were treated as valid.

10. Also other kind of invalid ballots are not covered by the provided rules. A ballot containing a nonexisting candidate is invalid. The entire ballot, not only the invalid candidate, is ignored by the election algorithm. The Scottish Executive has advised that this occurrence would not be an issue in the May elections as any non-existing candidates on the ballot paper would simply be ignored.

11. Also forms containing a candidate twice are considered to be invalid and are ignored in the election process. However, such a form will be harmless in the election algorithm. When the second occurrence of the candidate is considered by the algorithm the candidate has either been elected or eliminated. In both situations the candidate number will be ignored by the algorithm.

12. In general an STV election contains the possibility for candidates to withdraw themselves. In the Scottish elections this cannot occur. Some test cases taken from other STV elections contain withdraw candidates. Programs iut A and ri handles this correctly, iut B does not handle this. Since candidates cannot withdraw themselves in the Scottish elections, these test cases are ignored.

7   Test Results

During the tests we found a large number of issues. These issues can be grouped as indicated above. In this Section we indicate the issues found by source.

7.1   The Law

The Scottish law on these elections [10] specifies in an imperative way how a human being can compute the election result. On a number of minor points the law is not absolutely clear:

1. It is specified how to handle invalid ballots, but not how to handle an invalid ballot. Obvious possibilities are ignoring the ballot altogether, move it to the nontransferable pile immediately, treating it as an empty ballot, and using the part of the vote that is valid (if any).

2. Rule 48 states that numbers must have 5 decimal places precision and numbers must be truncated rather than rounded. It is unclear whether this must be done after each step, or after an entire computation. A representative of the Scottish executive indicated that the last interpretation is preferred.

3. Rule 50 allows two possible interpretations on the necessity of vote transfer if after the elimination of some candidate the remaining number of vacancies is equal to the remaining number of candidates. As indicated above, this does not influence the elected candidates. All programs do the vote transfer.

7.2   The Reference Implementation

After building and testing ri on its own only one real change was necessary. As 'obvious' in a functional programming language like Clean we implemented the five digit numbers as an abstract data type and implemented the needed operators (addition, subtraction, multiplication and division) for this type. This implies truncation after each operation, but that is not the interpretation of the law preferred by the Scottish executive. Hence we had to turn the abstract type into an ordinary type and adapt the computation of the vote transfer.

Other modifications are layout details of the vote transfer table to make it textually identical to the details of the corresponding tables of iut A and iut B. This implies that there are two versions of this layout.

7.3   The IUTs

All other issues where due to problems with iut A and iut B. There were more problems as expected for a certification project. The iut B caused significantly more issues than iut A.

7.4   Execution Speed

Much to our surprise the execution speed of the ri was considerably higher than the execution speed of iut A. The speed difference was a factor 2 to 5, depending a little on the size of the input and the number of rounds needed in the election. This was unexpected since lazy functional languages are not famous for their speed. Especially since we have always chosen the simple and obviously correct solution instead of smart and efficient solutions we did not expect ri to be faster than any iut. We did nothing special to make ri efficient.

The speed difference between ri and iut B was striking: ri is about a factor 250 faster than iut B. This is partly caused by the fact iut B uses a database intensively. The amount of data to be maintained by the election software is not that large that a database is required.

This low performance was a bottleneck in the tests. It takes about 30 minutes for the ri to compute the results for a large test suite and to compare these with the results of the iut. The program iut B takes more than five days to process the entire test suite. Each time we find an error in the iut we have to repeat all tests in the entire test suite.

7.5   Choices

When the votes of a candidate must be transferred and there are two or more candidates having exactly the same amount of votes, also in all previous stages, the law states that a candidates must be chosen by lot. The interactive version of the iut's ask the user to indicate a candidate, iut A has to possibility to chose a candidate pseudo randomly.

In practise this is very rare. However, it is easy to generate test cases where n candidates have the same amount of votes. In the worst case there are $n!$ possibilities to eliminate them one by one (it is often not necessary to eliminate them all).

Our first plan was to generate all possible vote transfer tables and see if one of them is equal to the table generated by the iut. However it is obvious that this does not work for test cases with for instance 10 or more candidates with an equal number of votes. Hence we fixed the elimination order to be used in the test.

7.6   Vote Transfer Tables

In retrospect it would have been easier to transpose the vote transfer table. Now each line contains the votes of one candidate during all stages. If we find a difference it is the first candidate that has in some stage a different number of votes in the tables from the iut and the ri. In tracking down the source of such an issue it is much more practical to have an indication of the first stage that shows a difference. Although these versions of the tables are equivalent, a transposed version would have been more convenient if we could have anticipated the number of issues to investigate more accurately.

8   Conclusions

This paper reports on the certification of election software by black-box testing. Due to the absence of suited properties we tested the iut by comparing its results with a reference implementation. The test results indicate that testing was worthwhile for both implementations tested. None of the iuts was correct. The construction of the reference implementation and the tests also indicate some points of underspecification in the law regulating these elections. We compared handcrafted test suites extended by real election results with an automatically generated test suite. Both test suites were able to spot the same errors in the iuts. Neither of these test suites was significantly more effective in finding issues.

The trend we signal in this paper is the use of functional programs as reference implementation. Functional languages appeared to be very suited for this purpose, it is easy and fast to produce a reference implementation. We were very pleased that this program caused by far the least number of issues during the tests. Much to our surprise it was also clearly the fastest implementation, although we did nothing to make the reference implementation efficient.

Acknowledgement. We thank Steven Castelein for helping us to develop scripts to execute series of test runs automatically and Peter Achten for his feedback on draft versions of this paper.

References

1. Aslaksen, H., Mcguire, G.: Mathematical aspects of irish elections. Irish Mathematics Teachers Association Newsletter 105, 40–59 (2006)
2. Fishburn, P.C., Brams, S.J.: Paradoxes of preferential voting. Mathematics Magazine 56(4), 207–214 (1983)
3. Droop, H.: On methods of electing representatives. Journal of the Statistical Society of London 44(2), 141–202 (1881)
4. Farrell, D.M.: Comparing electoral systems. Prentice Hall/Harvester Wheatsheaf, London, New York (1997)
5. Koopman, P., Alimarine, A., Tretmans, J., Plasmeijer, R.: Gast: generic automated software testing. In: Peña, R., Arts, T. (eds.) IFL 2002. LNCS, vol. 2670, pp. 84–100. Springer, Heidelberg (2003)
6. Koopman, P., Plasmeijer, R.: Fully automatic testing with functions as specifications. In: Horváth, Z. (ed.) CEFP 2005. LNCS, vol. 4164, pp. 35–61. Springer, Heidelberg (2006)
7. Koopman, P., Plasmeijer, R.: Generic generation of elements of types. In: Proceedings of the 6th Symposium on Trends in Functional Programming, TFP 2005, Tallin, Estonia, September 23-24, pp. 163–178. Intellect Books (2005) ISBN 978-1-84150-176-5
8. Plasmeijer, R., van Eekelen, M.: Concurrent Clean language report (version 2.0) (December 2001), http://www.cs.ru.nl/~clean/
9. The Electoral Commission. Vote Scotland, http://www.votescotland.com
10. The Scottish Ministers. Scottish local government elections order 2007. Rule 45–52 (2006)
11. Wikipedia. Single transferable vote, http://en.wikipedia.org/wiki/Single_transferable_vote

Every Animation Should Have a Beginning, a Middle, and an End

A Case Study of Using a Functor-Based Animation Language

Kevin Matlage and Andy Gill

Information Technology and Telecommunication Center,
Department of Electrical Engineering and Computer Science,
The University of Kansas,
2335 Irving Hill Road,
Lawrence, KS 66045, USA
{kmatlage,andygill}@ku.edu

Abstract. Animations are sequences of still images chained together to tell a story. Every story should have a beginning, a middle, and an end. We argue that this advice leads to a simple and useful idiom for creating an animation Domain Specific Language (DSL). We introduce our animation DSL, and show how it captures the concept of beginning, middle, and end inside a Haskell applicative functor we call `Active`. We have an implementation of our DSL inside the image generation accelerator, ChalkBoard, and we use our DSL on an extended example, animating a visual demonstration of the Pythagorean Theorem.

1   Introduction

Consider the problem of specifying the corners of a rotating square that is also moving from one location to another. There are two fundamental things happening over time: rotation and translation. The location of the corners is simply the combination of both movements, without interaction or interference. When describing more complex animations, however, we want to model simple interactions, and more generally, causality. Specifically, we want to introduce concepts like termination and sequentiality, and be able to describe interactions as one thing happening *after* another. In this paper, we discuss a *composable* solution to this description challenge which uses a Domain Specific Language (DSL) on top of Haskell [1] to express values that change over time, and also have a beginning and an end.

The fundamental question when crafting any type-based DSL is figuring out the key types and the primitives for these types. When we look at our target application, educational animations, and also look at animation tools in PowerPoint and Keynote, we make the following two basic observations. First, animations take a finite length of time, with a specific start and end point. In a sense, animations have a presence inside time, in the same way as a square can be present

R. Page, Z. Horváth, and V. Zsók (Eds.): TFP 2010, LNCS 6546, pp. 150–165, 2011.
© Springer-Verlag Berlin Heidelberg 2011

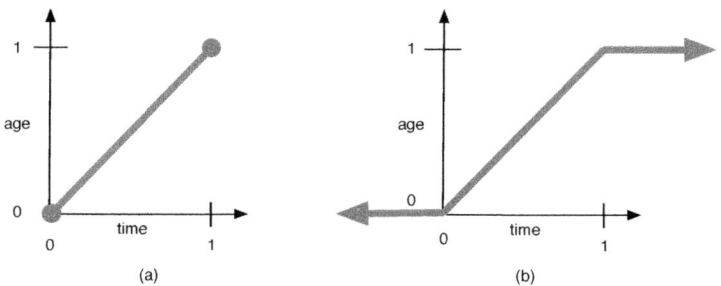

Fig. 1. The `age` combinator

on a 2D plane. We postpone considering infinite dynamic animations with our DSL, because we are explicitly attempting to build a language for scripting finite animations. Second, animations also often contain static, infinite elements, perhaps background images, that do not change for the duration of an animation. From these simple observations, we propose two primitives in our DSL, one that changes over time and is finite, and one that is static and infinite.

This paper presents these primitives, and a combinator-based language for creating dynamic animation using the primitives. We use an applicative functor [2] structure to implement this abstraction and incur other advantages, such as the clean and easy composition of animations (Section 2). We also provide a number of helper combinators and predefined functions for quickly creating functional animations (Section 4). Finally, we show how our language can be used to easily create practical, non-trivial animations (Section 5).

2   The Active Language

Our solution to this animation problem is the `Active` language. The conceptual framework behind the `Active` language is that all animations have a beginning, a middle, and an end. For every object in our language, we normalize the time component of an animation such that the value starts from 0 (the beginning of animation time), and ending at 1 (the end of animation time). This can be illustrated using the figure 1(a), where the dots are the beginning and end, and the line is the progression, or `age`, of an animation. The user of `age` does not need to be concerned about when each animation runs in the global time scale, but can instead build each animation with the assumption that it will act over its own 0 to 1 progression, and compose them later.

What happens before something is animated, or after animation? We *choose* to have an `Active` value be a constant before and after animation. Consider animating a object traveling; it is in one place before the animation, in transition during the animation, and one another place after the animation. We therefore choose our basic `Active` object to be of unit size in time (from 0 to 1), but also have a value before and after any animation. Figure 1(b) illustrates our realization of the representation in 1(a).

Our implementation of the `Active` language accomplishes this timing abstraction using a data type `Active` and a few primitive functions. The `Active` data type is defined (in Haskell) as:

```
data Active a                -- Dynamic Animation
   = Active Rational         -- start time
            Rational         -- stop time
            (Rational -> a)  -- what to do in this time frame
   | Pure a                  -- Static Animation
```

The first two `Rationals` are used to hold timing information, specifically the start and stop time of the current object. The function takes a `Rational` argument, representing time values between the start and stop times, and returns an animated value in the context of the time. The alternative constructor, `Pure`, is the way we represent an `Active` that is constant over time. The most primitive value in the `Active` DSL is age:

```
age :: Active UI
age = Active 0 1 f
    where f n | n < 0      = error $ "age value negative" ++ show n
              | n > 1      = error $ "age value above unit (1)" ++ show n
              | otherwise = fromRational n
```

age represents the most basic `Active`, which has a start time of 0 and a stop time of 1, as discussed above. This `Active` object also holds within it a basic function that returns the input `Rational` time value as a `UI`. A `UI` is simply a type synonym for `Float`, but is used to represent only those values on the interval [0,1]. Because the function stored within age returns a `UI`, age is of the type `Active UI`. Actions can then be mapped over this returned `UI`, but in order to do this, we must first define `Active` as a functor, given below for the curious reader. We also provide applicative functor capabilities. Specifically, applicative functors as used here allow for the declaration of a constant (static, infinite) `Active` value and the combination two `Active` values:

```
instance Functor Active where
    -- fmap :: (a -> b) -> Active a -> Active b
    fmap f (Active start stop g) = Active start stop (f . g)
    fmap f (Pure a) = Pure (f a)

instance Applicative Active where
    -- pure :: a -> Active a
    pure a = Pure a

    -- (<*>) :: Active (a -> b) -> Active a -> Active b
    (Pure a) <*> b = fmap a b
    (Active start0 stop0 f0) <*> (Pure a) =
            Active start0 stop0 (\ i -> (f0 i) a)
    a0@(Active start0 stop0 f0) <*> a1@(Active start1 stop1 f1) =
            Active (min start0 start1) (max stop0 stop1)
                    $ \ i -> f0 (boundBy a0 i) (f1 (boundBy a1 i))
```

When applying two animations, using the applicative functor <*> combinator, the interesting case is when combining two non-static animations. The first argument is a *function* which changes over time, the second is a value that changes over time, and the result is the application of the function to the argument, at every point in time. We choose to make this combined animation start at the earliest beginning of the two arguments, and finish at the last ending.

These definitions are particularly helpful in creating and combining animations. For example, the <*> operator allows for multiple animation functions to easily be applied to the same initial object. This ability can be really useful if, for instance, we wish to move an object while simultaneously scaling it. Active being an applicative functor is also helpful in creating combinators and predefined functions, as we will see in Section 4.

age is the primary method of creating an Active object. Once we have created an Active, all we have to do to get values over time is fmap a function over it. Generally for animation, this function would return an image so that we could display the returned images over time, creating an animation. The function can actually return any value, however, as shown by this definition for linear interpolation over time between two points:

```
simpleLerp :: (Float,Float) -> (Float,Float) -> Active (Float, Float)
simpleLerp (x1,y1) (x2,y2) = fmap (\ui -> lerp ui (x1,y1) (x2,y2)) age
       where lerp ui (x1,y1) (x2,y2) = ( x1+ui*(x2-x1) , y1+ui*(y2-y1) )
```

This Active will return values ranging linearly from (x1,y1) to (x2,y2) over time (though lerp would typically be a predefined library function). We can also begin to see some of the abstraction the Active DSL provides. Notice how the creation of this Active is completely independent from any timing information other than its own personal time progression. This same Active can be used to create a lerp that takes 1 second to complete or 100 seconds. The timing can be applied to each Active object separately, using either basic functions or built-in combinators. The primitive Active functions for handling timing effects are scale, mvActive, and after:

```
scale :: Float -> Active a -> Active a
scale _ (Pure a)           = Pure a
scale u (Active start stop f) = Active (scale u start) (scale u stop)
                                 $ \ tm -> f (tm / toRational u)

mvActive :: Float -> Active a -> Active a
mvActive _ (Pure a)           = Pure a
mvActive d (Active start stop f) = Active (toRational d + start)
                                          (toRational d + stop)
                                 $ \ tm -> f (tm - toRational d)

after :: Active a -> Active b -> Active a
after act@(Active low _ _) (Active _ high _) =
                       mvActive (fromRational (high - low)) act
```

When applied to an `Active` object, `scale` will stretch or shrink the amount of time that the object acts over. This can be used to make certain animations longer or shorter. It should be noted that this definition is actually an instance of a previously-defined `Scale` type class. This is not critical to understanding the details of `scale` except that it explains the call to `scale` within the body of the definition. This is a call to `scale`'s previously-defined `Rational` instance (which simply multiplies the two numbers).

`mvActive` is used for translating time values. When applied to an `Active` object, `mvActive` moves an animation forwards or backwards in time with regards to the rest of the scene. It can be used to put parts of an animation in the right place or offset animations to start at slightly different times.

The last basic timing function is the `after` function. It takes two `Active`'s as parameters and changes the time values of the first so that it will occur immediately after the second one finishes. This function is especially important for building up combinators to manage the ordering of animations in a scene, as we will see in Section 4.

3   ChalkBoard

The ChalkBoard project is an attempt to bridge the gap between the clear specification style of a language with first-class images, and a practical and efficient rendering engine. We will use ChalkBoard as an engine to display images generated using `Active`. The hook for ChalkBoard is that with the first-class status offered by pure functional languages comes clean abstraction possibilities, and therefore facilitated construction of complex images from many simple and compossible parts. This first-class status traditionally comes at a cost though—efficiency. Unless the work of computing these images can be offloaded onto efficient execution engines, then the nice abstractions become tremendously expensive. ChalkBoard was designed to bridge this gap by creating a functional image description language that targeted the OpenGL standard.

In order to understand the specifics of the ChalkBoard language, we need to think about types. In ChalkBoard, the principal type is a `Board`, a two dimensional plane of values. So a color image is a `Board` of color, or `RGB`. A color image with transparency is a `Board` of `RGBA`. A region (or a plane where a point is either in a region or outside a region) can be denoted using `Board` of `Bool`. Table 1 lists the principal types of `Board`s used in ChalkBoard.

The basic pattern of image creation begins by using regions (`Board Bool`) to describe primitive shapes. ChalkBoard supports unit circles and unit squares, as well as rectangles, triangles, and other polygons. The primitive shapes provided to the ChalkBoard user have the following types:

```
circle    :: Board Bool
square    :: Board Bool
rectangle :: Point -> Point -> Board Bool
triangle  :: Point -> Point -> Point -> Board Bool
polygon   :: [Point] -> Board Bool
```

Table 1. Boards and Type Synonyms in ChalkBoard

`Board RGB`	Color image
`Board RGBA`	Color image with transparency
`Board Bool`	Region
`Board UI`	Grayscale image of Unit Interval values
`type R = Float`	Represent real numbers
`type Point = (R,R)`	2D coordinate or point

To "paint" a color image, we map color over a region. Typically, this color image would be an image with the areas outside the original region being completely transparent, and the area inside the region having some color. This mapping can be done using the combinator `choose`, and the `<$>` operator:

```
choose (withAlpha 1 blue) transparent <$> circle
```

We choose the color blue with an alpha value of 1 for inside the region, and transparent for outside the region. The `<$>` operator is a map-like function which lifts a specification of how to act over individual points into a specification of how to translate an entire board. The types of `choose` and `<$>` are

```
choose :: O a -> O a -> O Bool -> O a
(<$>)  :: (O a -> O b) -> Board a -> Board b
```

where `O a` is an observable version of `a`.

As well as translating point-wise, ChalkBoard supports the basic spatial transformation primitives of scaling, moving, and rotating, which work over *any* Board.

```
scale  :: R     -> Board a -> Board a
move   :: (R,R) -> Board a -> Board a
rotate :: R     -> Board a -> Board a
```

Although there are many more functions and possibilities available in ChalkBoard, we should now know enough to begin talking about its use within the context of the Active DSL. Any additional required ChalkBoard information will be explained as needed, but for a better background understanding, see the original paper on ChalkBoard [3].

4 Active Combinators

Now that we have some of the most important functions in the Active language, we want to make using them with ChalkBoard easier. One natural way to do this is to create combinators that integrate common Active and ChalkBoard tasks. The first, and perhaps most essential, of these is the **over** function:

```
over :: Over a => Active a -> Active a -> Active a
over a1 a2 = fmap (\ (a,b) -> a 'over' b) (both a1 a2)

both :: Active a -> Active b -> Active (a,b)
both a b = pure (,) <*> a <*> b
```

The `over` function takes two `Active` parameters and combines them so that both animations are displayed one on top of the other (but not necessarily at the same time). `over` is actually an instance of the ChalkBoard `Over` type class, which helps explain the second reference to `over` in the body of the definition. This uses the ChalkBoard version of `over` to overlay two static objects, most notably boards with transparency, `Board RGBA`.

While `over` and our current timing functions let us combine animation pieces and display them in order, it can be verbose to specify a long sequence of animations that should all be overlaid and displayed at times relative to each other. This led us to create one of the main code structures that we have used repeatedly to manage our scenes. The main version of this structure uses the `flicker` and `taking` functions, though multiple derivatives of `flicker` have been created for managing time in different ways. The type of these functions and the general code structure can be seen here:

```
flicker :: Over a => [Active a] -> Active a
taking  :: Float -> Active a -> Active a

let anim = flicker [ animStep1
                   , taking 3 animStep2
                   , taking 0.5 animStep3
                   ]
```

The `flicker` function takes a list of `Active`'s and combines them into one `Active` object, with each animation in the list occurring immediately after its predecessor. Each successive animation is also placed on top of the previous ones, so parts of a scene can be built independently but displayed together. This is helpful in increasing the amount of abstraction in building a scene. Constructing each part separately allows for greater flexibility in changing certain aspects of a scene without affecting others, and managing the ordering of the scene without affecting what happens during each part.

`taking`, on the other hand, helps control the amount of *time* it takes to execute each of the individual animations. The `taking` function stretches or shrinks an `Active` so that it occurs in the amount of time specified by the `Float` argument. Generally, `taking` is easiest to use in close conjunction with the `flicker` function, as shown above, though it does not have to be. This just keeps most of the timing information in one place, even if one does not directly affect the other.

Now that we can manage the ordering and timing of an animation pretty well, we can start looking at some good combinators for common animation tasks. To help create many of these combinators, we use the `addActive` function:

```
addActive :: (UI -> a -> b) -> Active a -> Active b
addActive fn act = (fmap fn age) <*> act
```

This is a simple function we use to create many animation functions. Typically for animation, the a and b types are Board's of some variety. The function argument is then a representation of how we want to change a Board over time, and the Active argument contains a Board we want to change (though it may already be changing in other ways as well). addActive is especially helpful in adding new animations to existing ones, allowing us to avoid the systematic coding overhead of placing each new function into an Active and then applying it to the previous Active.

We use addActive to help create many of our predefined animation functions, including the standard 2D transformation functions from ChalkBoard (move, scale, and rotate) applied over time. As an example of this usage, the predefined move-over-time function in Active is:

```
activeMove :: (R,R) -> Active (Board a) -> Active (Board a)
activeMove (x,y) = addActive $ \ui -> move (ui*x,ui*y)
```

This function takes the ChalkBoard move command and turns it into a function over time as well. The move command in ChalkBoard simply moves a Board from its current position by a specified amount in the x and y directions. These amounts are given, respectively, in the ordered pair (R,R). The Active version of this function does the same thing, but applies this move over time. It will treat the input UI time value as a percentage and move the Board inside the Active argument step by step as the time value increases from 0 to 1, finally ending up displaced by a total amount of (x,y).

Other common actions defined using addActive are the remaining transformation functions (activeScale and activeRotate), as well as functions for making an Active appear/disappear (activeAppear, activeTempAppear, and activeDisappear). All of the Active versions of the ChalkBoard transformations (move, scale, and rotate) are versions of those functions that are applied over time. The appear/disappear functions tell a given Active whether it should only be visible once its time value is great than 0 (activeAppear), when its time value is in between 0 and 1 (activeTempAppear), or from the start of execution up until its time value is 1 (activeDisappear). Unless one of these functions is applied, all Active's will remain visible for the duration of the scene, regardless of when their animations execute (since they will still be receiving time values of 0 or 1). Example usage of these functions is the subject of the next section.

5 Case Study

While testing the current features and usability of Active, we decided to recreate an existing animation. This was done both to see how close we could get to the original, as well as how difficult it would be to do so. The animation we chose for this experiment was an animated proof of the Pythagorean Theorem that can

be found on Wikipedia at http://en.wikipedia.org/wiki/Pythagorean_theorem.
This example was visually pleasing, served a useful purpose, and was exactly
the type of animation we wanted to create easily in ChalkBoard. It also was
complicated enough that we felt like it would be a good test of ChalkBoard's
features, without being too complicated as to prevent new users, who haven't
seen any of these feature before, from following along.

In building this and other examples, a general structure for ChalkBoard animations using Active has begun to appear. It looks something like the following:

```
let animStep1  = ...
    animObject = ...
    animStep2  = ... f animObject ...
    animStep3  = ... g animObject ...

let wholeAnim = flicker [ animStep1, animStep2, animStep3 ]
```

First, the individual pieces of the animation are constructed. This stage consists of building all the separate Active Board's that will be the parts of the
final scene. These could be such things as an object moving, rotating, changing
colors, or a ton of other possibilities. The second stage of construction is string-
ing all of these smaller pieces together into a coherent whole using functions such
as flicker. After the animation is complete, it can then be played back, saved,
or manipulated however the user wishes. While creating animations using this
structure is by no means the only way to do so, it has proven to be effective
for the examples we have built thus far. Therefore, this case study will follow
the same structure, explaining how each stage was completed and some of the
functions that were used.

5.1 Stage 1: Building Animation Pieces

In beginning the Pythagorean example, we start by creating all of the different
Active animation pieces that will be used in the scene. The first of these is the
animation's background, which we just build to make about the same color as
the Wikipedia animation. The pure function is then applied to this background
board to lift it into the Active (Board a) space so that it can be combined
with the other Active Board objects we create for the animation.

Next, we build up a basic triangle in the middle of the screen, with code that
looks something like the following:

```
let (x,y)       = (0.2,0.15)
    (a,b,c)     = ((-x,y),(-x,-y),(x,-y))
    triangle345 = triangle a b c
    triLines    = pointsToLine [a, b, c, a] 0.004
    mainTriangle = (choose (alpha black) transparent <$> triLines)
                   'over'
                   (choose (alpha yellow) transparent <$> triangle345)
```

In doing this, we first create a 3-4-5 triangle by giving three points to the `triangle` constructor. This creates a `Board Bool` of our triangle. We also want a black outline around it in order to match the original animation. To do this, we use the `pointsToLine` function, which takes a list of points and a line width and draws a line between all adjacently listed points. Both `Board Bool`'s are then given their colors by using the `choose` function as shown. This makes the lines black over a transparent background (so we can see the triangle behind them) and the triangle yellow with a transparent background (to see the animation's background behind it).

While this code does create a simple triangle, the triangle itself is never actually displayed in the animation. Instead, this triangle is transformed in different ways to create the displayed triangles. For instance, the initial triangle shown in the animation is achieved by scaling `mainTriangle` by 1.5. The animation for shrinking and moving this new triangle into its final position is achieved by adding `Active` functions, as shown below:

```
let movingTriangle = activeMove (y,x) $ activeScale (2/3) $
                     pure $ scale 1.5 $ mainTriangle
```

First, the triangle is lifted into the `Active` world using `pure`. Then we start to add animation functions to it. In this instance, we apply an `activeScale` and an `activeMove`. This creates an animated triangle that shrinks slightly while also moving slightly up and to the right. Images of this resulting animation are in Figure 2.

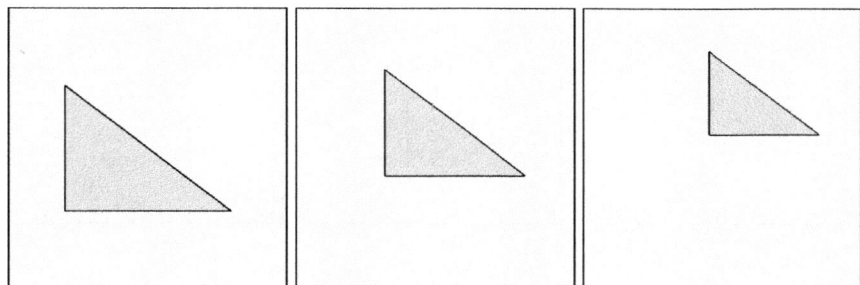

Fig. 2. movingTriangle animation

As a note, all of the text for this animation was actually added in last, separate from the geometry. In this case study, we will only be covering the creation of the geometric animation, and not the insertion of font. This is due to space constraints and because the only interesting font problem that involves the Active DSL is when to make the pieces appear and/or disappear (which we will already cover).

Moving on with the example, the next step is to create three identical but rotated triangles as displayed in the Wikipedia graphic. These are created using the list comprehension in `otherTriangles` (defined below), which simply rotates a moved version of the original `mainTriangle`:

```
let movedTriangle = move (y,x) $ mainTriangle
    otherTriangles = [ rotate (-i*pi/2) $ movedTriangle | i <- [1..3] ]
    addOtherTriangles = foldl1 over [ mvActive i $ activeAppear $ pure $ t
                                | (t,i) <- zip otherTriangles [1..] ]
```

These triangles are then made to appear when their animations start using the `activeAppear` function as described in Section 4. The next step, however, is getting them to appear *individually*. While they could each be treated as an independent animation piece and listed separately in the `flicker` portion of the program, we instead choose to apply the `mvActive` function to each of these new triangles in order to save time and make our code cleaner. As described in Section 2, this function (not to be confused with `activeMove`) simply moves the actions of a given `Active` backwards or forwards in time by the given value. Using the list comprehension in `addOtherTriangles` above, each new triangle is made to appear a little later in time than the previous. Finally, the list of `Active Board` objects, each element representing one new triangle appearing, is compressed into a single `Active Board` using `foldl1` with the `over` function. Figure 3 shows each of the new triangles being added individually to the animation.

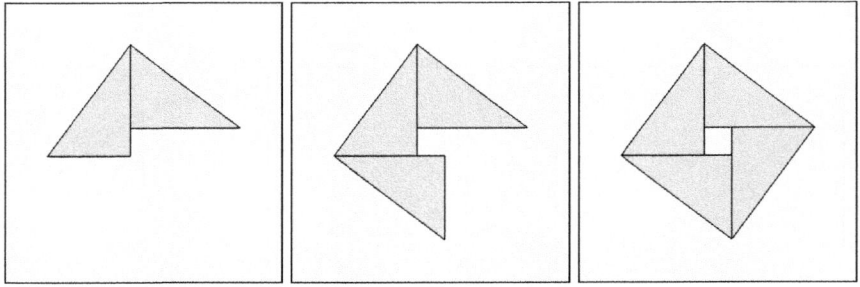

Fig. 3. addOtherTriangles animation

The next part of the animation is just adding in a couple missing pieces to the image so that the full area can be clearly seen. A small yellow square is added to the middle so that the larger square can be seen to have a size of $c \times c$. This larger square therefore has an area of c^2, as indicated by the accompanying text. The result of this small portion of the animation can be seen in Figure 4.

Next, we need to slide the top triangles down to match up with the lower triangles, as seen in Figure 5. We also want an outline of the old triangles to remain behind so we can see where they started (like in the original on Wikipedia). This is done in two parts, both of which are defined below:

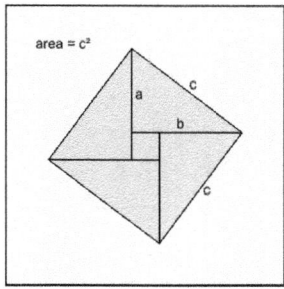

Fig. 4. fillSquare animation

```
let fadedTris = [ rotate (-i*pi/2) $ move (y,x) $
                  choose (withAlpha 0.6 white) transparent <$> triangle345
                | i <- [0,1] ]
    slideLeft = activeAppear $
                (activeMove (-2*y,-2*x) $ pure $ movedTriangle)
                'over' (pure $ head fadedTris)
   slideRight = activeAppear $
                (activeMove (2*x,-2*y) $ pure $ head otherTriangles)
                'over' (pure $ last fadedTris)
```

The first part is to fade the existing triangles to leave behind as outlines, and the second is to create the new triangles that will actually move. The first part is done by placing white triangles with alpha values of 0.6 over the two existing triangles so that they will appear faded. For the second part, we create the first slide by reusing `movedTriangle` (top right triangle) and applying an `activeMove` down to its final position on the bottom left. We do pretty much the same thing with the second slide, but grab the initial triangle from the head of `otherTriangles` (first rotated triangle on the top left) and slide it right.

The final part of the animation is simply changing the organization of the resulting shapes. Now that the triangles are in their final positions, two new squares can be drawn that cover the entire area. These squares have side lengths of a and b, and thus areas of a^2 and b^2. This in effect concludes the proof that $a^2 + b^2$ equals the original area of c^2. In order to animate this part, we use the same general strategy as fading out the two triangles in the last step:

```
let newSquares = (move (y, -y) $ scale 0.4 $ square)
                 'over' (move (-x, -x) $ scale 0.3 $ square)
    (s1, s2) = (x-y, x+y)
    newLines = pointsToLine [(-s1,-s2), (s2,-s2), ..., (-s1,-s1)] 0.004
    fadeInSquares = (fadeIn black 1 newLines)
                    'over' (fadeIn yellow 1 newSquares)

fadeIn :: O RGB -> UI -> Board Bool -> Active (Board (RGBA -> RGBA))
fadeIn rgb a brd = fmap fn age
     where fn ui = choose (withAlpha (o (ui*a)) rgb) transparent <$> brd
```

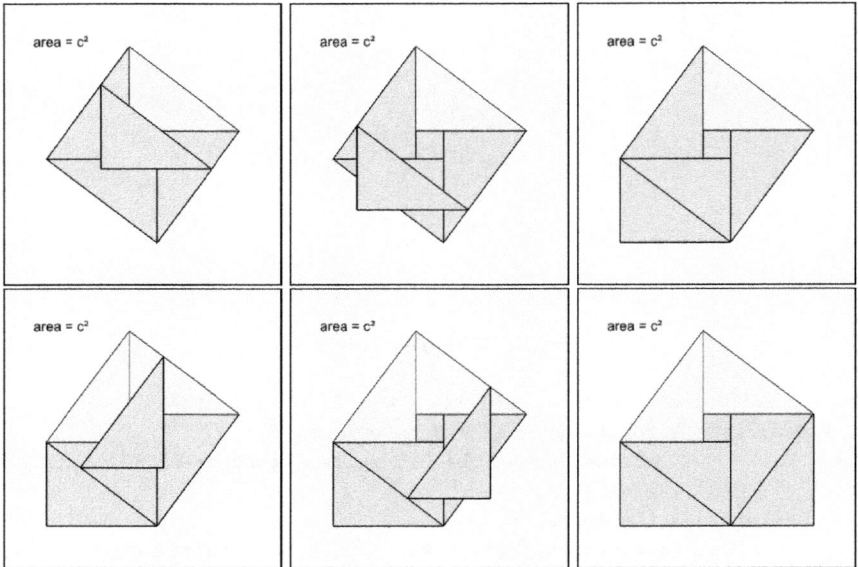

Fig. 5. slideLeft and slideRight animations

The main differences are that this time we use yellow squares with alpha values of 0.9 so that the new squares will be a darker yellow instead of a lighter one, and that we also draw lines around the new squares to make them clearer. The squares to be faded in are created as `Board Bool` shapes in ChalkBoard, like normal, and moved to the right locations. They are then faded in over time using the `fadeIn` function (predefined in `Active`, but included here for reference). This function simply creates an `Active` that fades a `Board RGBA` in from transparent to the given RGB and alpha value. The lines around the squares are also faded in over the squares at the same time, using the same function. This final piece of the animation is shown in Figure 6.

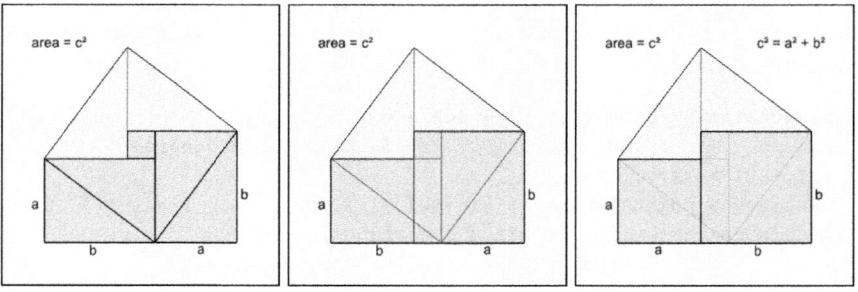

Fig. 6. fadeInSquares animation

5.2 Stage 2: Combining Animation Pieces

In this example, each part of the animation is created separately. The smaller animation pieces often use some of the same basic structures repeatedly, and this piecemeal construction strategy lends itself well to reuse. For instance, the originally defined `maintriangle`, which is never directly displayed, is rotated and moved around to create most of the triangles in the scene. While longer animations can be created directly using the `mvActive` function, we have found that it is generally much cleaner and easier to organize simple animations into a series using one of our combinators, such as `flicker`.

Using the `flicker` function in this way is the second major stage we discussed for creating an animation. With the `flicker` function, animations can be strung together, one after the other, stacking newer parts onto older ones. The time each individual animation component takes to be performed can be specified using the `taking` function, as described earlier. Our general structure looks like:

```
let anim = flicker [ taking 0.5 $ background
                   , taking 1 $ firstABC
                   , taking 1 $ movingTriangle
                   ...
                   , taking 1 $ fadeInSquares 'over' thirdABC
                   , taking 3 $ finalABC 'over' formula
                   ]
```

This use of `flicker` and `taking` is what we use to manage the majority of our ordering and timing for animations. It returns a single `Active Board` that can then be used to display the whole animation, or reused in turn to create an even bigger animation, hierarchically. In terms of displaying the animation, this will largely be done the same way for most animations:

```
sid <- startDefaultWriteStream cb "pythagorean.mp4"
playObj <- byFrame 29.97 anim

let loop = do mbScene <- play playObj
        case mbScene of
              Just scene -> do
                    drawChalkBoard cb $ unAlphaBoard (boardOf white) scene
                    frameChalkBoard cb sid
                    loop
              Nothing -> return ()
loop
```

First, the `Active Board` must be turned into a `Player` using the `byFrame` function (which also takes a desired frame rate). The `Player` is then passed to the `play` function to retrieve the next image of the animation (or `Nothing`, if the animation is finished). Finally, this retrieved image can be used in any way that ChalkBoard can use a `Board`. Traditionally, the image is displayed on the screen using `drawChalkBoard` or saved into a video file with `frameChalkBoard` (or both). After this, the process of calling `play` on the `Player` must be repeated to extract the next image. This is usually placed into a simple loop that extracts and then displays the returned frame, as shown above. We used this method to produce a video of the full animation created in this case study. The video can be seen online at http://www.youtube.com/watch?v=UDRGhTFu17w.

6   Related Work

There have been numerous image description DSLs using functional languages, many of them capable of animation. A lot of the image description languages similar to ChalkBoard are described in our earlier ChalkBoard paper [3].

In particular, the work of Conal Elliott had one of the largest influences on ChalkBoard. Elliott has been working on functional graphics and image generation for many years and has produced a number of related systems. These include Fran [4], Pan [5], and Vertigo [6]. ChalkBoard was heavily influenced by Pan and started from the same basic set of combinators provided in Pan.

In terms of animation and the Active DSL, some similar systems that have been created are Slideshow [7] and the function system presented by Kavi Arya [8]. One of the major differences between the Active animation system and these, however, is the treatment of time. Slideshow is predominately frame-based because of its goal of generating slides for presentations. Arya's system, meanwhile, can cue animations relative to one another or to object interactions. The Active DSL, on the other hand, is time-based. It allows the user to create functions mapped over a known time progression and then affect the time management of animations separately. While this management often includes cueing animations relative to others, similar to the two languages mentioned, it can also include stretching or shrinking animations and moving them forwards or backwards in time. A few of the Active combinators can also help provide a simple framework for reordering animations.

The closest related work to our Active DSL is Hudak's temporal media DSL [9], which was also used to specify change over time in a pre-determined manner, but was used to generate music, not images, and also did not codify the ability to use applicative functors. The Active DSL is also conceptually close to Functional Reactive Programming (FRP) [10], even though Active does not attempt to be reactive in the same sense as FRP. Both Active and (one implementation form of) FRP are mappings from time to value, however Active does not implement FRP Events, but rather an Active object has a start and an end. With Active being designed for presentations and similar educational animations, all of the actions in the Active DSL are explicitly specified ahead of time by the user, although they can be in relation to other animations.

Of course, there are many other animation languages and systems. Active is an attempt to combine the concept of first class functions over time (from FRP), width in time (like the temporal media DSL), and the idiom of packing such functions over time (as an analog to stacking boxes in space) to provide a clean starting idiom for animation specification.

7   Conclusions and Future Work

The `Active` language is a mathematically-based system where actions are the results of mapping functions over time values progressing from 0 to 1. It provides substantial abstraction for the different pieces that go into creating an animation, such as the drawing, timing, and ordering, and is useful in practice.

The biggest improvement we hope to make to the `Active` DSL in the future is the inclusion of some more precise combinators for the cueing and timing of animations. While the current structures have proven useful, there are some instances in which the current `Active` API could have been improved. Specifically, we hope to work on structures that will allow users to specify *when* animations should be visible. In this type of structure, the default may be for animations to only appear when they are currently active (progressing from 0 to 1), and have means of specifying which objects should be visible at other times.

Another improvement we hope to make is to increase the amount of internal sharing that is done by the ChalkBoard compiler in order to more efficiently create the animations it generates. In our animations, a lot of the same boards are often reused, just at slightly different positions on the screen. Because ChalkBoard treats each of these boards as a texture, the potential for reuse of these textures in animation is very high, they often just need to be remapped onto the scene at a slightly different location or size.

References

1. Peyton Jones, S. (ed.): Haskell 98 Language and Libraries – The Revised Report. Cambridge University Press, Cambridge (2003)
2. McBride, C., Patterson, R.: Applicative programing with effects. Journal of Functional Programming 16(6) (2006)
3. Matlage, K., Gill, A.: ChalkBoard: Mapping functions to polygons. In: Morazán, M.T., Scholz, S.-B. (eds.) IFL 2009. LNCS, vol. 6041, pp. 55–71. Springer, Heidelberg (2010)
4. Elliott, C.: From functional animation to sprite-based display. In: Gupta, G. (ed.) PADL 1999. LNCS, vol. 1551, p. 61. Springer, Heidelberg (1999)
5. Elliott, C., Finne, S., de Moor, O.: Compiling embedded languages. Journal of Functional Programming 13(2) (2003)
6. Elliott, C.: Programming graphics processors functionally. In: Proceedings of the 2004 Haskell Workshop. ACM Press, New York (2004)
7. Findler, R.B., Flatt, M.: Slideshow: functional presentations. J. Funct. Program. 16(4-5), 583–619 (2006)
8. Arya, K.: Processes in a functional animation system. In: FPCA 1989: Proceedings of the Fourth International Conference on Functional Programming Languages and Computer Architecture, pp. 382–395. ACM, New York (1989)
9. Hudak, P.: An algebraic theory of polymorphic temporal media. In: Jayaraman, B. (ed.) PADL 2004. LNCS, vol. 3057, pp. 1–15. Springer, Heidelberg (2004)
10. Elliott, C., Hudak, P.: Functional reactive animation. In: International Conference on Functional Programming (1997)

Functional Video Games in the CS1 Classroom

Marco T. Morazán

Seton Hall University, South Orange, NJ, USA
morazanm@shu.edu

Abstract. Over the past decade enrollments in Computer Science undergraduate programs have drastically dropped while simultaneously seeing demand for computer scientists in the job market increase. The reason for this disconnect is, in part, due to the perception new potential students have of programming as a dull activity requiring no creativity, very little social interaction, and endless hours of coding in front of a monitor. The question then is how can we capture the imagination of new students and perk their interest in a way that gets them excited while at the same time giving them a solid foundation in computer programming and Computer Science. This article puts forth the thesis that developing video games using functional programming should be a new trend in the CS1 classroom. The article describes the approach implemented at Seton Hall University using video game programming and Felleisen et al.'s textbook *How to Design Programs*. The first-year programming curriculum is briefly described and how to get students interested in programming through the development of a Space-Invaders-like game is illustrated. The presented development gives the reader a clear sense of how to use functional video games in the first semester classroom.

1   Introduction

Over the past decade enrollments in Computer Science programs have drastically dropped up to 70% in some countries [13]. According to CRA's most recent Taulbee Survey in the United States and Canada, the number of Computer Science and Computer Engineering newly declared majors has dropped from a high around 24,000 in the year 2000 to under 14,000 in the year 2008 [14]. In addition, the production of Bachelor's dropped from a high of over 20,000 in 2002 to under 12,000 in 2009. The Taulbee Survey also suggests that retention rates need to be improved. For example, in 2004 there were about 16,000 newly declared majors and, four years later, in 2008 there were under 12,000 Bachelor's produced.

The drop in enrollment is occurring while seeing demand for computer scientists in the job market increase. According to recent occupational employment projections for 2008-2018, computer and mathematical occupations are expected to grow by 22.2% [8]. This rate of growth is over twice as high as the average for all occupations. Among the fastest growing occupations are computer software engineers with demand for application developers expected to increase by 34% and demand for systems software developers to increase by 30.4%. The data

R. Page, Z. Horváth, and V. Zsók (Eds.): TFP 2010, LNCS 6546, pp. 166–183, 2011.

clearly suggests that there is and there will continue to be a high demand for Bachelor's in Computer Science. In addition to the expected demand, trends indicate that Computer Science majors are expected to be amongst the best paid professionals (e.g., software architects rank 8th with a median salary of US\$117,000), and amongst the professionals with the best quality of life (e.g., software developers rank 4th with 59% stating that there job has low stress) [10].

Being a field projected to remain in high demand and promising the potential for obtaining a high-paying low-stress job is not enough to attract students to and retain students in Computer Science. This seems counter-intuitive at first glance and can not solely be explained by the negative outlook caused by the dot com bust and the recent down turn in the economy. It is necessary to assess the perspective of students that enroll in the beginning courses. To this end, students enrolling in the introductory Computer Science course at Seton Hall University (the home institution of the author) have been interviewed over the past 8 years. From 2002 to 2007 this course was taught using Java as the language of instruction following the typical syntax-based approach of most textbooks with little emphasis on design and problem solving techniques. Uniformly across students, regardless of whether or not they continued as Computer Science majors, the sentiment was that Computer Science and programming were boring and required little or no creativity and social interaction. Programming was characterized as spending endless hours in front of a monitor debugging code. These sentiments were stronger in women which also exhibited lower retention rates. In 2008, the introductory course was taken over by the author and taught based on Felleisen's et. al's textbook *How To Design Programs* (HtDP) [4]. The outlook of students improved as well as retention rates, but students still characterized most of what they did as boring. Despite focusing on design and problem solving (instead of syntax), students felt that there was nothing really interesting or special about, for example, searching a list, computing the value of an integral, or sorting. The bottom line was that students felt it required no creativity and everyone was doing exactly the same thing and producing the same code. This sentiment to some degree is not unlike what students in other disciplines like, for example, Mathematics and Engineering face: the solution to a problem is the same for all students. There is, however, a difference with Computer Science that may signal why retention is harder. The typical assignment in Computer Science has a component that assignments seen by students in other disciplines do not have. Computer Science students must design, write, debug, and produce a working piece of software. That is, they must build an artifact of their discipline. It is a time-consuming process that beginning students in other disciplines do not have to face. This is not to say that other disciplines do not offer challenging and enlightening exercises to their students, but rarely, if ever, are beginning students in other disciplines asked to build an artifact of their discipline like beginning Computer Science students are asked to do on a regular basis. Given that beginning students can easily shop around and switch majors (at least in the USA), this represents a challenge that must be faced creatively by Computer Science departments to attract students to the major and to increase their retention.

The interviews with students at Seton Hall University identified one element that can help attract and retain students. Students across the board, regardless of whether or not they continued as Computer Science majors, qualified the design and implementation of video games (using the DrScheme's[1] universe teachpack [3]) as very interesting, as requiring creativity, and as fun to work in groups. In addition, students felt that requiring the design and implementation of a large video game by the end of the semester truly brought everything that they had to learn into focus which provided a sense of accomplishment and a sense of satisfaction with majoring in Computer Science. In 2009, the delivery of the introductory course was redesigned to incorporate more development of video games as motivation.

This article advocates that the design of functional video games should be a new trend in introductory Computer Science courses. Having beginning students develop *functional* video games means that they are liberated from reasoning about state and the sequencing of statements, because the code that they develop is assignment-free. Thus, students focus on how to design and implement a solution without having to focus on the overhead and dangers of using assignment. Our experience suggests that this approach facilitates the introduction and the understanding of recursion which usually is a fundamental topic in Computer Science that students struggle with in introductory courses. The use of video games has the added benefit that it has a built-in creative outlet. Students are able to customize their solutions to their personal preferences. The choice of graphics used, the level of difficulty preferred for the game, and the speed at which the game advances, for example, can vary from student to student. This provides students with the sense that not all solutions to a problem are the same and that they can creatively inject their own personality in the development and implementation of a solution. The reader can contrast this with the typical word problem found in a Mathematics or Engineering textbook. This ability to offer students problems with a creative outlet ought to be leveraged to engage, attract, and retain beginning students in Computer Science. The built-in creative outlet that video game development and implementation offers, for example, has proven an especially effective tool to make Computer Science and programming interesting to female students. Among young female students, the opportunity to be creative was the highest ranked characteristic. In contrast, male students ranked the ability to create competitive games the highest with creativity closely ranked behind it. Finally, the development of functional video games provides the opportunity to make core lessons in Computer Science and programming (e.g., design, recursion, sorting, and searching) relevant to the pop culture students are an integral part of. Much of what they learn ceases to be purely theoretical and can directly be applied to create something that not only are they interested in, but are also excited about.

The article first outlines the topics taught in the introductory courses at Seton Hall University and why the use of a functional language is ideal. The article then demonstrates how the design and implementation of a functional

---

[1] DrScheme has recently been renamed DrRacket.

video game, specifically a Space-Invaders-like game, can be used to motivate and teach students in CS1. The presentation aims to illustrate how functional video games can be used in the first-semester classroom and to serve as a road map that others can follow and adapt to their particular environment and students. The presentation also aims to demonstrate how relatively easy it is to develop a functional video game and to integrate functional video game development into the CS1 classroom. Finally, the article concludes with a discussion of related approaches and some conclusions.

2   Introduction to Computer Science and Programming

Introduction to Computer Science courses tend to focus on providing students with a solid foundation in programming [13]. This characteristic is justified, because teaching students about programming prepares them for the job market, programming tends to attract more students (both those majoring and those not majoring in Computer Science), and programming is a prerequisite for many upper-level Computer Science courses [12]. The debate of what should and what should not be included in an introduction to Computer Science and programming rages on. Instead of engaging in the futile exercise of systematically analyzing the list of potential topics to gain converts, the solution adopted at Seton Hall University is outlined below. The reader can decide decide if the choices made make sense for her institution and her environment.

It is noteworthy that this article is not advocating the presented methodology as absolute or rigid. As Computer Science evolves, so will the technologies, like video games, used to motivate students in introductory courses. The topics (e.g., structures, lists, and sorting) covered in such courses are also subject to change as Computer Science evolves, but at a much slower pace than vogue technologies. The primary lesson that should be drawn is that an interesting domain can be used to make the delivery of a solid foundation in programming fun and interesting for beginning students. Video game programming is such a domain for the foreseeable future.

2.1   Topics Covered in CS1 and CS2 at Seton Hall University

At Seton Hall University, all students must complete four years of study to earn a Bachelor's degree. During this time, students must fulfill general requirements as well as the requirements for their major. The Computer Science major requires 53-54 credits with the typical course being worth 3 credits and some courses being worth 4 credits. During their freshman year (i.e., the first year), students are expected to pass CS1 and CS2 which allows them to move on in their sophomore year (i.e., their second year) to courses focusing on designing classes. During their junior and senior year (i.e., their third and fourth years), students take upper-level Computer Science requirements as well as Computer Science electives most of which require programming.

It is our perspective that introductory Computer Science courses ought to focus on problem solving. Students should be empowered by helping them develop skills that take them from a problem statement to a *well-designed* solution. The emphasis is much more on designing the solution to a problem than the actual implementation of the solution. Although being able to follow through with the implementation of a solution is an important skill, it is the design of the solution that makes the implementation possible. Furthermore, it is the ability to design a solution to a problem that makes a Computer Science education relevant to other aspects of a student's life. Stated simply, solution design skills can be applied to problems beyond those solved using a computer and a programming language, because they make the thinking process explicit.

In addition to developing problem solving skills, students must also learn the rudimentary nomenclature of programming. At Seton Hall, there are two courses, CS1 and CS2[2], that serve as the introduction to Computer Science and Programming. Broadly speaking, CS1 covers the following topics (listed to make the connection with HtDP's Parts I-IV easy):

- Programming with primitive data (e.g., symbols, numbers, and pictures) and primitive functions (e.g., symbol equality, addition, and geometric drawing functions).
- Programmer defined functions and variables.
- Processing finite compound data (e.g., structures).
- Processing arbitrarily large compound data (e.g., structural recursion on lists, trees, and natural numbers).
- Abstraction (e.g., elimination of code repetition and functions as values)

Broadly speaking, CS2 covers the following topics (listed to make the connection with HtDP's Parts V-VIII easy):

- Generative recursion (e.g., quicksort).
- Iteration (i.e., accumulative recursion and loops).
- State-based computations (i.e., design using assignment).
- Distributed Computing (not a topic in HtDP).

Readers interested in a rationale for including the above topics in the curriculum for CS1 and CS2 are referred to the appropriate sections in HtDP. The abstraction techniques studied are specific to functional languages, but the focus is the reduction of errors by reducing code duplication. Students learn that common programming patterns can be captured as functions to make code more readable and less bug-prone. The distributed computing component introduces students to networks, a pervasive technology today, and provides the opportunity to design and implement a distributed application using the same language and software students have used throughout their first year.

These introductory courses aim to provide the foundation needed for students to go on and learn how to design solutions and write programs using any programming language. In fact, the skills acquired are directly transferable to designing programs using object-oriented languages such as Java. Although teaching languages with Scheme-like syntax are used in these courses, the goal is

---

[2] These courses are actually called Design of Programs I and Design of Programs II.

not teach students Scheme nor is the goal to make them functional programmers. In the interest of absolute clarity, we are not teaching our students Scheme nor do we advocate teaching beginning students Scheme. Scheme is a mature and powerful programming language with native support for many advanced features (e.g., continuations and hygienic macros) that are not addressed nor used in CS1 and CS2. Equally noteworthy is the fact that the emphasis is not on the syntax of any particular programming language although, of course, students must learn some Scheme-like syntax in order to implement solutions. Scheme-like syntax may not seem natural to students on the first day of class (e.g., prefix instead of infix notation), but it is useful in distinguishing Scheme from mathematics. Students may analyze a problem off-screen using mathematics written using infix notation, but must translate it into a programming language's syntax to implement a program. This is a process that is common to program development in general. One of the advantages of using Scheme-like syntax is that this translation is simple enough that it quickly becomes natural to beginning students using HtDP. Other reasons for using Scheme as the core behind the employed teaching languages are given in the preface of HtDP [4]. It is our estimation that the foundation we provide enables students to go on to learn about powerful abstractions provided by other languages (regardless of the syntax used) such as, for example, monads in Haskell, objects and inheritance in Java, and continuations and hygienic macros in Scheme.

In addition to the topics above, emphasis is placed on *iterative refinement*. It is important for students to understand that designs, solutions, and implementations evolve through a continuous cycle of enhancements. This lesson is a difficult one to convey especially when the programs students are asked to develop are small. Large projects, like the design and implementation of a video game, provide an excellent vehicle with which to emphasize iterative refinement.

3   The Functional and HtDP Advantages

The choice of a functional language for introductory courses can be controversial for some faculty members and for some students. This article will not digress too much into the objections raised by faculty members. These objections mostly boil down to not teaching a language used in industry and not focusing on teaching state-based problem solving. Teaching a particular language, even one used in industry, should not be the goal of an introductory course. Mostly focusing on teaching state-based problem solving fails to expose students enough to easy-to-use skills in the design of solutions and programs. In fact, assignment is harmful at the beginning. In our experience, students that start with state-based problem solving find it very hard to design solutions or to understand solutions that fail to mutate variables at every step. The sharp reader will have detected the concept of step (and sequencing) introduced into this text all of the sudden. This is precisely how students think of computation if they start with state-based problem solving: programs are a collection of sequenced assignments.

As any functional programmer knows, nothing can be farther from the truth and statements to this effect by students should not go unchallenged[3].

3.1   The Functional Advantage

Liberating students from reasoning about state and the machine, as mentioned before, is a formidable advantage offered by functional languages. Students are allowed to think about how to solve problems and do not have to reason about how to sequence mutations to solve a problem. They can build on their knowledge of high school algebra to design functions which brings problem solving into a domain that seems familiar to them. This approach has the added benefit that it makes mathematics relevant for students [6], improves the grades of students in mathematics courses [5], and builds on a natural synergy that more and more looks like an endangered species in the CS curriculum.

Functional languages can also–but not always–present students with a minimal amount of syntax that needs to be learned in order to solve interesting problems. Dynamically typed functional languages, for example, remove all syntax requirements associated with types which are required by statically typed languages. The observation is simple: the less time we spend discussing syntax the more problem solving and design principles we can actually teach.

Finally, as pointed out by Felleisen et. al [4], if an interpreted functional language is used, then Byzantine discussions about input and output are not necessary. Students do not have to be bogged down with how to input and output data–which has little or nothing to do with the solution to the problem they are implementing. Once again, students are liberated from side issues and allowed to focus on problem solving. Learning how to do I/O should not be a prerequisite to learn the basics of programming nor to take your first steps into the world of Computer Science.

3.2   The HtDP Advantage

An HtDP-based curriculum presents two major advantages for teaching introductory Computer Science and programming courses. The first is that it gives students a road map to follow from a blank screen to a working solution. This road map is based on what Felleisen et al. have coined the *design recipe*. A design recipe is a series of steps a student can follow in the design of a solution. In fact, there are several different design recipes all of which are variations on a theme depending on the type of problem being solved or the type of data being processed. The basic skeleton for developing a function for all the variations of design recipes is:

1. Problem analysis and data definitions.
2. Stating the contract, the purpose, and writing the function header.
3. Defining tests showing how a function should work.

---

[3] The author does not recommend challenging or trying to convince faculty members that express such a view in open debate. Let your results speak for themselves.

4. Development of a function template (derived from the data being processed) and an inventory of expressions that can be used to implement the function.
5. Defining the function.
6. Running the tests and making corrections if necessary.

At the beginning, students find the use of the design recipe cumbersome especially when the programs/functions being designed are small. In fact, many students feel it is overkill. It is important, however, to encourage them to develop good habits by following the steps in the design recipe even if they can see the solution before going through all the steps. The assignment of a non-trivial problem as homework and grading how well students follow the design recipe go a long way to bringing the point home.

The second major advantage an HtDP-based curriculum presents is that it is tightly-coupled with the DrScheme programming environment. This environment comes with a series a successively richer subsets of Scheme-like languages called the teaching languages. Each part of HtDP is associated with a teaching language. The teaching languages make available just enough syntax for students to learn to design solutions to the types of problems that they are being asked to solve. This hierarchy of teaching languages allows for meaningful error messages to be generated for mistakes that would otherwise be hard to decipher by a beginning student [4]. Our experience is that students suffer through much less frustration when compared to Seton Hall's old Java-based approach. In addition, DrScheme also comes with a rich set of libraries/teachpacks that simplify the implementation of solutions for different kinds of problems. One such teachpack is *universe* which defines an interface for writing animations (both interactive and non-interactive). Universe envisions an animation as a series of snapshots of an evolving world. There is a clock that at every tick displays the next snapshot of the world. Students must define the elements of the world and define functions for computing the next snapshot of the world when the clock ticks or when an external event, such as a keystroke or a mouse movement, occurs. Students must also define functions for drawing the world and for detecting the end of the animation. The code students develop can be functional (i.e., assignment-free) and free of any concerns about coordinating the display of snapshots. Readers interested in more details about the universe teachpack are referred to *How to Design Worlds* [3].

4   Video Games in CS1

Armed with the design recipe and with DrScheme's universe teachpack, instructors and (first-year) students can be ambitious and start developing a video game starting on the first day of class. At the beginning, of course, the video game is, shall we say, less than interesting. It lacks any real features video games have, because students still do not know how to do very much. The promise of developing a video game, however, is used to keep students motivated and students are encouraged as the process of iterative refinement adds dimensions to the game.

Fig. 1. A snapshot illustrating an implementation of Aliens Attack

Our attention will now focus on illustrating how to motivate topics in the CS1 curriculum by tying them in with the development of a Space-Invaders-like video game that we shall refer to as *Aliens Attack*. The presentation will display a series of different incarnations implemented during the iterative refinement process. In the game there is a defender at the bottom of the screen that the player may move left and right to shoot aliens. There are also one or more aliens in a grid-like formation that are trying to reach the bottom of the screen–presumably to conquer earth. All aliens move in the same direction–either left or right–and when an alien reaches the edge of the screen all aliens move down and start moving in the opposite direction. The game ends when either all aliens have been destroyed by the defender or an alien reaches the bottom of the screen. Figure 1 displays a visual representation of Aliens Attack.

4.1   Aliens Attack v0.0

On the first day of class, the assumption is made that students have no background in programming. Therefore, they are stumped by the task of creating a video game despite their enthusiasm to do so. They are told that the game will be developed using iterative refinement–not all at once, but little by little as they learn how to design programs. Nonetheless, the first version of aliens attack is developed. It is simply an empty scene of HEIGHTxWIDTH computer graphics coordinates where the game is to be drawn and played. A sample is generated by the code in Figure 2.

Students may be a little disappointed with this first version, but they are motivated to learn about defining constants, about primitive data, and about how to place images in a scene. In addition, students are encouraged to read the documentation to learn more about how place-image works. By the second class, most students are proud to show how they have modified the color

```
(define HEIGHT 650)
(define WIDTH 900)
(define E-SCENE
  (place-image (rectangle (* 2 WIDTH) (* 2 HEIGHT) 'solid 'yellow)
               0
               0
               (empty-scene WIDTH HEIGHT)))
```

Fig. 2. The code for Aliens Attack v0.0

and the size of the canvas to their liking. The stage is now set to learn about primitive data and primitive functions.

4.2 Aliens Attack v0.1

After gaining some programming experience with primitive data, students are brought back to the video game. The first enhancements tackled are drawing the defender in a scene and creating a defender in a new position. During problem analysis, students quickly realize that the defender can be represented by a natural number, n, such that $0 \leq n \leq$ WIDTH-1. This natural number represents the x coordinate of the defender. There is no need to represent the y coordinate nor the image of the defender as variable, because they can be defined as constants.

To draw a defender, students realize they need as input a defender and a scene and they need to return a scene in which the defender has been drawn in the given scene. This analysis leads to their contract and drawing function which may look as follows:

```
;;;    DATA DEFINITION: A defender is a natural number, n,
;;;                     such that 0 <= n <= WIDTH - 1
; EXAMPLE
(define OUR-HERO (/ WIDTH 2))

;;; draw-defender: defender scene --> scene
(define (draw-defender a-defender scn)
  (place-image DEF-IMG a-defender DEF-HEIGHT scn))
```

DEF-IMG and DEF-HEIGHT are the constants for the image and the y coordinate of the defender.

Naturally, the next task that students wish to tackle is getting the defender to move using keystrokes. This provides an opportunity to introduce students to conditional statements and booleans as the direction the defender moves in, if at all, depends on keystrokes. Data analysis reveals that computing a moved defender requires a defender and a direction[4] leading to a function to move the defender:

---

[4] Represented as a string corresponding to a keystroke in DrScheme.

```
;;; move-defender: defender string --> defender
(define (move-defender a-defender direction)
  (cond [(string=? direction "right") (+ a-defender DEF-DELTA-X)]
        [(string=? direction "left")  (- a-defender DEF-DELTA-X)]
        [else a-defender]))
```

DEF-DELTA-X is a constant representing by how much to move the defender with
each keystroke.

Testing the above function, however, reveals a bug. The defender can move off
the scene driving home early the importance of testing in software development.
Iterative refinement yields an improved function to move the defender:

```
;;; move-defender: defender string --> defender
(define (move-defender a-defender direction)
  (cond [(and (symbol=? direction 'right)
              (<= (+ a-defender DEF-DELTA-X) (sub1 WIDTH)))
         (+ a-defender DEF-DELTA-X)]
        [(and (symbol=? direction 'left)
              (>= (- a-defender DEF-DELTA-X) 0))
         (- a-defender DEF-DELTA-X)]
        [else a-defender])).
```

4.3   Aliens Attack v0.2

The next task is to introduce aliens each requiring an x and a y coordinate to
represent their position which motivates the need to represent finite compound
data. Such data is represented using structures. In this part of the course, some
students may stumble given that it is unlikely that they have studied functions
on compound data in any other course. Students start by studying a built-in
structure in DrScheme called a posn to represent a position in a scene. After
posn, students study how to define their own structures and how to design
functions for such structures.

A student's first attempt to represent an alien will typically define a structure
that only contains posn. The experienced programmer will notice that a structure definition is unnecessary, but its elimination is an optimization that can
pursued as a future refinement. There is nothing inherently wrong with defining
an alien as a structure that contains a posn.

Using compound data requires the development of a function template and
an inventory of expressions that can be used to access and manipulate the components of the compound data. For an alien in our video game, for example, the
results may be:

```
(define-struct alien (position)) ; where position is a posn
; EXAMPLE
(define ALIEN1 (make-alien (make-posn (/ WIDTH 2) (/ HEIGHT 2))))
; f-on-alien: alien --> ???
```

```
(define (f-on-alien an-alien)
  ; inventory
  ; (alien-position an-alien) = the posn stored in an-alien
  ; (posn-x (alien-position an-alien)) = the x-coordinate of
  ;                                      an-alien
  ; (posn-y (alien-position an-alien)) = the y-coordinate of
  ;                                      an-alien
  <the body of f-on-alien> )
```

This template can then be specialized by students to write functions to manipulate aliens akin to moving and drawing the defender. It is noteworthy to point out that students are not hacking code nor are they developing code using a blind trial and error strategy. Instead, they must think explicitly about the structures they are manipulating and understand that their structures influence the shape of the code they must develop.

Once students have some experience with structures and have written functions to draw and move the defender as well as the alien, they are ready to define a structure for the world and write the handlers for the first animation. The world is a structure that captures the elements that can change. In our video game there are three changing elements (so far): the defender, the alien, and the direction (left, right, or down) the alien is traveling. This leads to the following definition for world and its function template:

```
(define-struct world (def al dir))
; where def is a defender, al is an alien, and dir is a string
; EXAMPLE
(define INIT-WORLD (make-world OUR-HERO ALIEN1 "right"))

;f-on-world: world --> ???
(define (f-on-world w)
  ; inventory
  ; (world-def w) = the defender in w
  ; (world-al w) = the alien in w
  ; (world-dir w) = the string for the direction in w
  ; (alien-position (world-al w)) = the posn of the alien in w
  ; (posn-x (alien-position (world-al w)))
  ;    = the x coordinate of the alien in w
  ; (posn-y (alien-position (world-al w)))
  ;    = the y coordinate of the alien in w
  <BODY OF f-on-world>)
```

The game requires four event handlers for the animation: one to draw the world, one to process key strokes, one to compute the next world every time the clock ticks, and one to detect the end of the game. The above template is specialized by students to create the functions displayed in Figure 3 that serve as the event handlers. The code displayed is fairly easy to understand and uses auxiliary functions at-edge? to detect if the alien is at either the left or the right edge of

```
; draw-world: world --> scene
; Purpose: To draw the world
(define (draw-world w)
  (draw-alien (world-al w)
              (draw-defender (world-def w) E-SCENE)))

; process-key: world string --> world
; Purpose: To create a new world based on a keystroke
(define (process-key w k)
  (make-world (move-defender (world-def w) k)
              (world-al w)
              (world-dir w)))

; next-world: world --> world
; Purpose: To compute the next world (after a clock tick)
(define (next-world w)
  (make-world (world-def w)
              (move-alien (world-al w) (world-dir w))
              (cond [(and (at-edge? (world-al w))
                          (not (string=? (world-dir w) "down"))) "down"]
                    [(and (over-r-edge? (world-al w))
                          (string=? (world-dir w) "down")) "left"]
                    [(and (over-l-edge? (world-al w))
                          (string=? (world-dir w) "down")) "right"]
                    [else (world-dir w)])))

; game-over?: world --> boolean
; Purpose: To determine if the game is over (i.e., the alien has landed)
(define (game-over? w)
  (> (+ (posn-y (alien-position (world-al w))) ALIEN-DELTA-Y)
     HEIGHT))
```

Fig. 3. Functions to manipulate the world in Aliens Attack v0.2

the scene, over-r-edge? to detect if the alien is at the right edge of the scene, and over-l-edge? to detect if the alien is at the left edge of the scene.

Finally, students must provide the handlers to the universe interface to run the game. The syntax to do so is not cumbersome and easy to follow for students:

```
(big-bang INIT-WORLD
          (on-draw draw-world)
          (on-key process-key)
          (on-tick next-world)
          (stop-when game-over?))
```

4.4   Aliens Attack v0.3

Once students have a running video game with a moving alien and a defender that responds to keystrokes, the desire to add multiple aliens and shooting

```
; DATA DEFINITION
; A list of aliens, loa, is either
;   1. empty
;   2. (cons a l), where a is an alien and l is a loa.

; f-on-loa: (listof alien) --> ???
(define (f-on-loa a-loa)
  ; inventory
  ; (first a-loa) = the first alien in a-loa
  ; (rest a-loa) = a-loa minus its first alien
  ; (f-on-alien (first a-loa)) = the ??? from applying f-on-alien
  ;                               to the first alien in a-loa
  ; (f-on-loa (rest a-loa)) = the ??? from applying f-on-loa to
  ;                               (rest a-loa)
  (cond [(empty? a-loa) ...]
        [else (...(f-on-alien (first a-loa))
              ...(f-on-loa (rest a-loa)))]))

; move-loa: (listof alien) string --> (listof alien)
(define (move-loa a-loa direction)
  ; inventory
  ; (first a-loa) = the first alien in a-loa
  ; (rest a-loa) = a-loa minus its first alien
  ; (move-alien (first a-loa)) = the first alien moved
  ; (move-loa (rest a-loa)) = the moved (rest loa)
  (cond [(empty? a-loa) empty]
        [else (cons (move-alien (first a-loa) direction)
                    (move-loa (rest a-loa)))]))
```

Fig. 4. Recursive data definition for a list of aliens, recursive template for a list of aliens, and a specialization of the template to move a list of aliens in Aliens Attack v0.3

capabilities quickly arises. Student analysis reveals that there can be zero aliens, if all have been destroyed by the defender, or there can be one or more aliens that still need to be destroyed. Thus, the introduction of multiple aliens motivates the need for data of arbitrary size and leads to the study of lists (and other recursively defined data definitions like trees). During this study, students design and implement, for example, searching, sorting, accumulating (e.g., summing the elements of a list), and filtering algorithms. Throughout, it is emphasized that students exploit the structure of their data to determine the structure of their code. For example, a self-reference in the data definition translates to a recursive call in their function. In this manner, students learn quite naturally how to exploit structural recursion.

Armed with some experience processing data of arbitrary size, students return to the design of the video game and create the recursive data definition and function template for a list of aliens displayed in Figure 4. It is noteworthy that students realize that a function that consumes an alien must be applied to the first alien in the list and that a function that consumes a list of aliens must be applied to the rest of the list. Furthermore, the reason for a recursive call is not a mystery–the self-reference in the data definition for loa translates to a recursive call–and students know in advance of writing any code that such will be the case. Figure 4 also displays a specialization of the function template to move a list of aliens. Students can now be charged with changing their definition of the world structure to incorporate the list of aliens and to incorporate shots. Such an exercise reinforces the lessons on designing structures as well as filtering and list processing in general given that shots and aliens that are hit and shots that go off the screen must be eliminated from the game.

4.5   Aliens Attack v0.4

The final component of CS1 introduces students to abstraction. At this point in the course, students have added shots to their video games and will have functions to move a list of aliens and to move a list of shots. Typically, a function to move a list of shots will look as follows:

```
; move-los: (listof shot) --> (listof shot)
(define (move-los a-los)
   (cond [(empty? a-los) empty]
         [else (cons (move-shot (first a-loa))
                     (move-los (rest a-los)))]))
```

Structurally, this function is similar to move-loa in Figure 4 and most students grow tired of having to write similar code as this over and over. This presents the opportunity to introduce students to abstraction using elimination of code duplication and code reuse as motivation to create shorter programs. After an introduction to abstraction, students return to the design of the video game and re-implement as follows:

```
; move-loa: (listof alien) string --> (listof alien)
(define (move-loa a-loa direction)
   (map (lambda (a) (move-alien a direction)) a-loa))

; move-los: (listof shot) --> (listof shot)
(define (move-los a-los) (map move-shot a-los)).
```

When seen side-by-side, students realize that these new functions are structurally similar and apply the design recipe for abstraction to them. This process yields the code in Figure 5. Students realize that the first function in Figure 5 is an abstract function to move a list of anything which can be used in the development of other video games and appreciate that it is short (i.e., one line of code), that it is not recursive, and that it is easy to use. In fact, most students can not believe how easy moving a list of anything is made through abstraction.

```
; move-list: (X --> X) (listof X) --> (listof X)
(define (move-list f a-list) (map f a-list))

; move-loa: (listof alien) string --> (listof alien)
(define (move-loa a-loa direction)
   (move-list (lambda (a) (move-alien a direction)) a-loa))

; move-los: (listof shot) --> (listof shot)
(define (move-los a-los) (move-list move-shot a-los))
```

Fig. 5. Abstract function to move a list of X and concrete functions to move a list of aliens and a list of shots

5   Related Approaches

There have been a several approaches to the use of video game programming in conjunction with functional languages to motivate beginning students. The developers of DrScheme and HtDP have described the technical implementation of I/O in the universe teachpack and have outlined how to implement, both non-distributed and distributed, small simulations based on that description [5]. Naturally, the work described in this article builds on the work done by the developers of HtDP and the universe teachpack. In contrast, the work presented in this article sets aside the technical discussion of I/O and presents a more detailed road map for the actual use of video games in the CS1 classroom. In essence, the work described in this article is for educators "in the trenches" focusing on the actual deployment of a functional video game strategy in the classroom. In addition to describing a larger more realistic application in a CS1 setting, the work described here closely knits together the use of video games in conjunction with CS1 topics.

Soccer-Fun, developed using Clean, aims to motivate students by having them write programs to play soccer games [1]. It has successfully been used in a sophomore-level course aimed to teach functional programming to students with imperative and object-oriented programming experience and in a high school setting to attract students to Computer Science. The developers of Soccer-Fun report no experience with it in CS1. Although soccer is the most popular sport on the planet, it is unclear if such a platform is effective with students that are not fans of the sport.

Yampa is a language embedded in Haskell used to program reactive systems such as video games [2]. Yampa, in fact, has been used to implement a Space-Invaders-like game. As Soccer-Fun, Yampa is mostly intended to help those already familiar with imperative/OO programming to learn functional programming techniques. Both Soccer-Fun and Yampa, nonetheless, have been effectively used to motivate students.

The use of Haskell itself to program a video game, inspired in the classical game *Asteroids*, has also been reported successful at motivating students [9]. The authors report that the popularity of their approach was due, in part, to the use of animated graphics. Furthermore, the authors report that students made great efforts to embellish their solutions with fancy graphics. This may be the earliest indicator that providing students a creative outlet to personalize solutions to problems is an important pedagogic technique in Computer Science education. As with Soccer-Fun and Yampa, the scope of the efforts was to teach functional programming.

Outside the realm of functional programming, Python is poised amongst the most popular languages used to motivate students using games. Python presents students with an interpreter for easy interaction, but is an object-oriented language that naturally carries all the difficulties of designing and implementing programs using assignment. Furthermore, textbooks using Python require almost immediately the use of assignment and looping constructs (e.g., see [7,11]). Thus, programming quickly moves away from the familiar domain of high school algebra.

6   Concluding Remarks

This article puts forth the thesis that programming functional video games should become a trend in the CS1 classroom. The strongest proof that can be presented for why this should be a new trend is two-fold. On one side, the reader hopefully agrees that the development of functional video games is an imaginative approach that is not beyond the scope of beginning students as evidenced by the development presented in this article. On the other side, although not quantified, we have the enthusiasm and interest in programming that developing video games sparks in students. It is the belief of the author that functional video games can be an effective tool to once again make Computer Science an attractive and popular major for beginning college students.

Unlike previous efforts in the classroom to use functional languages to program video games, the goal is not restricted to teaching functional programming to students with programming experience. Instead, the goals of using functional video games are to motivate a student's interest in programming and to provide a sound vehicle for the dissemination of a solid foundation in programming. Essential to such an effort in the CS1 classroom is providing an interface with minimal syntax and an easy to understand semantics. It is the expectation of the author that the described development of a functional video game, using HtDP and DrScheme's universe teachpack, has demonstrated how easily a solid programming foundation can be imparted to students using a domain they consider fun and interesting.

Future work includes demonstrating how functional video games can be an effective pedagogical tool for motivating and teaching generative recursion, accumulative recursion (i.e., iteration), state-based computations, and distributed programming. The approach will assume that students have a foundation using structural recursion as well as abstraction as outlined in this article.

Acknowledgements

The author thanks the plt-scheme and the plt-edu mailing list community for the many frank and eye-opening discussions about teaching programming, about HtDP, and about interesting programming projects for students. Special thanks are extended to Matthias Felleisen and Shriram Krishnamurthi for frequently and kindly engaging me in frank discussions about teaching programming to beginning students. I trust that our public discussions on the mentioned mailing lists have been mutually beneficial.

References

1. Achten, P.: Teaching Functional Programming with Soccer-Fun. In: FDPE 2008: Proceedings of the 2008 International Workshop on Functional and Declarative Programming in Education, pp. 61–72. ACM, New York (2008)
2. Courtney, A., Nilsson, H., Peterson, J.: The Yampa Arcade. In: Haskell 2003: Proceedings of the 2003 ACM SIGPLAN Workshop on Haskell, pp. 7–18. ACM, New York (2003)
3. Felleisen, M., Findler, R.B., Fisler, K., Flatt, M., Krishnamurthi, S.: How to Design Worlds (2008), http://world.cs.brown.edu/1/
4. Felleisen, M., Findler, R.B., Flatt, M., Krishnamurthi, S.: How to Design Programs: An Introduction to Programming and Computing. MIT Press, Cambridge (2001)
5. Felleisen, M., Findler, R.B., Flatt, M., Krishnamurthi, S.: A functional i/o system or, fun for freshman kids. In: Hutton, G., Tolmach, A.P. (eds.) ICFP, pp. 47–58. ACM, New York (2009)
6. Felleisen, M., Krishnamurthi, S.: Viewpoint: Why Computer Science Doesn't Matter. Communications of the ACM 52(7), 37–40 (2009)
7. Harris, A.: The L Line, The Express Line to Learning. In: Game Programming, Wiley Publishing, Inc., Hoboken (2007)
8. Lacey, T.A., Wright, B.: Occupational Employment Projections to 2018. Monthly Labor Review, 82–123 (November 2009)
9. Lüth, C.: Haskell in Space: An Interactive Game as a Functional Programming Exercise. J. Funct. Program 13(6), 1077–1085 (2003)
10. Money Magazine and Salary.com. Best Jobs in America. Money Magazine (2009)
11. McGugan, W.: Beginning Game Development with Python and Pygame: From Novice to Professional. Apress, Berkeley (2007)
12. The Joint Task Force on Computing Curricula. Computing Curricula 2001 Computer Science (December 2001),
    http://www.acm.org/education/education/education/curric_vols/cc2001.pdf
13. CS2008 Review Taskforce. Computer Science Curriculum 2008: An Interim Revision of CS 2001 (December 2008),
    http://www.acm.org//education/curricula/ComputerScience2008.pdf
14. Zweben, S.: 2007-2008 Taulbee Survey. Computing Research News (May 2009)

ComputErl – Erlang-Based Framework for Many Task Computing

Michał Ptaszek[1,2] and Maciej Malawski[1]

[1] Institute of Computer Science AGH, al. Mickiewicza 30, 30-059 Kraków, Poland
[2] Erlang Solutions Ltd., London, United Kingdom
michal.ptaszek@erlang-solutions.com, malawski@agh.edu.pl

Abstract. This paper shows how Erlang programming language can be used for creating a framework for distributing and coordinating the execution of many task computing problems. The goals of the proposed solution are (1) to disperse the computation into many tasks, (2) to support multiple well-known computation models (such as master-worker, map-reduce, pipeline), (3) to exploit the advantages of Erlang for developing an efficient and scalable framework and (4) to build a system that can scale from small to large number of tasks with minimum effort. We present the results of work on designing, implementing and testing *ComputErl* framework. The preliminary experiments with benchmarks as well as real scientific applications show promising scalability on a computing cluster.

Keywords: many task computing, Erlang, grid, distributed computing, parallelism.

1 Introduction

In modern times, when the magnitude of data that needs to be processed on the daily basis is often far too large to consider it to be suitable for a single workstation, the importance of taking advantage of machines that form a cluster or computing grid is increasing. In most cases grid systems are aimed at performing the *coarse* grained computations that last for a relatively long time. The typical usage is to employ a big number of loosely coupled workstations to perform a highly specified, number-crunching and computationally intensive job.

Erlang as a functional programming language, focusing on concurrency, distribution and robustness [1], has taken a measure of a tool that allows programmers to build a highly scalable systems. However, although Erlang has never had a strong position in the computational science, it has been used several times as a highly-scalable middleware layer responsible for coordination and message transport[1,2] as well as a tool acting as a key-value storage [2].

One of main goals for this work was to prove that Erlang is capable of handling a massive-scale computation coordination. We specifically focus on *fine-grained*

---

[1] http://www.heroku.com
[2] http://www.facebook.com/notes.php?id=9445547199

R. Page, Z. Horváth, and V. Zsók (Eds.): TFP 2010, LNCS 6546, pp. 184–197, 2011.
© Springer-Verlag Berlin Heidelberg 2011

computational tasks in so-called *many task* computing model [3] which is gaining importance in many petascale applications [4]. A *task* is a small part of computing job, operating independently on its own data chunk, executed in parallel with its siblings. In the system we focus on, the number of tasks within a single job is very high (thousands/millions), however the processing time of each one is short (up to few minutes).

In this paper, we present the *ComputErl* framework written in Erlang which allows researchers to perform distributed jobs computing in heterogeneous environment involving utilization of the common computation paradigms. In section 2 we describe the main goals and requirements of the *ComputErl* framework. The analysis of existing solutions for many-task computing problems is given in section 3. The main concepts of our solution are presented in section 4, with details on supported multiple computational models in section 5. Section 6 gives the example applications and tests, while section 7 concludes our discussions and outlines the future work.

2   Goals and Requirements of *ComputErl*

The main goals of our work are to investigate whether Erlang can be used to build a scalable, flexible and extensible system supporting many task computing model. These goals can be summarized as follows:

Enlarging the scale
 The system should be scalable to run on wide range of machine sizes: on a standalone desktop machine, on a local cluster, on top of computing grid systems (like Grid5000[3] or PL-Grid[4] infrastructure) as well in cloud environment (like Amazon EC2[5]).

Support for different computation models
 Most of the tools that are already available provide only a very limited support for commonly used computation models, such as master-slave or map-reduce. Jobs submitted to the grid systems have generally the same workflow/dataflow structure, thus the tool should support formalization of typical processing paradigms and combining them hierarchically in a customizable and configurable way to fit the application structure.

Transparency of execution
 Another requirement for the tool is to facilitate the adaptation to the new environment. Switching from several workstations to the large scale system is often painful and requires learning new interfaces of the grid middleware tools, rewriting job descriptors and sometimes even altering the whole architecture.

 In order to reduce this effort, the created framework should hide all the difficulties related to the system-specific part, allowing to simply acquire the

---

[3] https://www.grid5000.fr
[4] http://www.plgrid.pl
[5] http://aws.amazon.com/ec2

access to the grid resources and start the tool on them without changing the application descriptors.

Extensibility

Nevertheless, the aforementioned computational models might not be sufficient for some family of problems, so the architecture of the framework ought to be flexible and extensible to support new models. The possible extension may be to support yet another model for parallel computations (for instance sorting networks) as well as the meta extension used for expressing the workflow in the system (like loops or *if-else* blocks).

Preparing a new extension responsible for handling the desired paradigm should be limited only to providing new code units: the core of the system should not be modified.

Support for heterogeneous environment

As the system is intended to hide the underlying environment from the user, it should also be able to run on top of different hardware configurations. Since Erlang executes its applications inside of its own virtual machine, the language itself provides an abstraction layer for the framework. Moreover, taking advantage of possibility of selecting and implementing new load balancing strategies leads to better hardware utilization and general performance improvement.

Fault tolerance

Since the probability of a single node failure increases together with the size of the cluster, the framework must be resistant to the breakdowns. Crash of one of the machines must not interrupt the processing that is in progress on other workstations. Additionally, the lost fragments of jobs should be rescheduled to the different, healthy nodes.

Apart from hardware failures, system ought to also be able to handle the internal crashes. Since the number of Erlang processes is going to reach huge number, the unpredicted behavior of one of them should not disturb the others. In order to achieve the proper internal isolation, framework is built obeying standard OTP design principles [5].

3   State of the Art

Since grid research area is very active nowadays, there are several solutions that might be used for many task computing family of problems.

Swift[6] is a system created at University of Chicago that supports specification, execution and management of science and engineering workflows. The tool provides its own specification language used to express and describe operations that should be performed on the data [4]. Unfortunately, *Swift* uses *Globus Toolkit* [6] as a middleware, thus it is a tedious job to configure and run it on the local, non-grid environment.

DIANE[7] is a tool for controlling and scheduling of computations on a set of distributed worker nodes [7]. The system is not limited to the grid infrastructure

---

[6] http://www.ci.uchicago.edu/swift/index.php
[7] http://it-proj-diane.web.cern.ch

and may be used with local resources. Moreover, *DIANE* makes use of *Ganga* – a front-end for job definition and management, thus its adaptation to the new job submission system should not cause any major problems [8].

The last presented solution - *DiscoProject*[8], is an implementation of the *Map-Reduce* framework for distributed computing. Although the core of the system is written in *Erlang*, the *map* and *reduce* functions provided by user are implemented in *Python*. The project has a large and active community and is still under heavy development.

From all approaches, *DiscoProject* is the most similar solution to the *ComputErl* system, however it is focused only on the Map-Reduce computing model.

4   Main Concepts of *ComputErl*

The system follows the algorithmic skeleton approach as the parallel design pattern [9]. Skeleton itself describes "(...) the structure of a particular style of algorithm, in the way in which *higher order functions* represent general computational frameworks in the context of functional programming languages. The user must describe a solution to a problem as an instance of appropriate skeleton". According to the design, each skeleton is implemented and considered independently from the other.

The concept of the system is shown in Fig. 1. The general idea is to provide a possibility to transparently execute multiple jobs/tasks at the same time, distributing them on the available resources. System, as the coordinator, will be responsible for handling the load balancing and communication, assigning tasks to nodes and monitoring the processing. The implication of that fact is that several different jobs might occupy the same node and tasks belonging to the same job might be spread over the cluster and executed in parallel on different machines. As one of the major requirements for the framework is to hide the infrastructure complexity, from the user point of view there is no difference, besides the performance, if the system is running on single machine or is using a network of loosely coupled nodes.

Since *ComputErl* has been designed and implemented as a tool for users who do not necessarily have to be Erlang programmers, the system can be perceived as a black-box that should be fed with the job description files. Each computation request submitted to the system must be described by two parameters: configuration file and the input data location.

The first parameter - configuration - is an Erlang parsable file, i.e. *file:consult/1*[9] function should be able to read and interpret its contents. The configuration file should consist of a single root element specifying an entry point for the job: {*computation_type, Type, Conf*}. *Type* parameter is an atom defining the computational model used in the given execution phase. The third element of the tuple, *Conf*, is a list of arguments that will be provided as a configuration to the main

---

[8] http://discoproject.org
[9] http://www.erlang.org/doc/man/file.html#consult-1

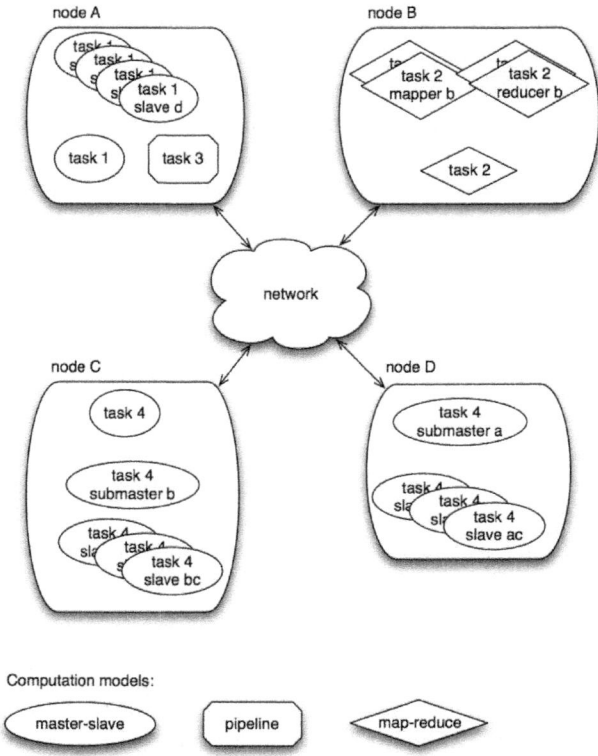

Fig. 1. Concept of the *ComputErl*: tasks belonging to multiple computation models are distributed over the computing nodes

process for the current step. The configuration parameters depend on the chosen computation model.

The programming language in which *ComputErl* has been written - Erlang - has been chosen because of the many reasons. The main advantages are:

lightweight processes – since the system is intended to be massively parallel, delegating well defined roles to the separate process instances simplifies the design and implementation. Developer does not need to bother about the operating system resources (each process consumes 331 words of memory at its startup), nor about creation time (circa 5-10 μs).

process isolation – together with the size of the system the probability of the failure grows. In order to avoid data loss or corruption, Erlang follows the *share-nothing* strategy. This means that no data (unless intentionally exposed) is shared between the processes. Crash in one of the processes does not cause the collapse of the whole system and is limited only to the small subset of processes which were linked to the erroneous one.

dynamic nature – in Erlang it is possible to inject new code without recompiling or stopping the whole system. Providing new computation models does not require changing the core of the system. To enable new functionality, developer ought to implement a set of callback modules for the given *Type* which will take care of processing the incoming data.

transparency of execution – since process identifiers encapsulate all the information needed for communication, hence from the code point of view there is no difference if the target process resides on the same node or is evaluating its code on the remote VM. In consequence a developer might implement the logic of the application without knowledge of process location.

well-defined system structure – as the scale of the system is far beyond the size of regular desktop application, the process relationship should be well-defined and structuralized. Following OTP principles regarding the architecture it is possible to design and implement a system that is clear and easy to maintain. All processes running within *ComputErl* system are grouped under special supervisor instances which, in turn, form a hierarchical arrangement called supervision tree.

5   Supported Computation Models

The *ComputErl* framework provides a possibility to express the application structure using a dedicated job description language based on the standard Erlang syntax. Although the system is able to follow whichever model user chooses, though - as a proof of a concept - three major approaches have been implemented. These are:

— master-slave,
— map-reduce,
— pipeline.

5.1   Master-Slave

The **Master-slave** computing model defines two types of execution units [10]:

— master processes, usually one for the whole computation, take care of coordinating the slaves work: distributing the data among them and collecting the results.
— slave processes that belong to one master, execute the requested command on the given data chunk and produces the results that are sent back to the caller. The number of slaves is configurable for each job.

When the computation begins, each worker process gets the data chunk assigned from its master. As soon as the processing of that data part ends, the slave returns the result and indicate that it is ready to handle the next task. Each master has also the dedicated *result saver* process attached, which is responsible for collecting the results and saving them to disk. When master's pending chunk queue is empty and all the slave processes finished their work, the whole process terminates and stops all the workers as well.

Because the amount of data chunks assigned to the single master might be very large, in order to avoid the potential bottlenecks several improvements to this model have been made.

To eliminate a situation when one process is flooded by the results from hundreds of workers, it is possible to define the maximum number of data chunks per master. When the boundary is exceeded, the coordinator process, instead of spawning the workers, creates an additional layer of master processes, dividing the data equally among them. New masters location is chosen by the *scheduler* process running on a master node. The algorithm is repeated until the number of tasks assigned to the single master is less than a given limit. A number of masters created on the new level is also parametrized.

The second improvement is related to the location of workers against the master. Since the system has been designed to handle a great number of small tasks at the same time, the overhead caused by the data marshaling and unmarshaling might level the profit of parallel execution. To avoid such a situation the workers are spawned on the same machine as masters.

This architectural decision implies a fact that the hardware parallelism is determined by the number of sub-masters. The workers themselves are used to take advantage of the CPU cores available within the assigned node.

5.2   Map-Reduce

Map-reduce - computational paradigm originally designed by Google to support the parallel large data sets processing [11]. Users provide two functions that are operating on the inputs:

- *map* - takes an input chunk and emits a set of intermediate key/value pairs.
- *reduce* - accepts the intermediate key and a set of values connected to it. *Reduce* function should merge its input data usually into zero or one output values.

The outputs of the reduce functions are treated as the outputs of the whole computation process. In *ComputErl* there are three types of processes involved in the map-reduce phase:

- *coordinator* - a finite state machine that distributes the data among the children processes and is responsible for grouping the map outputs by the key,
- *mappers* - group of processes that execute the configured mapping function,
- *reducers* - group of processes that execute the configured reducing function.

Both number of mappers and reducers can be configured separately.

Since the communication between the job coordinator and mapper/reducer processes is not very intensive (both input data and computation results are passed as a single message), both mappers and reducers are spawned on the remote nodes in the cluster.

5.3 Pipeline

Pipeline - a meta-pattern for connecting and scheduling the subsequent phases of more complex computations. When using that model a user describes a flow of the data within the system.

The flow is basically a list of subtasks that should be executed in the given order. The processing starts from the first subtask, which is fed with the original input data. Then, the result of each phase becomes an input for the next one. Outcomes of the last step become a result of the whole pipeline flow.

In this model, each subtask might be computed using any of the available models: master-slave, map-reduce, pipeline or the one provided by the user. When using that model, only one coordinator process is created.

6 Sample Applications

In order to prove the correctness of the framework, it has been tested using four benchmarks, representing typical applications.

6.1 Sleep Benchmark

This benchmark has been used only to prove the tool is able to distribute the job parts over the workers without dropping on the performance. *Sleep* task accepts as an input an integer which is a number of seconds that worker process should sleep for. As a result the script yields a string containing hostname where it has been executed, time on that host and the assigned sleep interval. The computation model chosen to accomplish the goal was master-slave. The configuration describing such a job is presented in Fig. 2

In order to verify the correctness, benchmark has been run on up to 100 physical machines. The parallel efficiency and speedup plots are presented in Fig. 3.

```
1   {computation_type , master_slave ,
2    [{output_file , "/tmp/sleep_output . out"},
3     {script , "scripts/sleep.sh"},
4     {max_tasks_per_master , 1},
5     {slaves_no , 1}]}.
```

Fig. 2. Sleep benchmark configuration

6.2 Mandelbrot Set Generation

The second benchmark *ComputErl* framework has been tested on is a job that renders the Mandelbrot set.

The job for in this benchmark is for a given image size to produce a file consisting of pairs: X, Y, R, G, B; where X, Y are the coordinates of each point

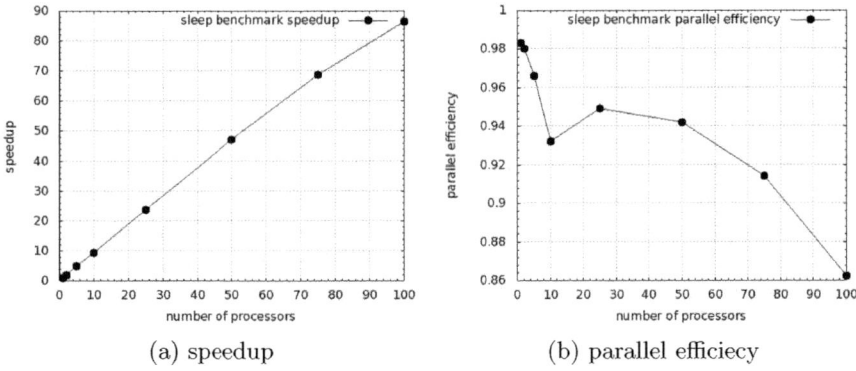

(a) speedup   (b) parallel efficiecy

Fig. 3. *sleep* benchmark speedup and parallel efficiency plots

on the picture, while R, G and B are the color coefficients in the RGB color representation model. All values are non-negative integers. Each task is defined as a computation of RGB value for a given pixel. The executable file uses *Python* programming language to implement the algorithm.

The job consists of two phases: input data generation – that is producing a list of all possible (X, Y) pairs and, in second step, computing the actual pixel color.

The chosen computation model for this job was pipeline that links two master-slave subprocesses. First master takes an image size as a parameter and creates a file with pixel coordinates $(X, Y$ pairs) - one for each row. A reference to this file is passed to the second phase master which distributes the data inside to the linked workers. Each worker computes the color of the assigned point and returns it back to the coordinator.

Since the number of tasks grows very fast (for *MxN* pixel image its number reaches $M \cdot N$) the single master would be overloaded with the slaves result submissions and next chunk requests. Because of that there is a need to spawn at least one more masters layer in the master-slave tree.

The configuration used for those tests is presented in Fig. 4.

6.3   Distributed Grep

Next benchmark has been introduced in order to check how good the *map-reduce* paradigm implementation is. The purpose of the application is to extract and point out the lines in the huge sets of text files that match a given pattern. However, if the pattern we are looking for does not occur more than a specified number of times in the same file, that particular file should not be listed in the results.

The job consists of two Python scripts implementing map and reduce functions. The first script, *grep.py* iterates over a given file and for each line that matches the pattern given in the regular expression format, emits a pair: *(filename, line*

```
1  {computation_type , pipeline ,
2        [[{computation_type , master_slave ,
3            {slaves_no , 1}]},
4          {output_file , "/tmp/coords.out"},
5          {script , "scripts/coords.py"}],
6
7          [{computation_type , master_slave ,
8           {result_delimiter , "\n\n"},
9
10           {max_tasks_per_master , 20},
11           {masters_per_level , 3},
12
13           {slaves_no , 8}]},
14
15        {output_file , "/tmp/mandelbrot.out"},
16        {script , "scripts/mandelbrot.py -2 -1 1 1"}
17        ]
18  ]}.
```

Fig. 4. Mandelbrot benchmark configuration

number). The second one - *reduce.py* - accepts two parameters: the filename and a list of line numbers in which the pattern has been found. If the length of the list is greater than a given threshold, an output line in format *filename:line number* is produced.

As an input 3800 text files from *Project Gutenberg*[10] have been used. Total size of the input reached 1.6 GB. In the sequential approach processing time for the whole set came to 542 seconds.

The best results has been achieved when using the configuration in Fig. 5.

```
1  {computation_type , map_reduce ,
2    [{mappers_no , 40},
3     {mapper_params ,
4      [{script , "scripts/grep/grep.py"}]},
5
6     {reducers_no , 20},
7     {reducer_params ,
8      [{script , "scripts/grep/reduce.py"}]},
9
10     {output_file , "/tmp/dist_grep"}]
11  }.
```

Fig. 5. Distributed grep benchmark configuration

---

[10] http://www.gutenberg.org/

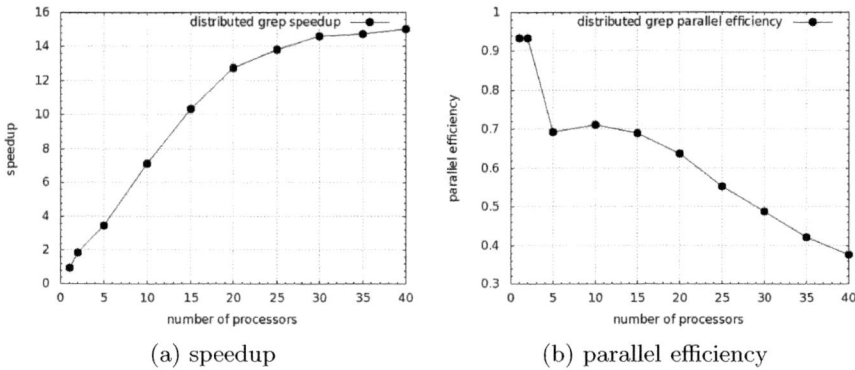

(a) speedup   (b) parallel efficiency

Fig. 6. *distributed grep* benchmark speedup and parallel efficiency plots

The preliminary results of the testing are presented in Fig. 6. The tests were run on a cluster of machines (Zeus at ACC Cyfronet AGH), each node having 2 Xeon Quadcore 2.5 GHz processors with 16 GB of RAM and 10 Gb/s inter-node connection. The nodes use a shared Lustre filesystem[11].

We expect that further performance improvements may be possible by introducing a distributed filesystem which allows to exploit data locality [11]. In the current configuration all data access requires network transmission, which limits the performance of data-intensive computing.

6.4   Bioinformatics Application

The last benchmark approach was to test *ComputErl* framework on a real application from bioinformatics domain. The application predicts the active sites of proteins based on FOD model [12]. The scripts that are used during the tests has been provided by the scientists who are using them on the daily basis. Apart from the implementation the job also requires the data files containing protein structure.

The tests were executed using all possible scale-input data configuration, which gave 162792 single script runs (7752 inputs, 21 different scales). Job has been divided into 7752 tasks: a single task has been defined as a multiple profile generator for all the available scales (21 subproblems) for the given input data (protein description). Every script execution produced 21 generated profiles. Total size of output files exceeds 3.5 GB of disk space. Since the total size of the all output data produced was too big for a single process to handle, the additional data savers were attached to each master process.

In order to accomplish the goal, the simple configuration for master-slave has been used. Its listing shows that preparing *ComputErl* to execute new job is fast and easy.

The configuration used for this application can be found in Fig. 7.

---

[11] http://wiki.lustre.org/

```
1  { computation_type , master_slave ,
2    [{ script , "scripts/profiles.sh "} ,
3      { output_file , "/tmp/profiles.out "}
4    ]
5  } .
```

Fig. 7. Bioinformatics application configuration

Tests have been performed using the default settings for master-slave model: having 10 slaves under each master, maximum 100 tasks for each of the coordinator and spawning 10 new master processes per new level.

The graphical representation of results obtained on the same machine as the grep benchmark (Zeus cluster) is available in Figure 8.

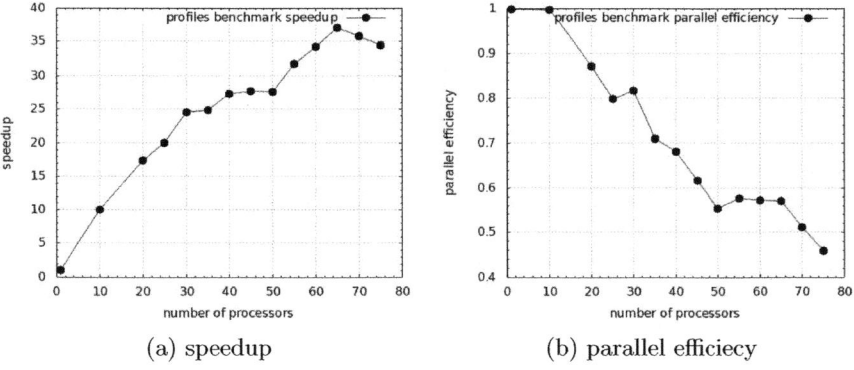

(a) speedup   (b) parallel efficiecy

Fig. 8. *profiles* benchmark speedup and parallel efficiency plots

7   Conclusions and Future Work

All the tests have been successfully executed and they have demonstrated that the framework does scale well on the large clusters of machines, and is capable of handling massive number of tasks at the same time.

Thanks to the OTP principles, controlling a highly concurrent, dynamic and parallel system turned out to be manageable: the supervision tree structure allowed building a clear and simple process' relationship graph, Erlang's built-in lightweight process support helped forget about the complexity of native operating system threads handling and synchronizing and finally the dynamic nature of language created an easy way to extend the existing solution via the user-provided callback modules. *ComputErl* turned out to be a very flexible utility, which can be run on top of potentially any of the modern computing grid systems or local clusters.

Nevertheless, *ComputErl* is still in its early days and a lot of work must be done before the tool would be regarded as a mature and competitive solution to the existing ones. Planned future work includes:

- Implementing and testing more meta-patterns, such as *if-else* branches, *for* or *while* loops. Having those structures may allow users to build more flexible and sophisticated data flow graphs for their computations.
- Load balancing strategy optimizations. One of the most interesting directions to go is to employ the existing tools to do the measurements (like *Ganglia* [13]) and basing on them, choose the least loaded target machine to deploy a given task on.
- Fault tolerance improvements. Using some kind of the persistent storage it should be possible to save (*checkpoint*) the intermediate data in between the phases of the computations. The persistence layer ought to protect the computed data from getting lost because of some unpredicted events, such as hardware failure. The framework, right after a failure detection, would be responsible for restarting the lost parts of the job on the other node, starting from the last snapshot that has been saved.

The *ComputErl* framework is available to the public as an open-source project at: http://bitbucket.org/michalptaszek/gridagh

Acknowledgments. The authors express their thanks to Katarzyna Prymula for providing the bioinformatics application for testing. The experiments were conducted on the Zeus cluster at ACC Cyfronet AGH. The research presented in this paper has been partially supported by the European Union within the European Regional Development Fund program no. POIG.02.03.00-00-007/08-00 as part of the PL-Grid project (http://www.plgrid.pl) and AGH grants 11.11.120.865 and UDA-POKL.04.01.01-00-367/08-00. We would also like to thank Jan Henry Nyström for his help on reviewing the paper.

References

1. Cesarini, F., Thompson, S.: Erlang Programming. O'Reilly Media, Sebastopol (2009)
2. DeCandia, G., Hastorun, D., Jampani, M., Kakulapati, G., Lakshman, A., Pilchin, A., Sivasubramanian, S., Vosshall, P., Vogels, W.: Dynamo: Amazon's highly available key-value store. In: SOSP 2007: Proceedings of twenty-first ACM SIGOPS Symposium on Operating Systems Principles, vol. 41, pp. 205–220. ACM, New York (2007)
3. Foster, I.: Many Tasks Computing: What's in a Name? (July 2008)
4. Wilde, M., Foster, I., Iskra, K., Beckman, P., Zhang, Z., Espinosa, A., Hategan, M., Clifford, B., Raicu, I.: Parallel scripting for applications at the petascale and beyond. Computer 42(11), 50–60 (2009)
5. AB Ericsson: OTP Design Principles User's Guide (February 2010)
6. Foster, I.: Globus toolkit version 4: Software for service-oriented systems. In: Jin, H., Reed, D., Jiang, W. (eds.) NPC 2005. LNCS, vol. 3779, pp. 2–13. Springer, Heidelberg (2005), http://dx.doi.org/10.1007/11577188_2

7. Mościcki, J.T.: Diane - distributed analysis environment for grid-enabled simulation and analysis of physics data. In: Nuclear Science Symposium Conference Record, vol. 3, pp. 1617–1620. IEEE, Los Alamitos (2003)
8. Mościcki, J.T., Brochu, F., Ebke, J., Egede, U., Elmsheuser, J., Harrison, K., Jones, R.W.L., Lee, H.C., Liko, D., Maier, A.: Ganga: a tool for computational-task management and easy access to grid resources. Computer Physics Communications (June 2009)
9. Cole, M.: Algorithmic Skeletons: Structured Management of Parallel Computation. MIT Press, Pitman (1989)
10. Shao, G., Berman, F., Wolski, R.: Master/slave computing on the grid. In: Heterogeneous Computing Workshop, pp. 3–16 (2000)
11. Dean, J., Ghemawat, S.: Mapreduce: simplified data processing on large clusters. Commun. ACM 51(1), 107–113 (2008)
12. Bryliński, M., Prymula, K., Jurkowski, W., Kochańczyk, M., Stawowczyk, E., Konieczny, L., Roterman, I.: Prediction of functional sites based on the fuzzy oil drop model. PLoS Comput. Biol. 3(5), e94 (2007)
13. Massie, M.L., Chun, B.N., Culler, D.E.: The Ganglia Distributed Monitoring System: Design, Implementation, and Experience. Parallel Computing 30(7) (July 2004)

Monad Factory: Type-Indexed Monads

Mark Snyder and Perry Alexander

The University of Kansas,
Information and Telecommunication Technology Center,
2335 Irving Hill Rd, Lawrence, KS 66045
{marks,alex}@ittc.ku.edu

Abstract. Monads provide a greatly useful capability to pure languages in simulating side-effects, but implementations such as the Monad Transformer Library [1] in Haskell prohibit reuse of those side-effects such as threading through two different states without some explicit work-around. Monad Factory provides a straightforward solution for *opening* the non-proper morphisms by indexing monads at both the type-level and term-level, allowing 'copies' of the monads to be created and simultaneously used within even the same monadic transformer stack. This expands monads' applicability and mitigates the amount of boilerplate code we need for monads to work together, and yet we use them nearly identically to non-indexed monads.

Keywords: monads, Haskell, type-level programming.

1 Introduction

Programming with monads in Haskell provides a rich set of tools to the pure functional programmer, but their homogeneous nature sometimes proves unsatisfactory. Due to functional dependencies in the Monad Transformer Library (`mtl`), an individual monad can only be used in one way in a fragment of code, such as using the `State` monad to store a particular state type. When a programmer wants to use a monad in multiple ways at once, some hack or work-around is necessary, such as using a record structure or carefully `lift`-ing through a specific monad transformer stack. While monad transformers allow us to combine the effects of different monads, we cannot directly use transformers to combine the effects of a particular monad multiple times. The problem grows as code from various sources begins to interact–when using existing code, a monad's usage might be "reserved" for some orthogonal use; should you edit that code, even if you can? Even when we give in and re-implement a common monad to differentiate between the uses, we must provide instances for a host of other common monads in defining the transformer, including providing an instance relating to the the copied monad–these details require more knowledge about monads than simply using them. We seek a more adaptable process for capturing monadic behavior, and expect some streamlining, re-usability, and a less error-prone process than some ad-hoc options that are commonly used. In particular, we expect to write fewer instances for transformer inter-operability.

R. Page, Z. Horváth, and V. Zsók (Eds.): TFP 2010, LNCS 6546, pp. 198–213, 2011.
© Springer-Verlag Berlin Heidelberg 2011

This paper introduces *type-indexed monads*, which allow for multiple distinct instances of a monad to coexist, via explicit annotations. A simple type class links the term-level index and the type-level index together, allowing both type inference and evaluation to differentiate between instances of monads.

An arbitrary number of these indexed monads can coexist, making monadic programming more modular and more flexible. This 'factory' approach solves some of the problems associated with non-indexed monads, and avoids the need for early design decisions on monad usage.

This approach tries to work with the existing implementation and existing code based on mtl, rather than propose massive re-writing. Perhaps most interestingly, the core technique may prove useful for other cases where a functional dependency causes instance selection to be problematic.

This work provides the following contributions:

- Particular monadic side-effects (such as state maintenance) may be used multiple times simultaneously, without affecting each other's usage.
- Type-indexed monads are compatible with existing monadic code, so we do not have to prepare our existing code to accomodate type-indexed monads. They can be stacked together in a monad transformer stack, also with the monads found in the Monad Transformer Library provided with GHC [2].
- Libraries that use common monadic effects don't need a local copy of any monad along with all the requisite instances. We discuss why that libraries might resort to re-implementing monads, providing a mechanism for removing the code duplication in favor of a re-usable solution. This saves effort and mitigates the error-prone process of monad implementation.
- When we combine monad transformers, we need an instance describing how every pair of transformers can be lifted through each other; this quadratic number of required instances is mitigated, as we provide instances that address the entire indexed family of monads. As long as type-indexed monads can define the needed semantics, there are no more instances to create.
- The State, Reader, Writer, RWS, and Error monads are implemented as type-indexed monads (available on Hackage [3]).

We identify the concept of a type-indexed monad, then build upon the initial definitions of monads to guide the type-indexed versions of monads. Type-indexed monads do not attempt to provide a simplified interface to monads. Rather, the point is to make heterogeneous monad usage simpler and more convenient for a programmer who has already overcome the hurdle of understanding monads.

2 Problem

Monads are a mechanism often used for simulating effectful computation in a pure language like Haskell. They are pervasive in Haskell programs, yet the mechanism used to define them in the Monad Transformer Library—type classes and the related instances—has drawbacks.

Type classes indicate that any given instance type has the overloaded functions defined for it. Consider the monad `State s`, and the associated type class `MonadState s m`.

```
class (Monad m) ⇒ MonadState s m | m → s where
  get :: m s
  put :: s → m ()

newtype State s a = State {runState :: (s → (a,s))}

instance MonadState s (State s) where
  get   = State $ λs → (s, s)
  put s = State $ λ_ → ((), s)
```

`MonadState` defines a set of 'non-proper morphisms', `get` and `put` (as opposed to 'proper' morphisms like `return` and `>>=`). We have an instance of `MonadState` defined for the `State` monad, meaning that we can use `get` and `put` to construct monadic values. The problem arises that `s` must be determinable by `m`. For a given monadic computation for some `m`, `get` always gets a value of a particular type. We can't use `get` and `put` to store multiple `s`'s, and we can't use them to store values of different types. The functional dependency `m→s` at once allows us to use `State` at various types for `s` in separate places in our code, and restricts us from using `State` at various types in the *same* code.

Example—Design Decisions, Implications. Suppose we are writing a library of monadic code. We want to provide some abstractions of operations that happen to maintain an environment of name-value pairs and pass around an integer as state; the actual purpose of the library is irrelevant. If we were free to be direct, we might actually use the `State` and `Reader` monads to manage our `[(String,v)]` and `Int` values for us. As we develop our library, we realize that we need some extra values to be kept in `State`; since we've already used `State`, we end up instead moving to a record as our state–indeed, many programmers would have started with this approach to avoid the tedious translation through the code. Now we can add to this record all the state we want, as long as we are designing the library and not just using it. An issue arises, in that `State` computations now have access to all fields of the record. Just as we would like to have separation in our processes' memory, we would like a guarantee of the separation of access to our different pieces of state. Some [4] use separate copies of the `State` monad to guarantee that separation. We will see that type-indexed monads are, at the type level, incapable of accessing or modifying each other's contents, and may be ideally suited to such work.

Our library will surely be exciting and popular, and we want to be savvy to our users' needs–they might want to use our library in their own monadic code that already uses `State` and `Reader`–so we create our own `MyLibM` monad (and transformer version) that provides the exact features of `State` and `Reader`, as well as the many `instances` needed for it to be a monad and be 'stackable' (combined via the monad transformers) with the original `State` and `Reader`.

As our library gains in popularity, some users want to expand on the state stored in our record–but it is *closed*–just as we can't add constructors to a `data` definition except at the source, we can't add fields to a record except in its initial definition. Another user decides they want to use our library in a way we hadn't anticipated–they want to use it for a few different things at once, and they have to play a rousing game of 'count the `lifts`' in order to use the `MyLibM` monad twice or more in the same transformer stack. Another user wants to use their own hand-written monad with ours, and has to write a few more instances to make the two interact appropriately, even though they already have instances for `State` and `Reader`.

Through this entire process, we find problems whenever we want to expand a monad's usage or re-use it. We have some closed definitions, code copies of some monads, and some unhappy library users that had to create their own work-arounds for our code. What if we could use a monad for its effects in multiple ways without having to resort to records (and other similar approaches, such as `HLists`)? What if we didn't have to create our own `State` and `Reader` monads just to make sure the library users still had free use of it?

Type-indexed monads aleviate these problems by allowing us to use different type-level indexes to differentiate between intended uses of a monad. In our library example, this means that we can have several `State` constraints over our code to thread different states through our code at once (whether or not the states' types happen to match). Instead of using a record type, we could just use another index of the monad if we chose. Instead of copying the functionality of monads into our own `MyLibM` monad, we can create an index to use; whether we export that index or not also gives us control over how the library may be used. The indexed versions are distinct from the original definitions, and they may be used together. The library users can now use `State` to their own liking (and multiple times as well) without interfering with library code. They can even use the library code at different indexes in the same code, and it only requires different type-indexes, and no tedious `lifting`, which can easily be abused. We also gain a guarantee of separation–we don't worry about one `get` affecting the wrong monad, as the types wouldn't line up–we gain this separation by the parametricity of the type-indexed monads' definitions. We can have one set of instances that work for any number of indexes, meaning if we can define our monad in terms of those offered in indexed style, we won't have any new instances to write, nor will users downstream. The number of instances is usually quadratic in the number of monads in the transformer stack, so this becomes more valuable as more monads are stacked.

3 Type-Indexed Monads

In order to provide a mechanism for type-indexed monads, we must account for differentiation between type-indexed monads at both the term-level for evaluation, and also at the type-level during typing. We consider some possible example uses to visualize type-indexed monad usage, and then provide details of a realizable implementation. The concept itself arose as a realization that McBride [5] uses type-level representations of numbers to create indexes that simulate terms at the type level; the dependent feel of explicitly indexing monads seems like a plausible avenue for type-level programming.

We use the `State` monad as our running example, though of course others are also implemented. Instead of using a non-proper morphism and expecting Haskell to infer the index we are using, we explicitly label each usage. If we relied on an inference mechanism (with no index argument), that would preclude the opportunity of using multiple copies of a monad that happened to operate on the same type, e.g. using two different `State` monads to store different sets of available registers in a compiler. If we are creating type-indexed monads, they should closely resemble usage of the original non-indexed version. We add the explicit indexing parameter as a first parameter to all non-proper morphisms. By convention, we add an 'x' (or 'X') to all labels to differentiate them from the original monad definition rather than rely on name qualifications. This explicit indexing will allow us to use different type-indexes with `StateX` to store the same type of state.

As an introduction to the syntax and feel of type-indexed monads, consider a basic monadic successor function, and a similar function that increases two separate states, using `StateX` monads:

```
succM :: (MonadState Int m) ⇒ m ()
succM = do n ← get
           put $ n+1

succ2M :: (MonadStateX Index1 Int m, MonadStateX Index2 Int m) ⇒ m ()
succ2M = do x ← getx Index1
            y ← getx Index2
            putx Index1 $ x+1
            putx Index2 $ y+1
```

Instead of providing separate `get1` and `get2` functions, we parameterize the `get` function to operate over the index as well. This feels similar to the record-as-state approach mentioned in the introduction, except that we can leave previous uses of `State` untouched. Also, this approach is open to further indexed uses. If we were to try to use `lift`s in order to use `State` twice, we might specify that `(put 1 >> lift (put 5)) :: StateT Int (State Int) ()`. To express this via constraints, the type may be written as `(MonadState Int (t m), MonadState Int m, MonadTrans t) ⇒ t m ()`. It's possible, but this gets messier as we add more constraints: we are specifying the transformer stack in our type. We would like to separate this concern, especially if we want to combine the code with code that has a more constrained type. We could perhaps use abstractions to hide the lifting, but this is still one more step that we have to do, and that we can get wrong. Phantom typing [6] won't help us here: an expression such as `(put 5)` doesn't give enough information to know into which `Int`-state to put the 5–either one would be plausible embedded in a do-expression, so there's no 'best' answer for the phantom to find or check for us.

Type-indexed monads clearly need to have distinct types. Haskell does not have dependent types, so our indexing must appear at the type level as well. Seeking openness, we express the type of a monadic computation by constraining it rather than constructing it. We define what characteristics a monadic computation must include, rather than directly defining it. The type of succ2M states that m is a monad exibiting the behavior of the (MonadStateX Index1 Int) instance, as well as the MonadStateX Index2 Int) instance. It is important to realize that succ2M can be used in any monadic computation that includes at least these non-proper morphisms. Other type-indexed uses may be later incorporated with use of succ2M.

3.1 Creating Type-Indexes

We want to create an index that exists at both the type and value level uniquely. The type-level representation is used in differentiating the type of one type-indexed monad from another, and the value-level representation is used in differentiating a value of one type-indexed monad from another. We also need a link between the two—type inference needs to know that a particular index value always refers to a particular type-level index, and constructing values of a particularly-indexed monad requires knowing how to represent the type-level index in order to generate a value of that type-indexed monad, for instance when returning a value. The Index type class exactly represents that correspondence between the term-level and type-level.

```
class Index ix where
   getVal :: ix
```

Creating a new type index comes in two predictable steps: we generate a simple atomic datatype, and provide an instance for Index.

```
data MyIndex = MyIndex deriving (Show, Eq)

instance Index MyIndex where   getVal = MyIndex
```

A singleton datatype and a trivial instance for each index are all we need for a new index to index into the monads. Template Haskell could be used to further-simplify the process, but it is already short. This simple addition of an index at both levels is all we need to completely introduce type-indexed monads. The idea is simple, direct, and gives us more options in how we use and think of monads.

We can now proceed to use these values at the type and term level interchangeably (via getVal and ::) in order to differentiate between instances of a monad.

3.2 Implementation

Just as in the implementation of the mtl monads, indexed monads will each require (i) a data constructor or newtype; (ii) an instance for the Monad type class;

(iii) a type class for the non-proper morphisms; (iv) an instance for the datatype at that type class; and (v) a transformer version that satisfies the MonadTrans type class in order to be combined with other monads in a transformer stack. We develop the StateX monad, showing how automatic a translation it is from the original definition of State. We will underline all indexing code—the remaining code would define the original, non-indexed monad. The type-indexed version should directly arise from this prescriptive process of adding indexes. The same process works on other monads such as Reader and Writer, but is not shown for brevity's sake.

The StateX Monad. We create the necessary data structure to represent a computation of the StateX monad, as well as a run function. We use newtype just as mtl does. We additionally define mkStateX to allow tagging the index type without directly ascribing a type, though this is only needed in the monad's definition and not in usage. We split the run function in two for the same reason.

The recurrent theme in indexing a monad is to have a value of the index type (its index value) be the first parameter to every non-proper morphism, and to include the index as a type parameter to the data structure and type class. The index is simply a label at the type level, and we use those labels to help identify which 'instance' of the monad is affected. The run function states that, given an index ix, a monadic computation of the *same* index of the monad and a starting state, we should execute the computation with that starting state. It is precisely the same as the original definition, except that we now index the monad at each usage.

```
newtype StateX ix s a = StateX {runStateX' :: s -> (a, s)}
mkStateX :: (Index ix) => ix -> (s->(a,s)) -> StateX ix s a
mkStateX _ v = StateX v
runStateX :: (Index ix) => ix -> StateX ix s a -> (s->(a,s))
runStateX _ m s = runStateX' m s
```

For StateX to be a monad, it must provide definitions for >>= and return. Again, notice we must always ensure the index matches. We also see the way in which the only function of the Index type class is used, to generate a value corresponding to a particular type, effectively converting the type down to the only value that inhabits the type (ignoring bottom). Otherwise, the code is quite similar to the State monad's Monad instance.

```
instance (Index ix) ⇒ Monad (StateX ix s) where
  return a = mkStateX (getVal::ix) $ λ s → (a,s)
  ((StateX x)::StateX ix s a) >>= f = mkStateX (getVal::ix) $ λ s →
                case (x s) of (v,s') → runStateX' (f v) s'
```

We also require a type class for the non-proper morphisms of our type-indexed monad, and we replicate the MonadState type class to handle our type-indexed versions.

```
class (Monad m, Index ix) => MonadStateX ix s m | ix m → s where
  getx :: ix → m s
  putx :: ix → s → m ()
```

The getx and putx functions are identical to those found in MonadState, except
for the extra parameter for the type index. We now provide the implementation
of the special effects of StateX to show how any StateX monad can perform
the special behavior of the MonadStateX class. As before, we repeat the original
definition's code, with our type-level indexing labels.

```
instance (Index ix) ⇒ MonadStateX ix s (StateX ix s) where
  getx (ixv::ix)   = StateX ixv $ λx → (x,x)
  putx (ixv::ix) s = StateX ixv $ λ_ → ((),s)
```

We now have the basic definition of a monad that we want. However, we have not
yet created a transformer version of the monad, nor have we handled the special
circumstances that arise when we use multiple monads of different indexes. Nor
have we enabled StateX to work alongside the original State monad. We turn
our attention next to handling these concerns.

The StateTX Transformer. We now create a transformer version of the
StateX monad, filling the same purpose as the StateT transformer does for
the State monad. We create a new data structure and run function. Again,
we must have the same type index to run the transformer. To complete the
definition of the StateTX monad, we must provide the relevant instances for
Monad, MonadTrans, and MonadStateX. Furthermore, to connect the StateTX
transformer to the StateX monad, we need an instance for the MonadStateX
type class in order to support the non-proper morphisms, and we need a means
of lifting monadic computations of the transformer.

```
newtype StateTX ix s m a = StateTX  runStateTX' :: s -> m (a,s)
mkStateTX :: (Index ix) => ix -> (s->m(a,s)) -> StateTX ix s m a
mkStateTX _ v = StateTX v
runStateTX :: (Index ix) => ix -> StateTX ix s m a -> s -> m (a,s)
runStateTX _ m s = runStateTX' m s

instance (Index ix, Monad m) ⇒ Monad (StateTX ix s m) where
  return a = mkStateTX (getVal::ix) $ λs → return (a,s)
  ((StateTX x)::StateTX ix s m a) >>= f = mkStateTX (getVal::ix)
                          $ λs → do (v,s') ← x s
                                    runStateTX' (f v) s'

--lifting a state transformer's operations
instance (Index ix) ⇒ MonadTrans (StateTX ix s) where
  lift x = mkStateTX (getVal::ix) $ λs'→x >>= λx'→return(x',s')

instance(Index ix,Monad m) ⇒ MonadStateX ix s (StateTX ix s m) where
  getx (ixv::ix)   = mkStateTX ixv $ λ(s1::s) → return (s1,s1)
  putx (ixv::ix) s = mkStateTX ixv $ λ_ → return ((),s)
```

By now this should look familiar. We have a transformer version of the StateX monad, and this transformer itself can be indexed. Up to this point, we haven't dealt with multiple indexes of a single kind of monad. This is the part that makes all the previous preparation worthwhile.

The following instance provides a way for index ix2 to provide the functionality of the index ix1 by explaining what to do when a getx x1 or putx ix1 computation is encountered. Note that the instance manually pipes its own state through behind the scenes by labeling the ix2 index's state (s::s2) in an abstraction, performing the computation from index ix1, and then returning the pair that further threads the ix2 index's state into the next computation. This is the key to separation of the two indexes' state.

```
instance (Monad m, Index ix1, Index ix2, MonadStateX ix1 s1 m )
   ⇒ MonadStateX ix1 s1 (StateTX ix2 s2 m) where
  getx (ixv::ix1) = mkStateTX (getVal::ix2) $ λ(s::s2) → do
                                         v1 ← getx (ixv::ix1)
                                         return (v1,s))
  putx (ixv::ix1) v1 = mkStateTX (getVal::ix2) $ λ(s::s2) → do
                                         putx (ixv::ix1) v1
                                         return ((),s)
```

In short, this defines how two indexes can coexist without affecting each other. It relies on the type information of the index, and *not* on the type information of what state is held by each monad. Each type-indexed monad could hold the same type of state and never be confused for another.

This does require GHC's OverlappingInstances pragma (among others) to be enabled. However, the overlap should only be required in the above instance to differentiate between two indexes that are easily tested for equality, and the pragma is not required at the site of usage.

Interoperability. One of our stated goals is to reuse particular monadic features with existing code that most likely uses the original definitions of monads. We should therefore be able to mix the indexed versions of a monad with the original. We show in this section how to mix the State and StateX monads. The indexed monads provided in the Hackage package all can be used with the mtl monads.

Even in the definitions of Haskell's library-provided monads, they must provide instances for each monad to interact with every other. These 'cooperation' instances occupy a large part of the mtl's codebase. We want the StateTX transformer monad to be able to provide the MonadState functionality, and we want the StateT transformer monad to provide the MonadStateX functionality. Each of these needs results in a new instance, simply defining the state management and adding the index labeling at the type level.

```
instance (MonadState s1 m, Index ix) ⇒ MonadState s1 (StateTX ix s2 m)
   where
  get   = mkStateTX (getVal::ix) $ λs → do n ← get
                                          return (n,s)
```

```
put v = mkStateTX (getVal::ix) $ λs → put v >>= return ((),s)
instance (Monad m, MonadStateX ix s1 m, Index ix)
    ⇒ MonadStateX ix s1 (StateT s2 m) where
  getx (ixv::ix) = StateT $ λs → do n ← getx (getVal::ix)
                                    return (n,s)
  putx (ixv::ix) (v::s1) = StateT $ λs → do putx (getVal::ix) v
                                            return ((),s)
```

Although the code is not included in this paper, there is of course a need for instances often provided by monad definitions: instances for Functor, MonadFix, and instances that let the transformer version provide the non-proper morphisms of all the other 'standard' monads such as IO, Error, Writer, and Reader. This is no different than the original definitions of monads in that there is an initial price to pay for interoperability when defining the stack of monads that combine to create the monad with the desired capabilities. Similarly, we only have to define these once in a library and then simply use them. If we only need to interact with one copy of a monad, we could still just write the instances for mtl; if we need two copies, we write instances for the indexed monads; if we need any more copies, there are no more instances to write–and the indexed monad instances are essentially identical to the mtl instances. This time we gain an unlimited number of monads from it, not just one. The indexed library could even provide a set of bindings mimicking the original definitions, but implemented via the type-indexed definitions — then the library could become a drop-in replacement for even easier use. By creating another index, we hook into that entire set of instances, and *any* type-indexed monad can fully participate with all other type-indexed monads and the original mtl monads without writing more instances.

This does not entirely mitigate the need for instances. In particular, any home-grown monad still needs its own set of instances. If it does not interact with multiple copies of any one monad then we are not required to write those instances, and so no extra work is required; we simply may write one more set of instances that corresponds to an unlimited number of monads. This only serves to highlight the need to support reuse of the monad definitions.

3.3   Separation of Type-Indexed Monads

We should briefly reason about why two type-indexed StateX monads cannot access each others' state. We are interested in ensuring that one type-indexed monad cannot access a differently-indexed monad's state. We can devise a simple argument based on the types involved. The only way to access or modify the state of a StateX monad is to use the non-proper morphisms with the given index, or to directly create a StateX X_1 s_1 v_1 value. By having a single value in the index-type, we exclude the possibility of two different indexes existing at the same type. Therefore, an expression like getx X_1 :: StateX X_1 s_1 v_1 has no means of accessing the state s_2, which is tied to values of type StateX X_2 s_2 v_2. Just as Haskell disallows indexing into a list with a Boolean (xs!!True), at the type level we are excluding the possibility of using the wrong type of index to access the state. This guarantee cannot be argued as succinctly when using a record that provides unfettered access to all of its fields. By looking at the type signature of a monadic function, we can tell definitively whether it is capable of seeing or modifying a particular indexed state.

We have checked a couple of properties over the indexed state monads using QuickCheck [7]. A problem arises in that the types change when we use different indexes. This property is great for understanding separation, but horrible for generating test cases. The approach was to design a small domain-specific language (DSL) for representing a computation, create our `Arbitrary` instances of that, and then translate it into a computation constrained with all of the indexes that we allowed in the DSL. This process is complex enough that it starts to obfuscate the properties being checked. In short, we looked at properties such as showing that using a `StateX` monad with the same operations will yield the same result as using just the `State` monad; we also tested that a put and get with a particular state monad (indexed or not), interrupted by any number of puts and gets from other distinct state monads, will still result in the originally placed value. We observed that the properties held, assuming we trust the DSL and its conversions. When a test approaches the complexity of the system on which we are checking properties, the value is not as clear.

3.4   Usage

Using indexed monads is virtually the same as using the original monads. We construct our computations using $>>=$ and `return` (or more familiarly, do-notation) and the non-proper morphisms, and then run the computation in a combination of the run functions of the monads involved. Type ascriptions are similar in necessity as when using the basic monads. We assume that `StateX`, `StateTX`, `ReaderX`, and `ReaderTX`, are all defined.

Using a type-indexed monad by itself is only distinguished by the addition of the index in using the non-proper morphisms and in ascribing the type. In this example, type ascriptions are voluntary.

```
comp::(MonadReaderX MyIndex Int m) ⇒ Int → m Int
comp x = do a ← askx MyIndex
            return (x+a)

runcomp :: Int → Int
runcomp x = runReaderX MyIndex (comp x) 4
```

Indexed monads also work with their ancestors (the non-indexed versions), and do not interfere with each other as they are independently defined. They can also work with other indexes of themselves, as this example also shows. Note that we use the original `State` monad with an integer for its state, and that two differently-indexed `StateX` monads also use integers as their state without disturbing each other. We also see another indexed `StateX` monad containing boolean state, showing that it does not prohibit heterogeneous usage between the type-indexed monads. Also, note that the run function stacks the original monad between the indexed monads. Type-indexed monads impose no additional restriction on the order in which you run them. The type ascriptions for quad and runquad are not necessary.

```
data Ix1 = Ix1 deriving (Show, Eq)
instance Index Ix1 where getVal = Ix1
-- and similarly for Ix2, Ix3.

quad :: (MonadStateX Ix1 Bool m, MonadStateX Ix2 Int m,
         MonadStateX Ix3 Int  m, MonadState Int m)
      ⇒ m Int
quad = do a ← getx Ix1
          b ← getx Ix2
          c ← getx Ix3
          d ← get
          return (if a then b+c else d)

runquad :: Bool → ((((Int,Int),Int),Int),Bool)
runquad b = flip (runStateX Ix1) b
          . flip (runStateTX Ix2) 2
          . flip runStateT 10
          . flip (runStateTX Ix3) 3
          $ quad
```

%> runquad True
((((5,3),10),2),True)
%> runquad False
((((10,3),10),2),False)

Next, we use two unrelated type-indexed monads to showcase their usage in conjunction with each other. Note e.g. that ReaderX and StateX can use the same index safely, as there is no confusion between which monad is referenced.

```
compM::(MonadReaderX Ix Int m, MonadStateX Ix String m) ⇒ Int → m Int
compM x = do  a ← askx MyIndex
              putx MyIndex $ "var"++(show a)
              return (a + x)

comp::Int → (Int,String)
comp x = flip (runReaderX Ix) 4  .  flip (runStateTX Ix) "" $ compM x
```

%> comp 5
(9, "var4")

We can use the ErrorX monad to throw and catch multiple errors in the same code. We use the ascribe function to streamline the examples — otherwise it would be unclear what instance to use to satisfy ErrorX ix e. We also use runIdentity — Just as there is no runError but only runErrorT, there is no runErrorX, only runErrorTX.

```
data Err = E1 | E2 Int | E3 String deriving (Show, Eq)

instance (Index ix) => ErrorX ix Err where
   noMsgx ix = E1; strMsgx ix = E3

ascribe::(MonadErrorX X1 Err m, MonadErrorX X2 String m) => m a->m a
ascribe = id

run = runIdentity . runErrorTX X1 . runErrorTX X2
```

```
%> run . ascribe $ return 5
   Right (Right 5)
%> run . ascribe $ throwErrorx X1 E1
   Left E1
%> run . ascribe $ throwErrorx X2 "no"
   Right (Left "no")
```

We can run our indexed ErrorX monads in whatever order we choose. Throwing the same X2 error but running the monads in different orders naturally affects the nesting of the resulting Either type.

```
throw2no = throwErrorx X2 "no"
```

```
%> runIdentity . runErrorTX X1 . runErrorTX X2 . ascribe$ throw2no
   Right (Left "no")
%> runIdentity . runErrorTX X2 . runErrorTX X1 . ascribe$ throw2no
   Left "no"
```

```
%> run.ascribe$ catchErrorx X1 (throwErrorx X1 (E3 "err3"))
                                (λ(E3 s) -> throwErrorx X2 s)
   Right (Left "err3")
```

The original mtl couldn't handle multiple errors at once — that could only be simulated with a closed datatype, as we did with Err. Indexed monads allow us to throw and catch various types of errors within the same monadic code.

We have seen that type-indexed monads are used nearly identically to non-indexed monads. We have gained the ability to extend our usage of particular non-proper morphisms without re-defining them; instead, we only must generate a new type index, a trivial task.

4   Related Work

Monad Transformers. Moggi [8] introduces monads as a model of computation, and others [9,10,11] continue this invaluable work to introduce and develop the idea of monad transformers. GHC [2] distributes with the Monad Transformer Library [1]. The current work with type-indexed monads and type-indexed monad transformers extends this work in a new direction, parameterizing the monads themselves (as opposed to parameterizing over monads), and allowing for more versatile use via indexing while leaving intact current patterns of non-indexed use. The new contribution is to *open* the monads in order to allow concurrent distinct instances of the monads to operate separately.

MonadLab. MonadLab [12] creates a domain-specific language utilizing Template Haskell [13] in order to encapsulate monad construction and abstract away implementation details. Being both a pedagogical tool for learning monads and a positive contribution to the expressivity and convenience of monads, Monad-Lab uses the meta-programming of Template Haskell to create an entirely new monad with the DSL-specified side-effects, replete with the required instances and regularly-specified non-proper morphisms. Type-indexed monads go in a different direction–rather than encapsulate and hide the details of monads, they expand on possible usage of the existing monads. Type-indexed monads provide a means to combine monadic code (avoiding index clashes rather than intersecting usage) and add more side-effects ad-hoc (via another indexed copy).

Parameterized Monads. Atkey [14] takes a categorical approach to monads that also introduces the notion of type-varying state. Rather than require that e.g. the `State` monad always inputs and outputs a particular state s, a `State` computation accepts state of type s1 and outputs state of type s2. This of course requires a multiplicative property that chained `State` computations' outputs and inputs align to compatible types. This does not afford the ability to store multiple pieces of state, but does relax our state requirements by allowing us to change throughout our computation exactly what type of state is stored. Similar ideas are spread throughout the Haskell-Cafe mailing list, notably by David Roundy and Oleg Kiselyov in late 2006.

Monatron. Jaskelioff [15] takes a ground-up approach to monad transformers, approaching the issue of the quadratic lifting instances by standardizing the lifting procedure between transformers. Monatron accomplishes this by separating the usage from the implementation of non-proper morphisms, meaning that we can lift through *any* transformer, as opposed to defining lifting instances through particular transformers. However, in order to re-use monadic effects as we've discussed, the user still must define the lifting-depth for each interacting use of the monadic effects; this does not enable using library definitions (written in Monatron) in multiple ways once the lifting depths are set.

Type-indexed monads do not solve the issue of quadratic lifting instances per se, but mitigate the issue by providing the instances as necessary, so long as the monad with the desired non-proper morphisms can be indexed. Jaskelioff discusses an example of two `Error` monads stacked with a `State` monad and the confusion between which errors to throw; this is a direct translation into type-indexed monads that implement `Error` and `State`.

HLists. One approach to opening the contents of e.g. `State` is to use an `HList` [16] as the state. `HLists` provide a way to use type-level programming to guarantee that an index into the structure will result in a value, and of a particular type. One could use this to gain some flexibility into the 're-use' of a monad by adding constraints on the state or environment to ensure a desired field is included. This decision still must be made initially, or else downstream uses cannot take the opportunity. Also, there is no guarantee of separation between the states, as all are available for modification. Type-indexed monads can still use a record at the values level instead of at the types level as for HLists, and yet we can still add more uses as well. By defining abstractions around usage of a type-indexed monad in a separate module and only exporting those abstractions and a few type synonyms, we can tell by the type of an expression whether it can access a particular state. HLists are concerned with heterogeneous lists themselves, and not in opening up usage of monads.

5   Conclusions and Future Work

We have introduced the notion of type-level indexes into monads to provide 'copies' of monads. We've shown how such an implementation compares to non-indexed monads to motivate their usefulness and approachability. We provided a reference of implementation details, and discussed how type-indexed monads allow us to reduce the amount of code necessary as well as reduce a source of possible errors by generalizing the process of duplicating particular side-effects.

Type-indexed monads provide a flexible framework for reusing monadic features. They open up the monad definitions with explicit indexing, allowing us to extend the use of non-proper morphisms without program-wide modification of existing uses. Indexed usage is added, rather than modifying current usage. Type-indexed monads solve the issue of using monads in library code by providing copies of monads, rather than manually generating a copy of needed monads along with all the instances. This both enhances code re-use while minimizing the chances for error introduction. Type-indexed monads also mitigate the number of instances that we need for monad transformers when multiple distinct monads can be replaced by indexed variants rather than hand-coded semantic copies of monadic functionality. If a stack of monads can be defined in terms of type-indexable monads, then all instances are already provided. Even if this is not so, one set of instances now applies to an unlimited number of monads. We write interfaces between kinds of monads, instead of between each implementation of a particular set of side-effects. Type-indexed monads are used in nearly identical fashion to non-indexed monads, providing a familiar interface that should aid in adoption. The reference implementation is available from the Hackage repository [3], an indexed approach to the mtl package. We would like to see type-indexed monads for even more monadic definitions in the future.

Acknowledgements

We'd like to thank the reviewers for quite helpful insights and suggestions, and we'd also like to thank Tom Schrijvers for some very helpful correspondence.

References

1. Gill, A.: mtl: The Monad Transformer Library (September 2010),
   http://hackage.haskell.org/package/mtl-1.1.1.0

2. GHC: The Glasgow Haskell Compiler, http://haskell.org/ghc/
3. Snyder, M.: mtlx: Monad transformer library with type indexes, providing 'free' copies (October 2010), http://hackage.haskell.org/package/mtlx-0.1.5
4. Harrison, W.L., Hook, J.: Achieving information flow security through precise control of effects. In: CSFW 2005: Proceedings of the 18th IEEE Workshop on Computer Security Foundations, pp. 16–30. IEEE Computer Society, Washington, DC (2005)
5. McBride, C.: Faking It - Simulating Dependent Types in Haskell. J. Funct. Program 12(5), 375–392 (2002)
6. Cheney, J., Hinze, R.: First-class phantom types. Technical report, Cornell University (2003)
7. Claessen, K., Hughes, J.: QuickCheck: a lightweight tool for random testing of Haskell programs. In: ICFP 2000: Proceedings of the Fifth ACM SIGPLAN International Conference on Functional Programming, pp. 268–279. ACM, New York (2000)
8. Moggi, E.: An Abstract View of Programming Languages. Technical Report ECS-LFCS-90-113, Dept. of Comp. Sci., Edinburgh Univ. (1990)
9. Wadler, P.L.: Comprehending Monads. In: Proceedings of the 1990 ACM Conference on LISP and Functional Programming, pp. 61–78. ACM, New York (1990)
10. Wadler, P.: The Essence of Functional Programming. In: Conference Record of the Nineteenth Annual ACM SIGPLAN-SIGACT Symposium on Principles of Programming Languages, Albequerque, New Mexico, pp. 1–14 (1992)
11. Jones, M.P.: Functional Programming with Overloading and Higher-Order Polymorphism. In: Jeuring, J., Meijer, E. (eds.) AFP 1995. LNCS, vol. 925, pp. 97–136. Springer, Heidelberg (1995)
12. Kariotis, P.S., Procter, A.M., Harrison, W.L.: Making Monads First-Class with Template Haskell. In: Haskell 2008: Proceedings of the First ACM SIGPLAN Symposium on Haskell, pp. 99–110. ACM, New York (2008)
13. Sheard, T., Jones, S.P.: Template Meta-Programming for Haskell. SIGPLAN Not 37(12), 60–75 (2002)
14. Atkey, R.: Parameterized Notions of Computation. In: Proceedings of Workshop on Mathematically Structured Functional Programming (July 2006)
15. Jaskelioff, M.: Monatron: An Extensible Monad Transformer Library. In: Castagna, G. (ed.) ESOP 2009. LNCS, vol. 5502, pp. 64–79. Springer, Heidelberg (2009)
16. Kiselyov, O., Lämmel, R., Schupke, K.: Strongly Typed Heterogeneous Collections. In: Haskell 2004: Proceedings of the ACM SIGPLAN Workshop on Haskell, pp. 96–107. ACM Press, New York (2004)

Author Index

Batch number: 09490872

Printed by Printforce, the Netherlands